A USA-BASED STORE THAT PUTS THE CUSTOMER FIRST.

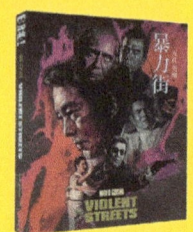

★★★★★

A+ LEGENDARY!

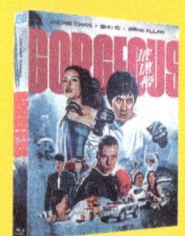

★★★★★

The eBay character limit is too small to properly covey how amazing this seller is. Really makes the customer and purchase feel valued. Will absolutely buy again!!

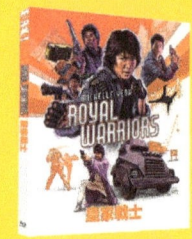

★★★★★

ABSOLUTELY SUPERB! Lightning fast safe and secure shipping! Great customer service! Thank you! Highly recommended! A+++!!!

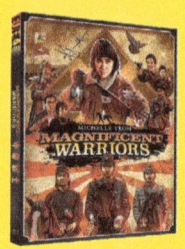

100% REAL FEEDBACK LEFT BY ACTUAL CUSTOMERS.
VISIT OUR FEEDBACK FORUM FOR MORE.

SEE OUR ADVERTISEMENTS AT CITYONFIRE.COM

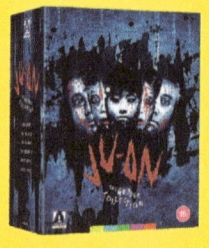

THE GOODIE EMPORIUM™

https://www.ebay.com/str/goodieemporium

Editorial

Enter the Dragon is a martial arts movie that has left an indelible mark on cinema history. Its cultural significance was recognised in 2004 when it was selected for preservation in the US National Film Registry. But for many of us who grew up watching it, the movie is more than just a film. It is a seminal moment in our childhood, a high watermark for the ideals of a life well-lived, and a source of inspiration that continues to resonate today.

Bruce Lee's Enter the Dragon was a game-changer in the world of martial arts movies. It opened a doorway to Chinese cinema that had remained closed to all but a few for so long, and effortlessly bridged the gap between western and eastern cinema. The movie propelled Bruce Lee to the highest echelons of worldwide fame, but his untimely death only days before the film's release imbued it with a special ingredient, something intangible and ethereal. It was as though we were witnessing a man at the absolute pinnacle of what was possible for one man to achieve, and his performance was so profound that his light was extinguished by the sheer effort of it.

Enter the Dragon defined martial arts movies for the western world. It introduced a physical language to the common man, where fighting was no longer about the scrabble of two drunken men clawing at each other in the garbled mess of a bar room brawl. Fighting became a beautiful acrobatic dance between two highly skilled proponents, highly trained in their art and at the peak of physical perfection. A movie fight became something that could be savoured and experimented with.

The impact of Enter the Dragon is still felt today. Without it, audiences around the world may not have craved for more Chinese superstars such as Jackie Chan, Jet Li, and Donnie Yen, and the multitude of films that were produced in the same vein. Action stars of today that show deadly precision and skill in the martial arts may have been less physically capable or less desired. The intricate choreography of fight scenes in modern western cinema would seem cumbersome and slow compared to today's feast of razor-sharp martial arts exponents as displayed in films like The Bourne series and even Batman.

Bruce Lee's influence can be seen in countless stars who owe much of their success to him. Jean Claude Van Damme, Steven Segal, Jackie Chan, and many others would not have existed, at least not in such a successful guise, were it not for the grand master himself.

For many of us who grew up watching Bruce Lee movies, using them as a way to cement our ideals of manhood, honour, and physical prowess, Enter the Dragon was more than just a movie. It was a source of inspiration, a call to live a life of honour, strength, and determination. Bruce Lee's philosophies and his martial arts continue to inspire generations to this day.

In conclusion, Enter the Dragon deserves its place in history as a seminal martial arts movie that defined the genre for the western world. Its impact can still be felt today, and its influence on cinema and popular culture is undeniable. For those of us who grew up watching it, Enter the Dragon will always hold a special place in our hearts, as a source of inspiration and a reminder of the ideals that we should strive to live by.

Hope you enjoy this issue.

Rick

THE KING OF VILLAINS

The Legendary Shih Kien
By Rick Baker

Shek Wing-cheung, better known by his stage name Shih Kien, was a Chinese actor who was born on January 1, 1913 in Hong Kong. He was known for his roles as villains and antagonists in a number of early Hong Kong wuxia and martial arts films, which date back to the black-and-white era.

Shih was raised by his stepmother and was a sickly child. He decided to practise martial arts to improve his health and trained for nine years. Shih trained at Shanghai's Chin Woo Athletic Association and was among the first generation of students at the school to be certified as instructors. After becoming certified to teach styles, including Eagle Claw and Choy Li Fut, he decided to start his career as an actor. However, the outbreak of the Second Sino-Japanese War caused his studies to be disrupted. Shih and his friends travelled between Guangzhou and Hong Kong to stage drama performances, in order to raise funds as part of the anti-Japanese movement. Besides acting on stage, Shih also participated in back-stage activities, such as makeup and arrangements of lighting and props.

In 1940, Shih officially entered the entertainment industry as an apprentice of the Cantonese opera makeup artist Sit Kok-Sin, before becoming an actor. Shih starred as a Japanese secret agent in his debut film Flower in the Sea of Blood that year. Nine years later, Shih was invited by film director Wu Pang to work with him on a series of Wong Fei-hung-related films. Shih gained fame for his portrayal of the villains in those films, and continued to play the role of the antagonist in several films during the first 20 years of his career. Shih's iconic "villain laughter" in the films was later mimicked and parodied by several actors.

In 1973, Shih was chosen to portray the villain in Bruce Lee's martial arts movie Enter the Dragon, in which he played Han, a one-handed triad boss who is highly skilled in martial arts (his character's voice was provided by Keye Luke). His character had a final showdown with Lee's character in the ending climax of the film. His performance as the primary villain, Han, in the 1973 martial arts film "Enter the Dragon" starring Bruce Lee, is perhaps his most famous role and the one that brought him recognition in the

Western world.

In 1975, Shih joined the Hong Kong television station TVB, and appeared in several wuxia-themed television series, playing villains most of the time. However, he had also played the roles of gentlemanly, kind and fatherly characters, such as: Cheung Mo-kei's godfather Tse Shun in The Heaven Sword and Dragon Saber (1978), Lung Koon-sam in The Good, the Bad and the Ugly (1979), So Tai-pang in The Brothers (1980), and a grandfather in The Feud of Two Brothers (1986). Shih also shone in dramatic roles in non-wuxia films as well, such as Hong Kong 1941. Later in his career, Shih took on a comedic role with Jackie Chan in The Young Master. In 1980, Shih was invited to participate in filming a television commercial to promote Ricola's mint candy products with his popular image as a villain.

Shih Kien's career in film spanned over

six decades, known for his gracious and kind demeanour. He was a true professional and a beloved figure in the world of Chinese cinema Shih Kien was a highly respected actor in the Hong Kong film industry, and his talent and dedication to his craft earned him a devoted fan base. Despite his success, Shih Kien remained humble and was known for his gracious and kind demeanour. He was a true professional and a beloved figure in the world of Chinese cinema. Known for his gracious and kind demeanour, he was a true professional and a beloved figure in the world of Chinese cinema.

Shih retired from the entertainment industry in 1992, with the

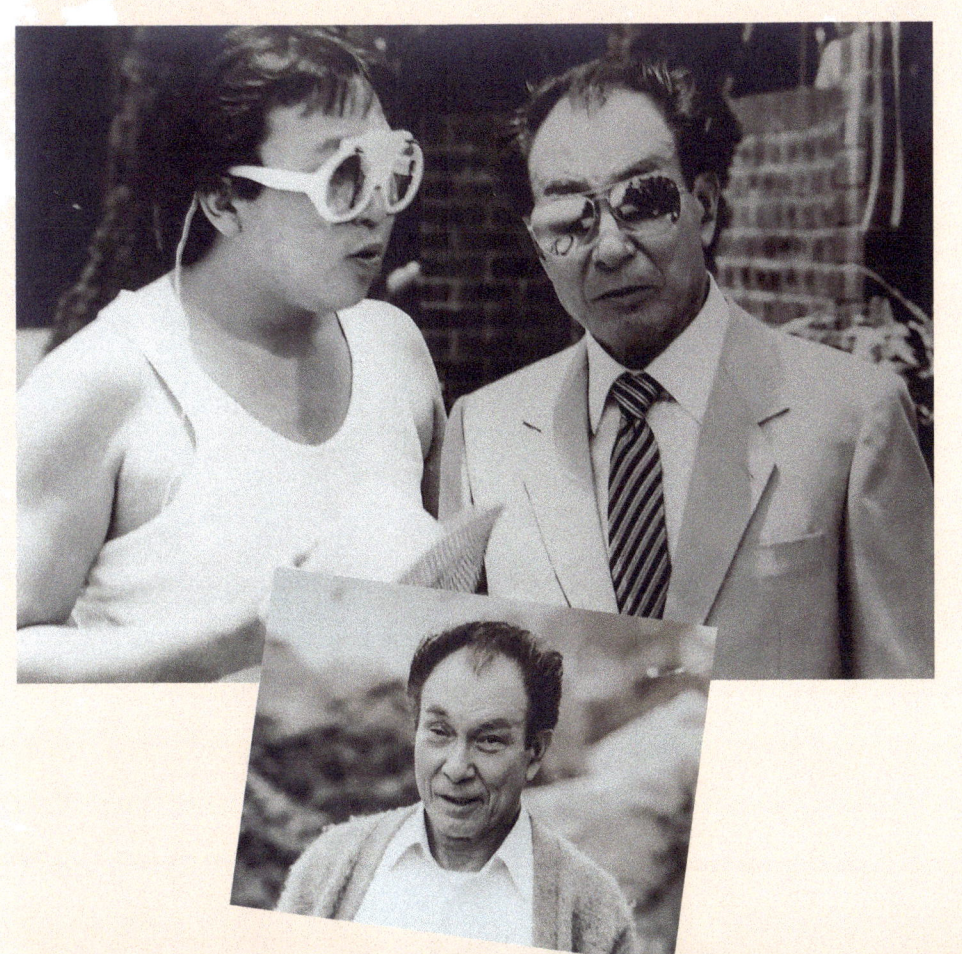

1994 film HK Adam's Family specially dedicated to him. He appeared in the 2003 documentary Chop Socky: Cinema Hong Kong at the age of 90.

Shih received the Life Achievement Award in 1996 at the Golden Bauhinia Awards. Seven years later in 2003, Shih received the Professional Achievement Award at the 22nd Hong Kong Film Awards with Cho Tat-wah, who portrayed the protagonist or hero in several of the films they starred together in. In 2006, Shih donated one of his properties to the entertainment industry in support of the development of the industry. Between January and February 2007, the Hong Kong Film Archive showed 13 of Shih's films that were preserved at the archive.

Shih died of kidney failure on 3 June 2009 at the age of 96. At the time of his death, Shih was believed to be one of the oldest living successful actors in Hong Kong, but his legacy as a talented and versatile actor lives on. His contributions to the film industry will not be forgotten, and he will always be remembered as one of the greats of Hong Kong cinema.

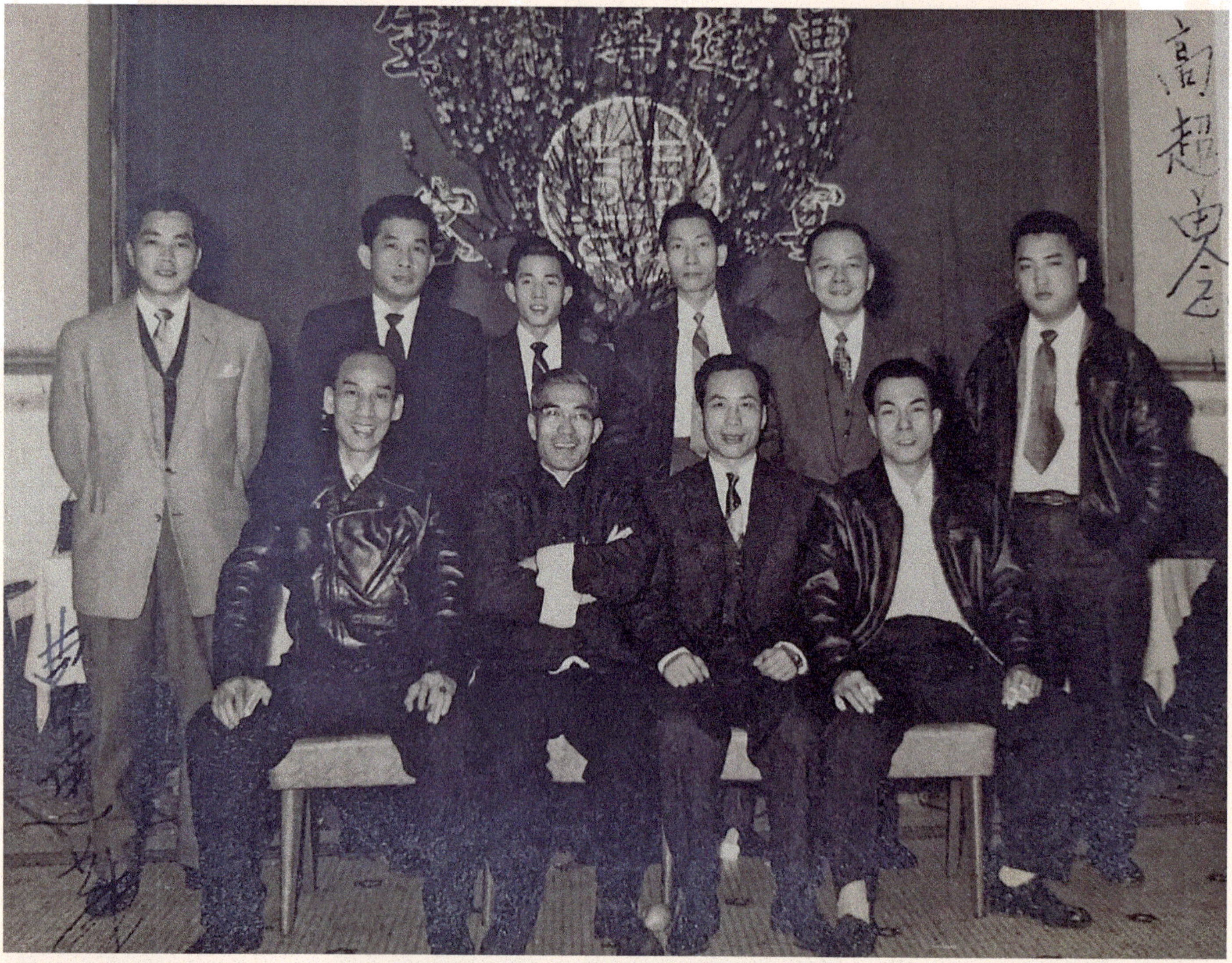

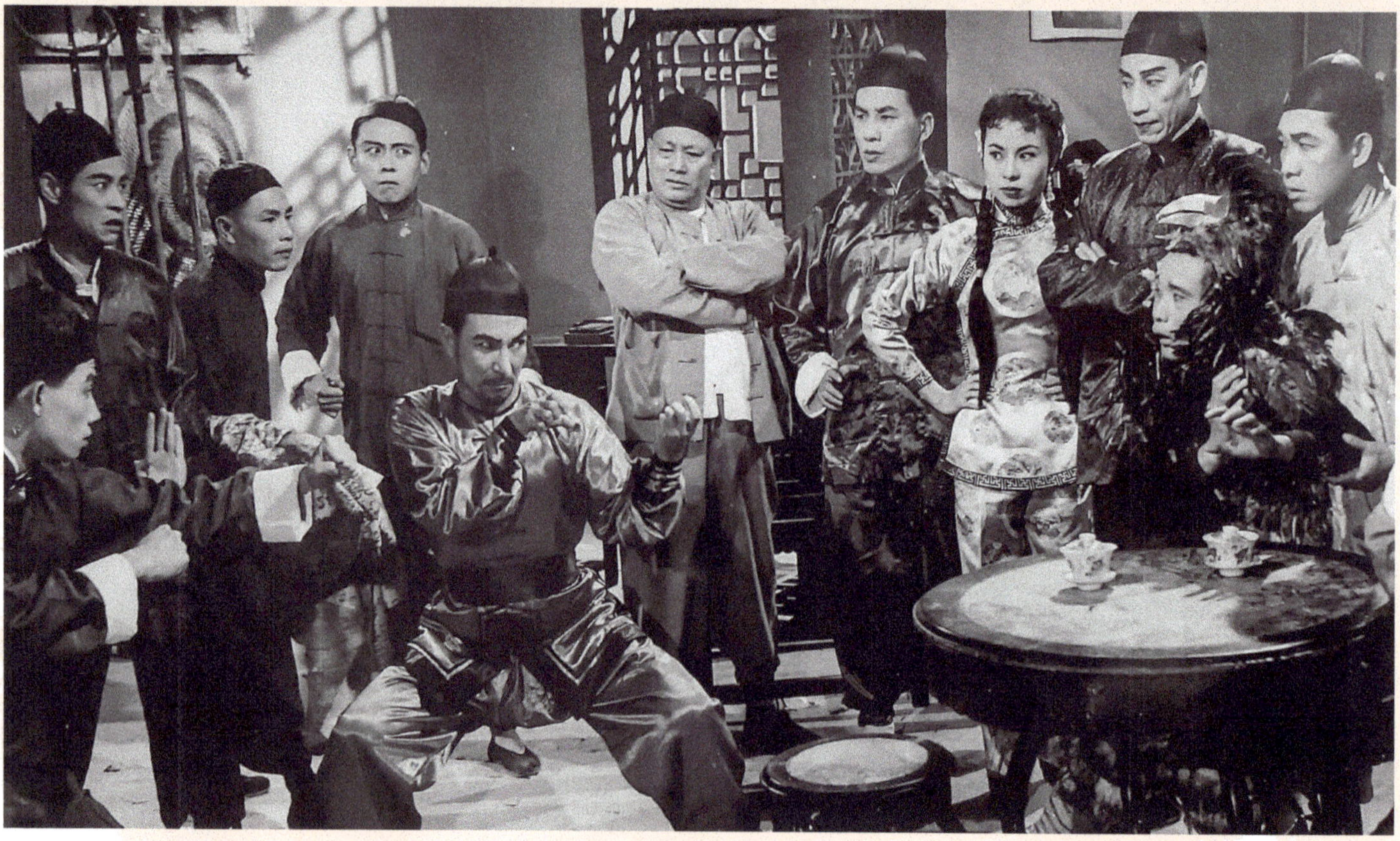

Selected Filmography
(partial list of films)

Xuehai Hua (1940) – Japanese Spy
Dijiu Tianchang (1940)
Gui lai yan (1948)
Na Zha mei shan shou qi guai (1949) – White Gorilla
The True Story of Wong Fei Hung (1949, part 1, 2) – Gray Hair Fu
Hong Hei Koon huit chin Lau ga chun (1949) – Lau Sum-yim
Zhujiang lei (1950) – Cheung Kau
Hao men qi fu (1950)
Huo shao Shao Lin si (1950)
Fang Shi Yu xue zhan Yin Yang Dong (1950) – Priest Pak Mui
Dadao Wang Wu Xuezhan Xiao Bawang (1950)
Lu A Cai (1950)
Lei dian zhui feng jian (1951)
Huang Fei Hong chuan da jie ju (1951)
Dadao Wang Wu Yuxue Jinchou Ji (1951)
Yi fan feng shun (1951) – Lo Kin-ping
Hu dan ying hun (1952) – Chiu Fu
Jia (1953) – Ko Hak-ming
Feng liu tian zi (1953)
Ye du Yuan Yang jiang (1953)
She qing gui (1953)
Huang Fei Hong yi gun fu san ba (1953) – Wong Kwong-Jun
Chun (1953) – Ko Hak-ming
Qiu (1954) – Ko Hak-ming
Bin cheng yan (1954)
Huang Fei Hong yu Lin Shi Rong (1954) – Lui Kung-Cheung
Cheng da sao (1954)
Ai xia ji (1955)
Liang Kuan yu Lin Shi Rong (1955) – Ng Dai Pang
Xu Huang Fei Hong zhuan (1955) – Iron-Pellet Lee
Chang sheng da (1955) – Cheng Nam San
Tian chang di jiu (1955)
Huang Fei Hong hua di qiang pao (1955) – Suen Kwan-Lun
Huang Fei Hong wen zhen si pai lou (1955) – Suen Kwan-Lun
Hou chuang (1955) – Fitness instructor
Huang Fei Hong chang ti jian ba (1955)
Huang Fei Hong da nao Fo Shan (1955) – Wu-So Yung
Huang Fei Hong huo shao Daoshatou (1956) – Drunk Cheong
Huang Fei Hong du bei dou wu long (1956) – Duk-Kok Lung
Fang Shi Yu yi jiu Hong Xi Guan (1956) – Lee Sam-yeh
Huang Fei Hong san xi nu biao shi (1956) – Pak Wing Fu
Huang Fei Hong yi jiu long mu miao (1956) – Bully Biu
Huang Fei Hong nu tun shi er shi (1956) – Pang Jan
Huang Fei Hong fu er hu (1956) – Yeung Fei-Fu
Huang Fei Hong xing shi hui qi lin (1956) – Sek Wang
Huang Fei Hong tie ji dou wu gong (1956) – Fung Lo-Ngau
Huang Fei Hong long zhou duo jin (1956) – Dai Mung Bing
Huang Fei Hong Shamian fu shen quan (1956) – Big Mole Mak
Huang Fei Hong heng sao Xiao Beijiang (1956) – Cheung Boon
Huang Fei-hong gong chuan jian ba (1956)
Bu xia xiang wei zhui hun biao (1956)
Huang Fei Hong yong jiu mai yu can (1956) – Bean Curd Hing
Huang Fei Hong Guanshan da he shou (1956) – Flying Spider
Bi xue en chou wan gu qing (1956)
Bai hao ying xiong chuan (1956)
Tie sha zhang san hui ying zhao wang (1956)
Huang Fei-hong tian hou miao jin xiang (1956) – Rocky Koo
Huang Fei Hong shui di san qin Su Shulian (1956) – Rat Tak
Huang Fei-hong qi shi hui jin long (1956)
Huang Fei Hong da nao hua deng (1956) – Kwok Hung Pau
Na Zha nao dong hai (1957) – East sea Dragon King
Huang Fei Hong Henan yu xie zhan (1957)
Nanhai quan wang ye dao mei hua ma (1957)
Huang Fei Hong shi wang zheng ba (1957)
Shui hu zhuan: Zhi qu sheng chen gang (1957) – 'Winged Tiger' Lui Wong
Huang Fei Hong die xie ma an shan (1957) – Lee Lung
Huang Fei Hong da po fei dao dang (1957) – Yuen Yiu Nam
Heng ba qi sheng sheng zi qi (1957)
Yan zhi ma san dou Huang Feihong (1957)
Huang Fei-hong ye tan hei long shan (1957) – Huen Muk
Huang Fei-hong xie jian su po wu (1957) – Crooked-Nose Biu
Jian qing (1958) – Old Master Lau
Huang Fei Hong wu du dou shuang long (1958) – Bearded Hung
Huang Fei Hong long zheng hu dou (1958)
Huang Fei Hong da po jin zhong zhao (1958)
Huang Fei Hong da nao Feng Huang Gang (1958) – Cheung Dai-Lung
Dai chat ho see gei (1958)
Huang Fei Hong lei tai dou wu hu (1958) – Mount Chuen Tiger
Huang Fei Hong fu qi chu san hai (1958)
Huang Fei Hong hu xue jiu Liang Kuan (1958) – Ma Yu Foo
Story of the Vulture Conqueror (1958–1959) – Wong Yeuk-see
Sword of Blood and Valour (1958–1959) – Wan Ming-san / Man Tsi-wah
Da po tong wang zhen (1959) – Tang Che
Qi xia wu yi ye tan chong xiao lou (1959) – Tang Che
Story of the White-Haired Demon Girl (1959, 3 parts)
Huang Fei Hong bei kun hei di yu (1959) – Ma Yu Fu
Shi xiong di (1959) – General
Huang Fei Hong hu peng fu hu (1959) – Yeung Fei Foo
Lu (1959)
Qi jian xia Tian Shan (1959)
Huang Fei Hong yi guan Cai hong qiao (1959) – Kam Si Kei
Huang Fei Hong lei tai zheng ba zhan (1960) – Yeung Fei Foo
Shi xiong di nu hai chu mo (1960)
Xing xing wang da zhan Huang Fei Hong (1960) – Wong Tak HIn
A Li Ba Ba yu si shi da dao (1960)
Zui hou wu fen zhong (1960)
Mi mi san nu tan (1960) – Lung Si Yeh
The Book and the Sword (1960)
The Story of the Great Heroes (1960–1961, 4 parts)
Huang Fei Hong yuan da po wu hu zhen (1961) – Flying Tiger Wong
Bu bu jing hun (1961) – Chow Chi-Hong
Tian shan long feng jian shang ji (1961)
Yuan yang dao shang ji (1961)
Yuan yang dao xia ji (1961)
Tian shan long feng jian xia ji (1961)
Mo quan zhui xiong (1961) – Kiu Yat Pu
Kun lun qi jian dou wu long (1961)
Kun Lun san nu xia (1961) – To Fu Kit
Ru yan jing hun (1962) – Sze Fu
Yu shi fei shi (1962) – Ma Yu Lung
Shuang jian meng (1962)
Shuang jian meng xia ji da jie ju (1962)
Mo ying jing hun (1962)
Huang mao guai ren (1962) – Cheung Yan Lai
Xian he shen zhen xin zhuan shang ji (1962)
Xi xue shen bian (1963)
The Black Centipede (1963)
Gu rou en chou (1963) – So Pak-Kin
Yi tian tu long ji shang ji (1963) – Golden Lion Tse Siu
Yi tian tu long ji xia ji (1963) – Golden Lion Tse Siu
Guai xia yan zi fei (1963) – Chow Cho-Kei
Nan long bei feng (1963) – Luk Fong-ho
Lei dian tian xian jian (1963) – Ma Lui
Hao men yuan (1963) – Hong Ngai-Chung
Story of the Sword and the Sabre (1963, 1965, 4 parts) – Xie Xun
Luoyang qi xia zhuan (1964) – Pui Tai-Pau
Bai gu li hun zhen shang ji (1964) – Lai Chun-Wah
Bai gu li hun zhen xia ji (1964) – Lai Chun-Wah

The Flying Fox (1964) – Yumyang Gwaisao
Hong jin long da zhan bian fu jing (1964)
Liu she dao (1964) – Chung Tin-bao
Xuehua shenjian (1964) – Shi Mau-Duen
Qing xia qing chou (1964)
Man tang ji qing (1964)
The Flying Fox in the Snowy Mountains (1964) – Yim Kei
Devil's Palm: Part 1 (1964)
Liu zhi qin mo (1965) – Lo Sing Hung
Gui gu shen nu (1965)
Dao jian shuang lan (1965)
Huang jiang san nu xia (1965)
The All-powerful Flute: Part 1 (1965)
Ru lai shen zhang nu sui Wan Jian Men (1965)
Te wu yi ling yi (1965)
Treasure Hunt (1965)
Tit gim jyu han seung jaap (1965)
Yat gim ching (1966) – Shek Dai-Hung
Bi luo hong chen shang ji (1966)
Wen jie men shang ji (1966)
Wen jie men xia ji (1966)
Sheng huo xiong feng shang ji (1966)
Sheng huo xiong feng xia ji (1966) – Hung Jan Tin
Jin ding you long (1966)
Zhen jia jin hu die (1966) – Chong Tak Ming
Jin ding you long gou hun ling (1966)
Jie huo hong lian shang ji (1966)
Yu nu jin gang (1967)
Bi yan mo nu (1967)
Yu mian nu sha xing (1967) – Wu Wan Lung
Kong zhong nu sha shou (1967)
Mao yan nu lang (1967)
Yu nu fei long (1967) – Wong Chong
Story of a Discharged Prisoner (1967) – One-eyed Dragon
Hak ye mau ba hoi yeung wai (1967)
Qi jian shi san xia (1967) – Iron Head Snake / Zen Master Fearless
Hong fen jin gang (1967)
Fei zei jin si mao (1967)
Huang Fei Hong hu zhao hui qan ying (1967) – Mang Fu
Sha shou fen hong zuan (1967)
Tian jian jue dao Shang ji (1967) – Tso Kam-pak
Wu di nu sha shou (1967)
Hei sha xing (1967)
Li hou zhu (1968)
Huang Fei Hong wei zhen wu yang cheng (1968)
Du yan xia (1968)
Ru lai shen zhang zai xian shen wei (1968)
Huang Fei Hong xing shi du ba mei hua zhuang (1968) – Cheung Hing-Fui
Xue ying hong deng (1968)
Lan ying (1968) – Lam Kei
Fang Shi Yu san da mu ren xiang (1968)
Tai ji men (1968) – Kuan
Huang Fei Hong zui da ba jin gang (1968) – Iron Palm
Duo ming dao (1968)
Fei xia xiao bai long (1968)
Shen bian xia (1968)
Sha shou jian (1968) – Gor Kong Lung
Huang Fei Hong rou bo hei ba wang (1968) – Pak Foo
Xiao wu yi da po tong wang zhen (1968) – Chief Guard Fang Lui-ying
Huang Fei Hong: Quan wang zheng ba (1968) – Tai Tin Pau
Xia sheng (1968)
Tie er hu (1968) – To Chan-ping
Tian lang zhai (1968) – Scarface Wolf
Duo ming ci xiong jian (1969)
Huang Fei Hong qiao duo sha yu qing (1969)
Fei zei bai ju hua (1969)
Shen tou zi mei hua (1969) – Ho Pau
Huang Fei Hong shen wei fu san sha (1969) – Ko San Fu
Long dan (1969)
Yin dao xue jian (1969)
Du yan xia du chuang jian hu (1969)
Sam chiu liu (1969)
E Mei ba dao (1969)
Jiang hu di yi jian (1969)
Huang Fei Hong yu xie liu huang gu (1969) – Bat Leung
Tong pi tie gu (1969) – Shek Tin-Geng
Yu mian sha xing (1969)
Du bei shen ni (1969)
Huang shan ke (1969)
Yu nu jian (1969)
Xiao wu shi (1969)
Huang Fei Hong hu de dou wu lang (1969) – Ma Tin Lung / Fei Tin Leung
San sha shou (1970)
Nu jian kuang dao (1970) – Chang Si Fang
Shen tan yi hao (1970)
Huang Fei Hong yong po lie huo zhen (1970)
Cai Li Fo yong qin se mo (1970)
Shi wang zhi wang (1971)
Ri yue shen tong (1971)
Fei xia shen dao (1971)
The Comet Strikes (1971)
Jin xuan feng (1972)
Ji xiang du fang (1972) – Li-shan Ho
Shi hou (1972)
Wang ming tu (1972) – Master Xi – village leader
Tian ya ke (1972)
Enter the Dragon (1973) – Han
Fan mai ren kou (1974)
Er long zheng zhu (1974) – Tiger
Lang bei wei jian (1974)
Two Graves to Kung Fu (1974)
Huang Fei Hong yi qu Ding Cai Pao (1974) – Master Shen Chiu Kung
Hou quan kou si (1974) – Chow Li Ming – Charles Ming
Yinyang jie (1974)
Long jia jiang (1976) – Patriarch Lung
Hua xin san shao sao Yin Jie (1976)
Hua sheng san shao bo yin jie (1976)
The Private Eyes (1976) – Gow-suk – Uncle 9
Xia liu she hui (1976) – Boss Shih
Yin xia en chou lu (1978) – Lo Tien-fung
Xing gui (1979)
Long xing mo qiao (1980) – Master
The Young Master (1980) – Chief Sang Kung
She mao he hun xing quan (1980)
Bruce King of Kung Fu (1980)
Ru lai shen zhang (1982) – Heavenly Foot
Hua xin da shao (1983) – Mo Yan-sang
Gan yan gwai (1984) – Jian Ren – Uncle Ghost
Hong Kong 1941 (1984) – Chung Shin
Dian feng kuang long (1984)
Hong Kong Godfather (1985) – Szetu Han
Aces Go Places 4 (1986) – Interpol Hockey Teach Coach
Millionaire's Express (1986) – Master Sek
E nan (1986) – Man in Picture
The Magic Crystal (1986) – Sergeant Shi
Mao shan xiao tang (1986) – Kent of Mount Mao
Wo yao jin gui xu (1986)
Duet ming ga yan (1987) – Fung's Father
Nan bei ma da (1988) – Mr. Guan
A Better Tomorrow 3 (1989) – Mun's father
Hu dan nu er hong (1990) – Liu Lung
Wu ye tian shi (1990) – Grandpa
Huang Fei Hong xiao zhuan (1992) – Old Master
Jian ren shi jia (1994) – Kan San
Xiang Gang lun xian (1994) – Himself
Sap hing dai (1995) – Uncle Three (final film role)

TV series
The Legend of the Book and the Sword (1976) – Cheung Chiu-chung
The Heaven Sword and Dragon Saber (1978) – Tse Seun
Chor Lau-heung (1979) – Lung Sing-saam
Demi-Gods and Semi-Devils (1982) – Xiao Yuanshan
The Legend of the Condor Heroes (1983) – Kao Chin-yan
The Return of the Condor Heroes (1983) – Kao Chin-yan
The Other Side of the Horizon (1984) – Fu Chin-san
The Smiling, Proud Wanderer (1984) – Wong Yuen-ba
Sword Stained with Royal Blood (1985) – Muk Yan-ching
The Flying Fox of Snowy Mountain (1985) – Seung Kim-ming
Man from Guangdong (1991)

BATTLE WITH HAN PHOTO GALLERY

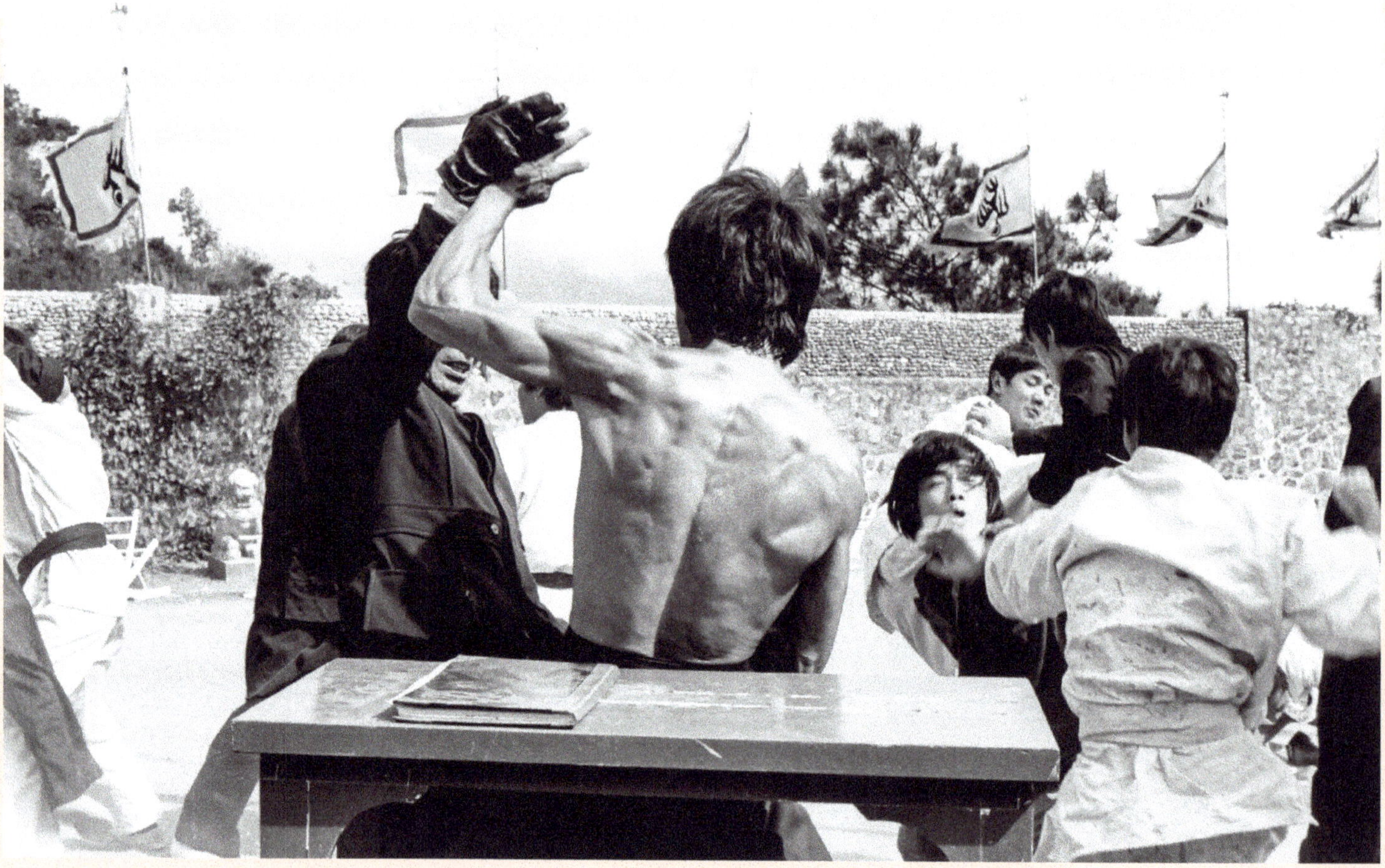

Page: 12

Page: 13

Page: 14

Page: 15

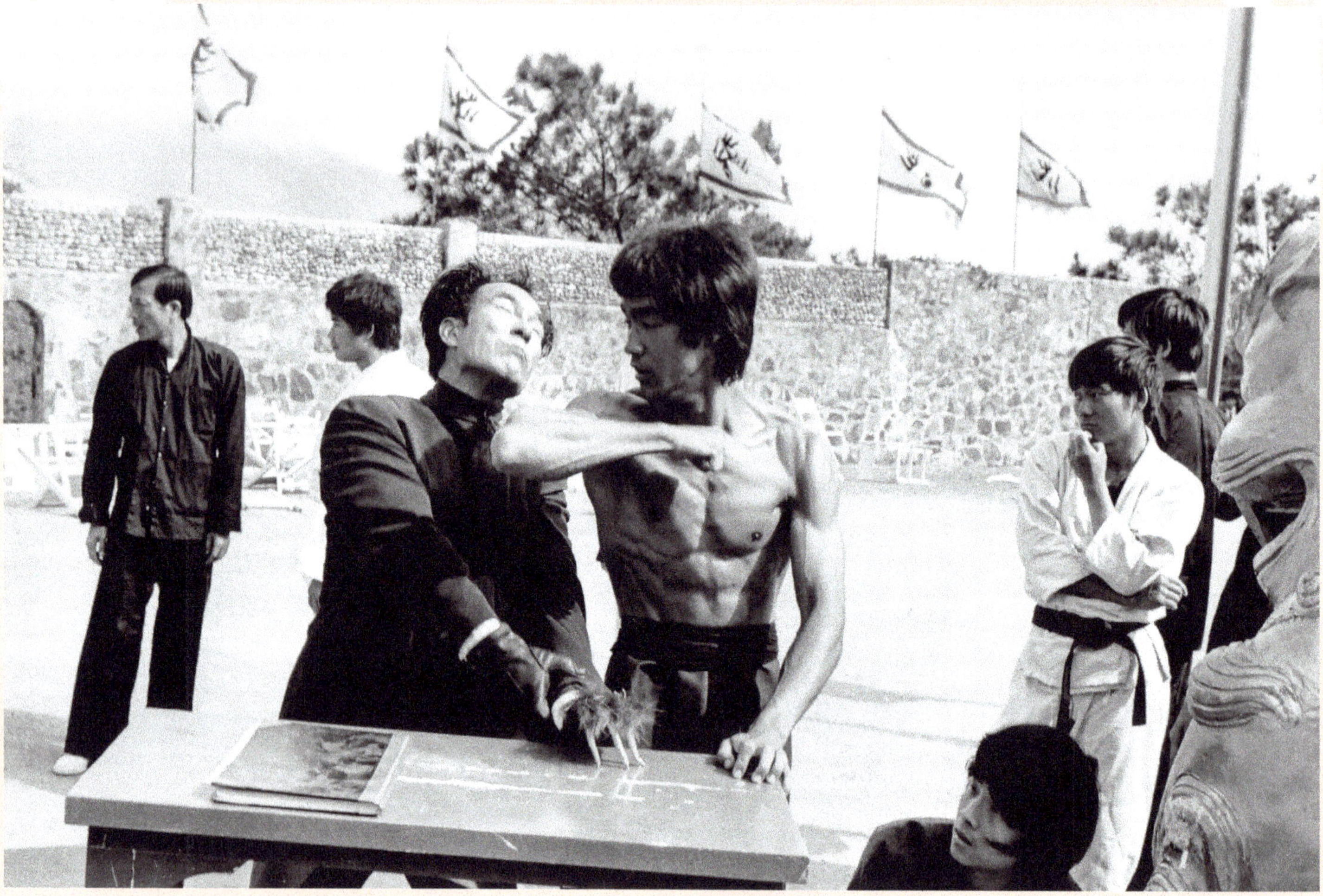

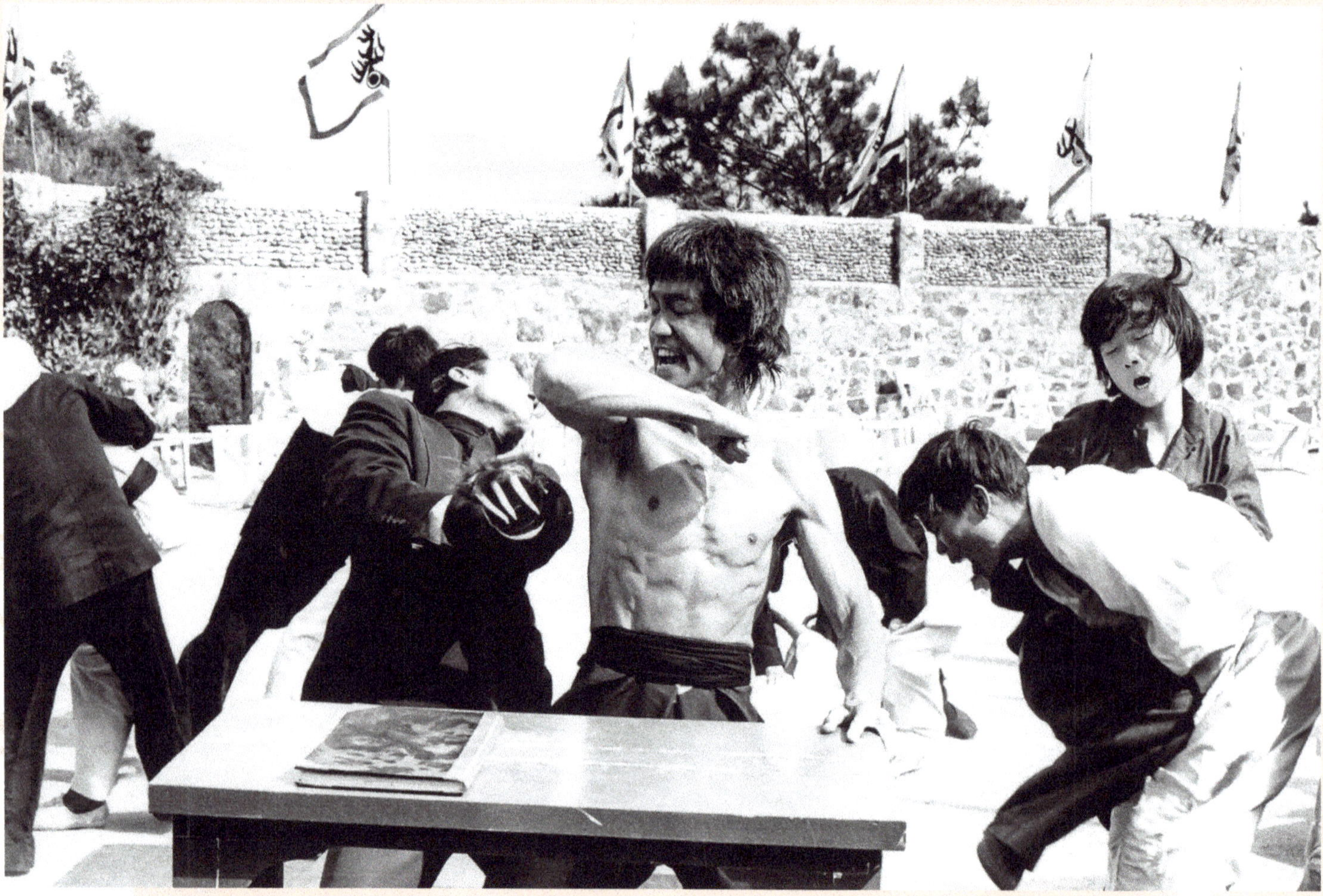

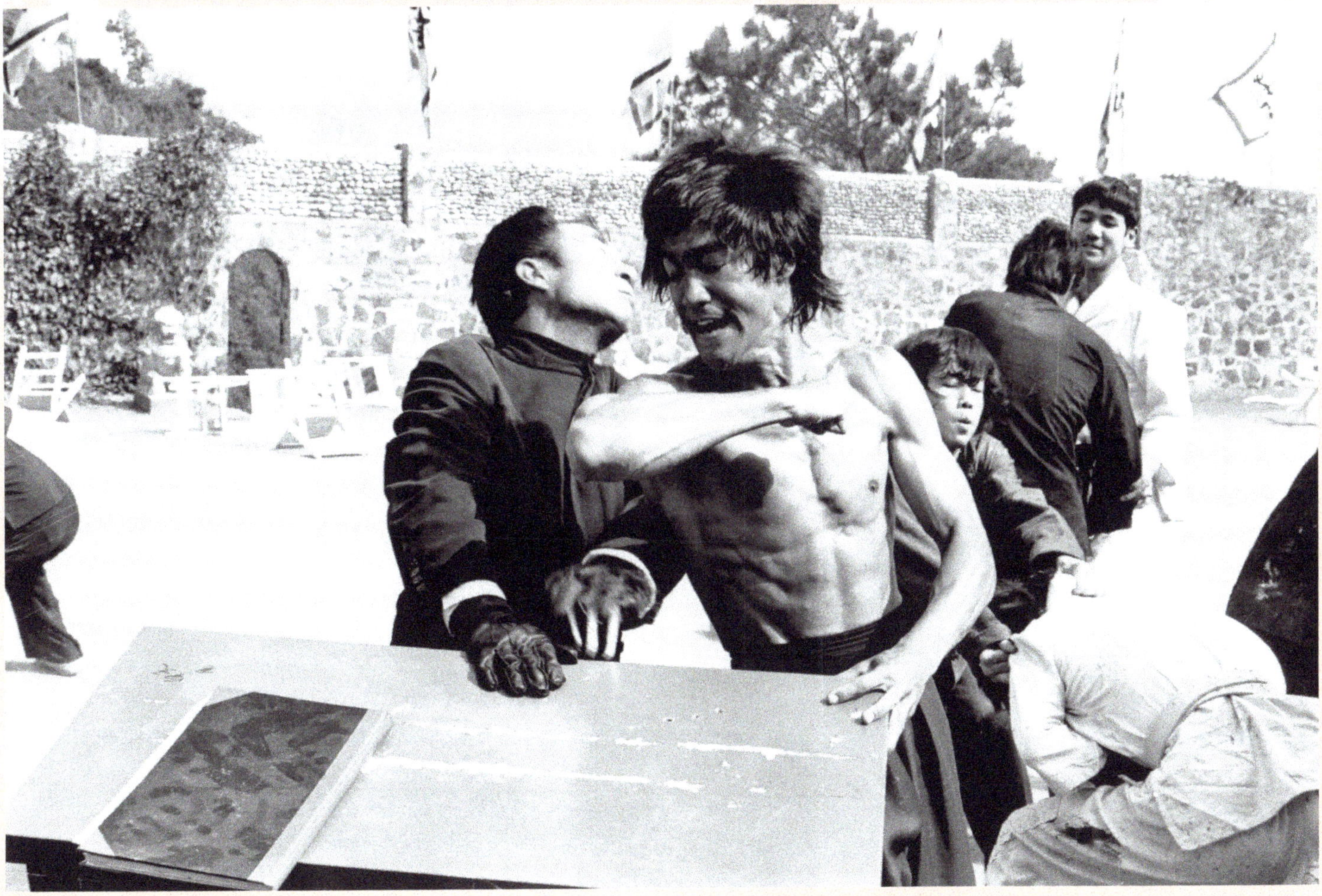

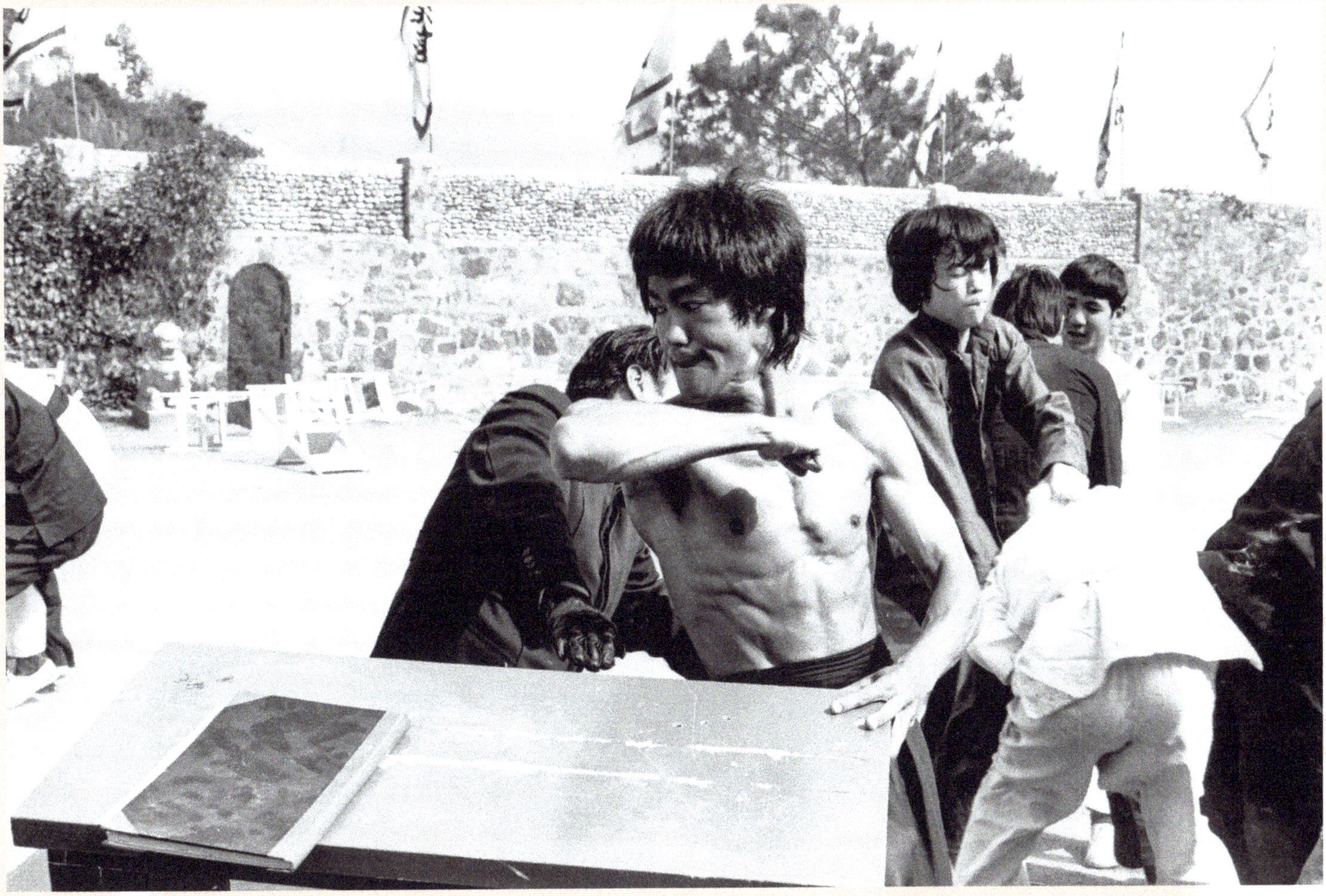

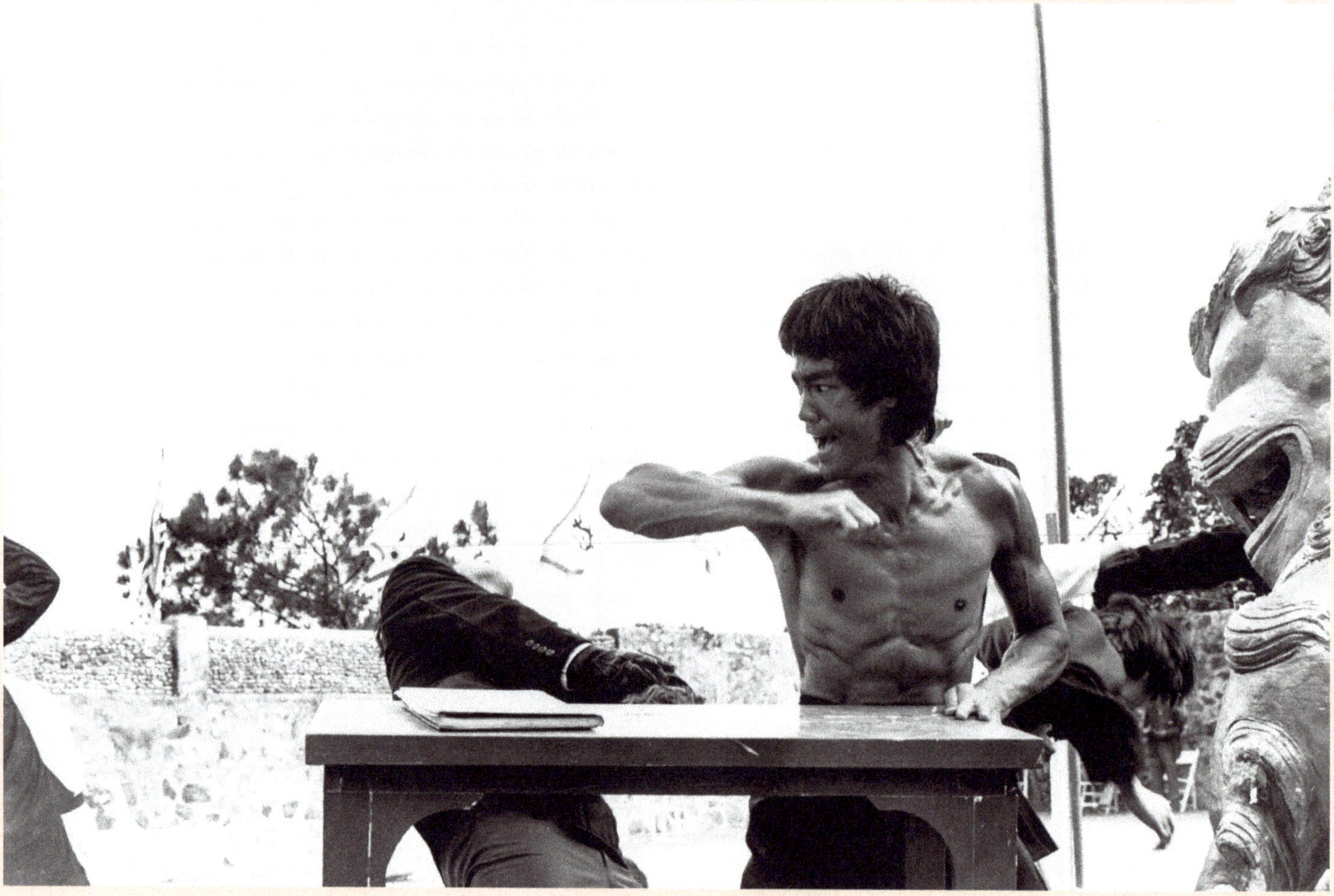

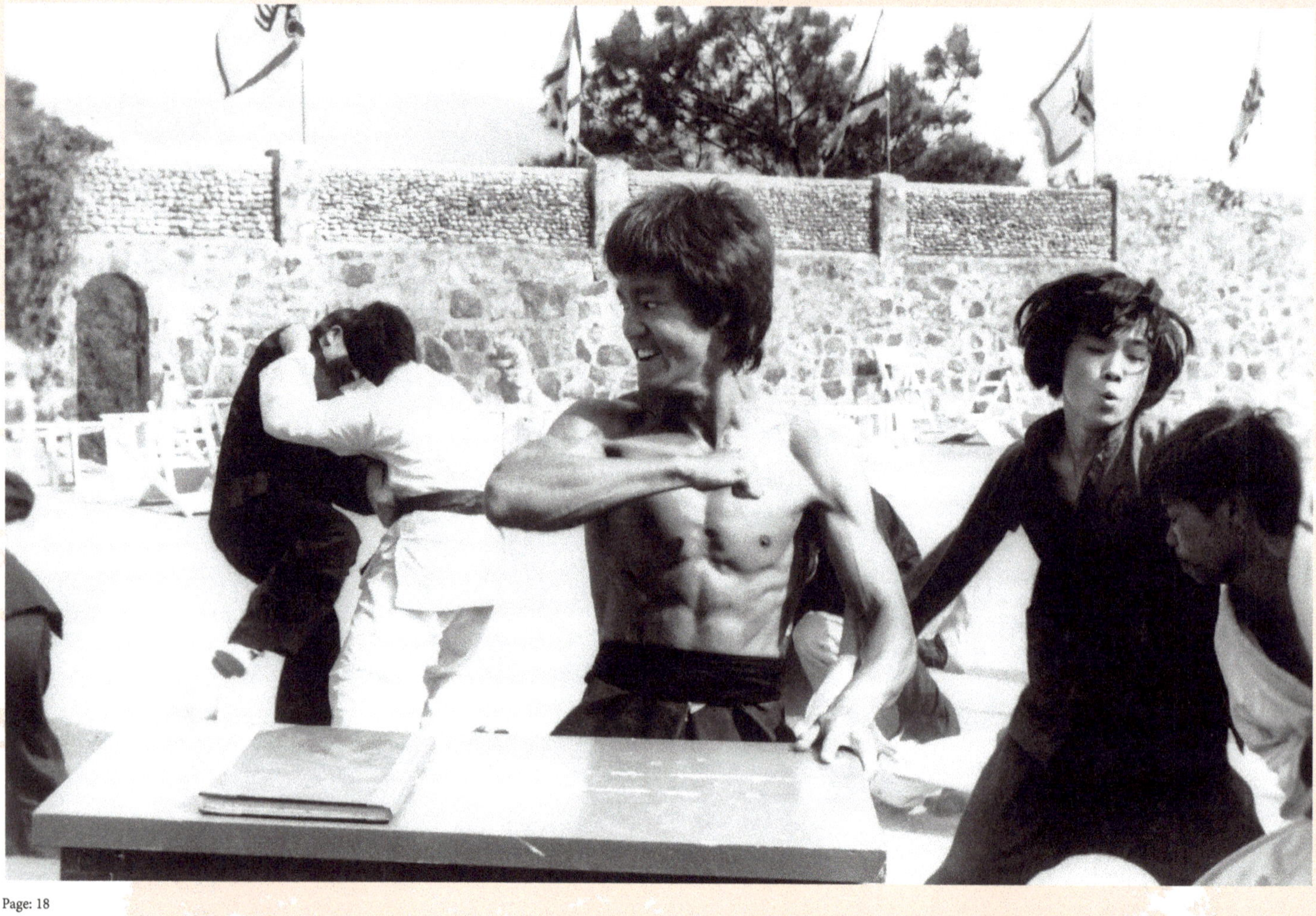

BEYOND MARTIAL ARTS

"An In-Depth Academic Analysis of '*Enter the Dragon*' and Its Impact on Hollywood Filmmaking"

Rick Baker asks the questions to film professor Dalton Regilt

How did the director, Robert Clouse, manage to balance the themes of martial arts and espionage in "Enter the Dragon"?

One of the key elements of "Enter the Dragon" is the way that Clouse balances the themes of martial arts and espionage. To achieve this balance, Clouse draws on a range of techniques, including the use of visual symbolism, character development, and action sequences.

The martial arts tournament serves as a cover for Lee's character's true mission, which is to gather intelligence on the criminal organization operating on the island. This blending of martial arts and espionage allows Clouse to explore the themes of loyalty, betrayal, and the nature of power through both the physical and psychological dimensions of combat.

Clouse also employs visual symbolism to reinforce the themes of the film. For example, the final confrontation between Lee and the villainous Han takes place in a room filled with mirrors. The mirrors serve to emphasize the duality of the characters and the theme of self-discovery that runs throughout the film. The use of mirrors also creates a visual representation of the idea that martial arts and espionage are two sides of the same coin, each relying on strategy and skill to overcome one's opponent.

The film's central characters are all martial artists, but they each have different motivations for participating in the tournament. Some are there for glory, while others are seeking revenge or trying to escape their past. Clouse uses these motivations to create complex characters that are not simply archetypes of the martial arts genre but rather individuals with their own unique motivations and goals.

Finally, the action sequences in "Enter the Dragon" are well choreographed to blend martial arts and espionage. The fight scenes are not simply displays of physical prowess but are also strategic battles that showcase the characters' ability to outthink and outmanoeuvre their opponents. This blending of physical and mental prowess reinforces the idea that martial arts and espionage are interconnected and that success in either field requires a balance of both. This blending of themes creates a film that is both a classic martial arts movie and a compelling espionage thriller.

What was the significance of Bruce Lee's role with his input as writer and choreographer in the film, and how did it influence the final product?

Lee's role in these aspects of the production had a significant impact on the final product and the legacy of the film.

First, Lee's involvement in the writing of the film allowed him to shape the character of his own role, as well as the overall direction of the story. Lee's character was not simply a one-dimensional hero but a complex and multifaceted individual who grappled with issues of identity, loyalty, and justice. Lee's writing also helped to establish the themes of the film, including the idea that martial arts is not simply about physical strength but also about mental discipline and self-awareness. In addition to his role as a writer, Lee's choreography of the fight scenes was another key element of the film's success. Lee's background as a martial artist allowed him to bring a level of authenticity and precision to the action sequences that had not been seen before in martial arts films. He also introduced a more fluid and dynamic style of fighting that incorporated elements of different martial arts disciplines, such as Wing Chun, boxing, and fencing.

Lee's choreography also emphasized the strategic and tactical aspects of martial arts, as opposed to simply showcasing physical prowess. The fight scenes in "Enter the Dragon" were not simply displays of violence but were also battles of wits and strategy, with each character using their unique skills and abilities to gain an advantage over their opponents.

The impact of Lee's involvement in the writing and choreography of "Enter the Dragon" cannot be overstated. The film's complex characters, intricate plot, and

Page: 19

dynamic fight sequences set a new standard for martial arts films and influenced countless filmmakers in the years that followed. Lee's influence can be seen in everything from the "ninja craze" of the 1980s to the rise of mixed martial arts (MMA) in the 21st century.

This was significant in shaping the film's direction, themes, and action sequences. His contributions elevated the film above other martial arts movies of the time and established a new standard for the genre. Lee's influence can still be felt today in the continued popularity of martial arts films and the enduring legacy of "Enter the Dragon."

How did Bruce Lee's own martial arts philosophy and technique come across in his portrayal of the character of Lee in the film?

Bruce Lee's martial arts philosophy and technique were deeply intertwined with his portrayal of the character of Lee in "Enter the Dragon." Lee's approach to martial arts was rooted in his belief that the ultimate goal of martial arts was not simply to defeat an opponent but to achieve a state of self-awareness and self-mastery.

In the film, Lee's character is depicted as a martial artist who has achieved a level of physical and mental discipline that allows him to move beyond the realm of competition and into a state of self-realization. Lee's fighting style is characterized by its fluidity, speed, and precision, as well as its emphasis on using an opponent's energy against them. These elements are all hallmarks of Lee's own martial arts philosophy and technique.

His approach to martial arts was deeply influenced by his study of Wing Chun, a Chinese martial art that emphasizes close-range combat and the use of quick, efficient movements. This is evident in the way that Lee's character moves and fights in the film, as he is constantly shifting and adapting to the movements of his opponents, using their own energy against them.

In addition to his physical prowess, his character also embodies the mental and spiritual aspects of martial arts. He is shown as a deeply introspective and disciplined individual, who is constantly striving to achieve a state of self-awareness

and self-mastery. This is evident in his interactions with the other characters in the film, as well as his own internal dialogue and reflections.

Lee's portrayal of his character in "Enter the Dragon" is a reflection of his own deeply held beliefs about martial arts and its potential to transform the individual. His emphasis on the mental and spiritual aspects of martial arts, as well as his innovative approach to technique and strategy, he set a new standard for martial arts films and influenced countless practitioners in the years that followed set a new standard for the genre and continues to inspire practitioners to this day.

What was the impact of Enter the Dragon on the careers of the supporting actors, such as John Saxon and Jim Kelly?

John Saxon was cast as of Roper in the film, a suave and streetwise American who is enticed to participate in a martial arts tournament on a mysterious island. Saxon was already an established actor before appearing in "Enter the Dragon," having starred in a number of films and TV shows throughout the 1960s and 1970s. However, his performance in "Enter the Dragon" helped to increase his popularity and cemented his status as a leading man.

Jim Kelly played the character of Williams in "Enter the Dragon," a martial artist and former Green Beret who is recruited by Lee's character to participate in the tournament. Unlike Saxon, Kelly was not an established actor before appearing in "Enter the Dragon," However, "Enter the Dragon" helped to raise Kelly's profile significantly. His portrayal of Williams was well-received by audiences and helped to establish him as a charismatic and talented actor. Kelly went on to star in a number of martial arts films throughout the 1970s, including "Black Belt Jones," "Three the Hard Way," and "One Down, Two to Go." While his career did not achieve the same level of longevity as Saxon's, Film and television director and producer Reginald Hudlin described Kelly's enduring identity: "The iconography that Jim Kelly established as the cool martial artist with the giant 'fro resonates to this day. If within only a few films you can create an image that has lasted over the years, you must have done something really right. And he did.

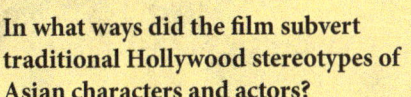

In what ways did the film subvert traditional Hollywood stereotypes of Asian characters and actors?

The film has been praised for subverting traditional Hollywood stereotypes of Asian characters and actors, particularly through its portrayal of Bruce Lee's character and its casting of a diverse group of actors. Traditionally, Hollywood has depicted Asian characters and actors in limited and stereotypical ways. Asian characters were often portrayed as villains or as submissive and passive, while Asian actors were often relegated to minor roles or relegated to playing the same stereotypical characters repeatedly.

"*Enter the Dragon*" subverted these traditional Hollywood stereotypes in a number of ways. Firstly, Bruce Lee's character, Lee, is portrayed as a complex and multifaceted character. Lee is a skilled martial artist who is confident and assertive, but he is also portrayed as a sensitive and introspective person. This portrayal of Lee helped to challenge the traditional stereotype of Asian men as submissive and passive.

Secondly, the film's diverse casting also helped to subvert traditional Hollywood stereotypes. Alongside Bruce Lee, the film featured a number of actors from different ethnic backgrounds, including John Saxon, Jim Kelly, and Ahna Capri. The casting of a diverse group of actors helped to challenge the traditional Hollywood stereotype of Asians as being a monolithic group and provided representation for actors from different backgrounds.

Finally, the film also subverted traditional Hollywood stereotypes through its depiction of the martial arts. "Enter the Dragon" portrayed martial arts as a powerful and dignified art form, rather than as a source of violence or savagery. This depiction of martial arts helped to challenge the traditional Hollywood stereotype of Asian martial artists as being violent or threatening, the film's impact on the industry cannot be overstated, as it paved the way for a more diverse representation of Asians in Hollywood films.

How did the film's exploration of themes of betrayal and revenge reflect the social and political context of its time?

The United States was going through a period of social and political upheaval, marked by protests against the Vietnam War, civil rights struggles, and a general sense of disillusionment with the

government and traditional institutions.

The film's exploration of themes of betrayal can be seen as reflecting this sense of disillusionment. Throughout the film, characters are shown betraying one another, with hidden agendas and secret motivations. The character of Han, the film's primary antagonist, is revealed to have betrayed his own country by selling military secrets to foreign powers. This theme of betrayal reflects the general sense of distrust and disillusionment that many Americans were feeling towards their government and institutions at the time.

Themes of revenge can also be seen as reflecting the social and political context of its time. In the film, characters seek revenge for past wrongs, whether it is the murder of a family member or the betrayal of a friend. This theme of revenge reflects the sense of frustration and anger that many Americans were feeling towards their government and society. Many people felt that they had been wronged and were seeking a form of justice or revenge for past injustices.

Furthermore, the film's depiction of martial arts as a means of seeking revenge can also be seen as reflecting the social and political context of its time. Martial arts, with their emphasis on discipline and self-defence, were seen as a means of empowerment and resistance for many Americans, particularly those from marginalized communities. The film's use of martial arts as a means of seeking revenge can be seen as reflecting this sense of empowerment and resistance.

"*Enter the Dragon*" explores themes of betrayal and revenge, which can be seen as reflecting the social and political context of its time. The film reflects the general sense of disillusionment and distrust that many Americans were feeling towards their government and institutions, as well as the sense of frustration and anger that many were feeling towards their society. The film's use of martial arts as a means of seeking revenge can also be seen as reflecting the sense of empowerment and resistance that many Americans were feeling at the time. What can the film's portrayal of masculinity and gender dynamics teach us about the cultural values of the 1970s?

The film's portrayal of masculinity is marked by a strong emphasis on physical strength and martial arts prowess. The

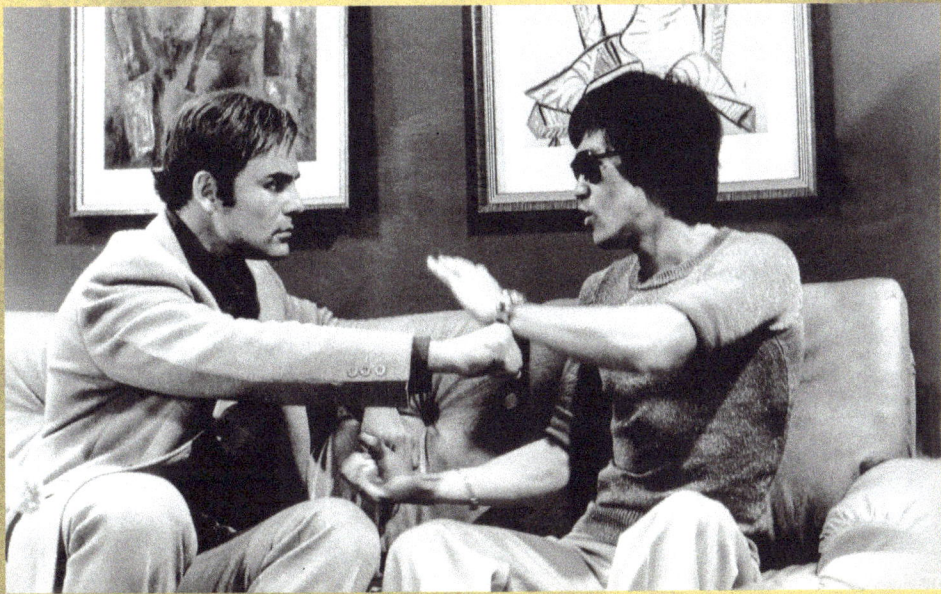

male characters in the film are all skilled fighters who rely on their physical abilities to achieve their goals. This portrayal of masculinity reflects the cultural values of the 1970s, which were marked by a strong emphasis on physical fitness and athleticism.

However, the film also presents a nuanced view of masculinity. The character of Lee, played by Bruce Lee, is portrayed as a sensitive and introspective man, who is deeply committed to his martial arts practice. Lee's portrayal challenges traditional gender stereotypes by showing that men can be both physically strong and emotionally sensitive.

The film's portrayal of gender dynamics is also marked by a sense of change and shifting social norms. The female characters in the film, while not central to the plot, are portrayed as strong and capable. For example, the character of Tania, played by Angela Mao, is a skilled martial artist who is able to hold her own in a fight. This portrayal of female strength reflects the changing role of women in society, as more women began to challenge traditional gender roles and assert their independence.

However, the film is not without its problematic gender dynamics. The female characters in the film are often objectified and sexualized, particularly in the scenes set in Han's private chambers. This objectification reflects the lingering cultural values of the 1970s, which were still marked by a strong sense of male entitlement and objectification of women.

The film's portrayal of physical strength and athleticism reflects the cultural emphasis on physical fitness and athleticism, while the portrayal of sensitive masculinity challenges traditional gender stereotypes. The film's portrayal of female strength reflects the changing role of women in society, but the objectification of female characters also reflects lingering cultural values of male entitlement and objectification of women.

How did the film's success in the US and internationally shape the reception and perception of martial arts cinema in the West?

Prior to the release of "Enter the Dragon," martial arts cinema was a relatively niche genre that was largely unknown to Western audiences. However, the success of "Enter the Dragon" helped to introduce Western audiences to the genre and sparked a wave of interest in martial arts cinema. The film's popularity led to a number of other martial arts films being released in the United States and around the world, helping to

establish the genre as a mainstream form of entertainment.

The success of "*Enter the Dragon*" also had a significant impact on the perception of martial arts in the West. Prior to the release of the film, martial arts were often seen as a mysterious and exotic art form that was largely misunderstood by Western audiences. However, the popularity of "Enter the Dragon" helped to demystify martial arts and introduced Western audiences to the principles and techniques of the art form. The film's emphasis on discipline and training also helped to establish martial arts as a form of physical fitness and self-improvement, rather than simply a source of violence or aggression.

Furthermore, the success of "Enter the Dragon" also had a significant impact on the film industry as a whole. The film's innovative use of martial arts choreography and editing techniques influenced a generation of filmmakers and helped to establish martial arts cinema as a legitimate and respected form of filmmaking. The film's influence can be seen in a number of subsequent martial arts films, as well as in other genres such as action cinema and superhero films.

"*Enter the Dragon*" had a profound impact on the reception and perception of martial arts cinema in the West. The film helped to introduce Western audiences to the genre and sparked a wave of interest in martial arts. The film's emphasis on discipline and training also helped to establish martial arts as a legitimate and respected art form. Finally, the film's innovative use of martial arts choreography and editing techniques influenced a generation of filmmakers and helped to establish martial arts cinema as a legitimate and respected form of filmmaking.

In what ways did Bruce Lee's own life and experiences inform the character of Lee in "*Enter the Dragon*"?

Bruce Lee's own life and experiences played a significant role in the development and portrayal of the character he played in the movie "Enter the Dragon." Lee drew on his personal experiences as a martial artist, actor, and philosopher to create a complex and multifaceted character that reflected his own beliefs and values.

One way in which Bruce Lee's life informed the character of Lee in "Enter the Dragon" was through his personal philosophy of martial arts. Lee believed that martial arts were not just about physical fighting, but also about personal development, self-improvement, and the pursuit of inner peace. This philosophy is evident in the character of Lee, who is portrayed as a wise and philosophical martial artist who values discipline, focus, and self-control.

Furthermore, Lee's own experiences as an Asian-American immigrant in the United States shaped the character of Lee in "Enter the Dragon." Lee experienced discrimination and racism throughout his life, and he used his platform as an actor and martial artist to challenge stereotypes and promote Asian culture. In the movie, Lee's character is portrayed as a proud and confident Asian man who is not afraid to challenge Western stereotypes of Asian masculinity.

In addition, Lee's experience as a martial artist and teacher informed the character of Lee in "Enter the Dragon." Lee was known for his innovative and practical approach to martial arts, and he believed in adapting his techniques to suit each individual fighter's strengths and weaknesses. This approach is reflected in the character of Lee, who is shown teaching his students to adapt and improvise in combat, his experiences as an Asian-American immigrant, and his approach to martial arts training and teaching, Lee created a complex and

"*Enter the Dragon*" is one of the most important films in the history of martial arts cinema, and it has had a profound impact on the genre and popular culture more broadly. The film's enduring popularity is a testament to its influence and cultural significance.

One of the key reasons for the film's success is the central performance of Bruce Lee. Lee was a charismatic and talented martial artist, and his performance in "Enter the Dragon" helped to elevate the film above other martial arts movies of the time. The film also showcased Lee's unique approach to martial arts, which emphasized speed, agility, and adaptability, and his innovative techniques have continued to influence martial artists around the world.

In addition to Lee's performance, the film's mix of genres and styles also contributed to its success. The film blended elements of martial arts, spy thriller, and blaxploitation genres, creating a unique and compelling cinematic experience. The film's use of locations, costumes, and music also added to its appeal, giving viewers a glimpse into a world that was both exotic and exciting.

Furthermore, the film's message of cross-cultural understanding and unity resonated with audiences around the world. At a time when racial tensions were high and cultural divides seemed insurmountable, "Enter the Dragon" offered a vision of a world where different cultures and backgrounds could come together and find common ground.

Today, "*Enter the Dragon*" remains popular because of its enduring appeal and cultural significance. The film continues to inspire martial artists and filmmakers around the world, and its message of cross-cultural understanding and unity is as relevant today as it was when the film was released in 1973. The film's influence can be seen in the countless martial arts movies, video games, and other media that have been released in the decades since its release. Ultimately, "Enter the Dragon" has become an enduring cultural touchstone that continues to captivate and inspire audiences around the world.

nuanced character that reflected his own values and beliefs.

How did the film's combination of martial arts, spy thriller, and blaxploitation elements create a unique cinematic experience, and what was the cultural significance of this hybridization?

How do you feel about Bruce Lee's experience working with Robert Clouse would have shaped Bruce's own filming and directing abilities had he lived?

Bruce Lee's experience working with Robert Clouse on the film "Enter the Dragon" would have undoubtedly had a significant impact on his own filming and directing abilities. However, it is difficult to speculate precisely how his experience would have shaped his future work, as Lee tragically passed away just before the release of "Enter the Dragon."

Despite this, there are several ways in which Lee's experience working with Clouse may have influenced his own filmmaking approach. For one, Clouse was a seasoned director with years of experience in the film industry. Working with someone of Clouse's caliber likely provided Lee with valuable insights into the filmmaking process, including camera angles, lighting, and sound design.

Additionally, Clouse's experience working with Hollywood studios may have given Lee a better understanding of how to navigate the film industry and negotiate creative control over his projects. Lee was known for his uncompromising artistic vision, and working with Clouse may have helped him learn how to assert that vision while still working within the constraints of the industry.

Furthermore, Clouse's approach to storytelling may have also influenced Lee's future work. "Enter the Dragon" was a combination of martial arts, spy thriller, and blaxploitation elements, and Clouse deftly blended these genres to create a compelling and engaging film. Lee may have taken inspiration from this approach and incorporated a similar mix of genres and styles into his own future projects.

Overall, while it is impossible to know precisely how Bruce Lee's experience working with Robert Clouse would have shaped his own filming and directing abilities had he lived, it is clear that working with such an experienced and talented director undoubtedly provided Lee with valuable insights and knowledge that he would have likely applied to his future work.

In a final question for the interview can you sum up the importance of Enter the Dragon and how it has not only become the world's most successful martial arts film but why it is as popular today as it was when it was released in 1973

THE BRUCE LEE CENTER IN PHILADELPHIA

By Chris Poggiali

Philadelphia has been the home to at least two world-famous fighters, one real (Joe Frazier) and the other imagined (Rocky Balboa), but for a decade after Fists of Fury opened at the Milgram Theatre on May 16, 1973, the City of Brotherly Love couldn't get enough of Bruce Lee, the man the Philly newspaper ads had ballyhooed as "the one and only wild man of kung-fu!" The Milgram was one of four theaters located on the 1600 block of Market Street in downtown Philly. On the corner was the Fox (1600 Market), a 2100-seat theater with 70mm projection capabilities. In 1971 the theater's dressing rooms and stage area were converted into the 400-seat Stage Door, with a separate entrance and box-office around the corner on 16th and Ludlow Streets. Next door to the Fox was the Milgram (1620 Market Street) with 1457 seats. Both of these theaters were owned by Milgram Theatre Inc. The next two theaters were a couple of steps down in quality. The Studio (1632 Market Street) had 416 seats and had been an all-night grindhouse for years by the time it switched to porno in the early '70s. The same can be said for the Center (1638 Market Street), a 445-seat dive right next door that would eventually become known as the Bruce Lee Center – despite the fact that it never played an actual Bruce Lee movie.

However, the Milgram-owned theaters up the block always did well with Lee's films. The Chinese Connection played first-run at the Fox and made $70,000 its opening week. Return of the Dragon set an all-time house record for the Milgram, raking in $85,000 for a five-day opener and $165,349 its first 19 days. After Bruce died, the Fox ran a double feature of Enter the Dragon and The Chinese Connection for 24 hours straight as a tribute beginning at midnight

on August 27, 1973. The Fox was also the second theater in the world to get Larry & Marco Joachim's feature film of The Green Hornet (with Bruce's screen test as a bonus attraction) on October 23, 1974. It made $34,000 its first weekend – pretty impressive for several episodes of a seven year-old failed television series.

The first 'Bruceploitation' movie hit Market Street on December 11, 1973 when Queen Boxer opened at the Fox with newspaper ads that falsely trumpeted leading actress Chia Ling as "Judy Lee, the sister of Bruce Lee." The film's distributor, Aquarius Releasing, returned to the Fox two years later with Goodbye Bruce Lee: His Last Game of Death, which they shadily tried to pass off as Lee's unfinished Game of Death. Moviegoers drawn in by advertising that promised "a new full-length film with Bruce Lee vs. Kareem Abdul Jabbar" were so angered by the deception that dozens of them complained to the Pennsylvania Bureau of Consumer Protection, which filed a lawsuit requesting a permanent injunction against the ads. Because of a court order issued by Philadelphia Common Pleas Court Judge Eugene Gelfand, the Fox Theatre had to post a sign at the lobby box-office stating "Bruce Lee is not in this film. It is a tribute to his remarkable career and to his memory." An injunction against the film's ad campaign was granted statewide, so when Goodbye Bruce Lee played in Pittsburgh, Harrisburg and other areas of Pennsylvania, all advertising had to clearly state that the film was actually "a tribute to Bruce Lee."

Despite this controversy, the Fox opened the real Game of Death with continuous 24-hour showings and free Bruce Lee posters given out to the first 500 attendees

at the midnight kickoff on May 23, 1979. The management advertised this event as a "world premiere," even though the film had opened in Hong Kong, Japan and Germany over a year earlier and in the U.K., France and other countries the previous summer. Game of Death was a moneymaker, but also the last Bruce Lee film to play the Fox; in August of '79, a realtor announced that it would be purchasing the entire 35,000 square foot parcel of land housing the Fox, Milgram, and Stage Door theaters from Milgram Theater Inc. and raze it for a 39-story office building.

All three theaters were shuttered by spring 1980, leaving their sleazier porno neighbors, the Studio and Center, the only surviving movie houses on the 1600 block of Market Street. Both venues were under intense scrutiny for attracting an undesirable criminal element, particularly the Center, where a moviegoer had been stabbed 37 times by a deranged vagrant who attacked him in the men's room in June 1979 during a double bill of Porn Brokers and Bad Penny. In an attempt to stop the city scum from creeping into the suburbs, the Pennsylvania state legislature amended the obscenity statutes in 1980, making it a crime for an individual or business to exhibit, display or distribute any material deemed to be obscene. This immediately put the Center in the crosshairs. Built in the mid '30s as a Warner Bros theater, "The Center of Attractions," as it was nicknamed, opened on March 5, 1937 with The Gold Diggers of 1937. By the 1960s it was an all-night grindhouse running second- and third-run major studio pics while the bigger downtown theaters were booking the newest and most popular movies. The Center's last legitimate program was Chastity paired with It Takes All Kinds on February 11, 1970. The next day, the theater reopened with a double bill of Inga and The Best House in London, the first program of the new "adults only" policy that would remain unchanged for over a decade.

In January 1981, a few weeks after the new Pennsylvania state obscenity laws had gone into effect, detectives from the Philadelphia DA's office raided three movie houses and six adult bookstores, arresting nine people and seizing boxes of films and magazines. Additional raids in February hit the Studio and another porn theater a few blocks down Market Street (and right across from City Hall), the Apollo. Fearing they would

be next, the owners of the Center decided to switch their policy from porno to martial arts overnight; on February 12, 1981, they ran their last X-rated program – a double bill of Caged Virgins and Teenage Intimacies – and by the next day had changed the name of the theater to the Bruce Lee Center and were showing two movies from Larry Joachim's Trans-Continental Film Corp., Call Me Dragon and Dirty Chan, for the admission price of 99 cents. Over the next 14 months, the Bruce Lee Center ran dozens of martial arts movies, but not a single one starring the real Bruce Lee. When Enter the Dragon was re-released by Warner Bros on May 23, 1980, it bypassed the Bruce Lee Center in favor of the Budco Goldman 2 a few blocks away, on 15th Street near Chestnut. Columbia's reissue of Fists of Fury and The Chinese Connection also played the Budco Goldman 2 a year later (May 8, 1981).

Below is a week-by-week rundown of all the double features that played the Bruce Lee Center between February 13, 1981 and the end of April 1982, when the theater turned off its projector, popcorn warmers and marquee lights for the last time.

February 13, 1981
Call Me Dragon (aka Bruce Lee Against Supermen)
Dirty Chan (aka Man of Iron)
February 20, 1981
Call Me Dragon (aka Bruce Lee Against Supermen)

Dirty Chan (aka Man of Iron)
February 27, 1981
Black Samurai
The Tattoo Connection
March 6, 1981
Bruce Lee: His Last Days, His Last Nights (aka I Love You, Bruce Lee)
The Three Avengers (aka The Lama Avenger)
March 13, 1981
Duel of the Iron Fist (aka The Duel)
Master Killer (aka The 36th Chamber of Shaolin)
March 20, 1981
The Revenge of the Patriots (aka The Ming Patriots)
Black Magic

March 27, 1981
The Kid with the Golden Arm
Chinatown Kid
April 3, 1981
The Deadly Angels
The 5 Deadly Venoms
April 10, 1981
The Unbeatable Dragon (aka Invincible Shaolin)
Fortress in the Sun

April 17, 1981
The Savage 5
Street Gangs of Hong Kong (aka The Delinquent)
April 24, 1981
The Bodyguard
Soul of Chiba (aka Soul of Bruce Lee)
May 1, 1981
The Godfathers of Hong Kong (aka The Mandarin)
The Thunder Kick

STARTS TODAY!

FIRST RUN ALL NEW MARTIAL ARTS FILMS

HIS HANDS ARE DEATH!

BRUCE LI Call me Dragon

Distributed by TRANS CONTINENTAL FILM CORP. IN COLOR

PLUS **DIRTY CHAN** R IN COLOR

99¢ TILL NOON
BOX OFFICE OPENS 9:30 A.M.

CONTINUOUS FROM 10:00 A.M.

BRUCE LEE CENTER
17th & Market • LO 4-4942

FIRST RUN! 2 ALL-NEW MARTIAL ARTS FILMS

GEORGE LAZENBY
JUDITH BROWN

GRAB The Gold! THE INTERNATIONAL ASSASSIN

PLUS **The Four Assassins**

99¢ MON TO FRI TILL NOON

CONTINUOUS FROM 10:00 AM

BRUCE LEE CENTER
17th & Market
LO 4-4942

May 8, 1981
The Street Fighter
Return of the Street Fighter
May 15, 1981
Bronson Lee, Champion
Jaws of the Dragon (aka The Fierce One)
May 22, 1981
The Executioners of Death (aka Executioners from Shaolin)
5 Masters of Death (aka Five Shaolin Masters)
May 29, 1981
Korean Connection
Single Fighter
June 5, 1981
Sister Street Fighter
The Black Street Fighter (aka Bogard)
June 12, 1981
Goodbye Bruce Lee: His Last Game of Death (aka I Love You, Bruce Lee)
The Tongfather
June 19, 1981
Penitentiary
The Black Dragon vs. the Yellow Tiger (aka The Growling Tiger)
June 26, 1981
Blood Beach
Queen Boxer (aka The Avenger)
July 3, 1981
The Golden Triangle
The Bloody Avengers (aka The Boxer Rebellion)
July 10, 1981
The Flying Guillotine
The Tattoo Connection
July 17, 1981
The Avenging Eagle
Bruce Lee: His Last Days, His Last Nights (aka I Love You, Bruce Lee)
July 24, 1981
Dynamo
The Three Avengers (aka The Lama Avenger)
July 31, 1981
The Incredible Kung Fu Master
Duel of the Iron Fist (aka The Duel)
August 7, 1981
The Incredible Kung Fu Master
Duel of the Iron Fist (aka The Duel)
August 14, 1981
The Four Assassins (aka Marco Polo)
Master Killer (aka The 36th Chamber of Shaolin)
August 21, 1981
Handlock (aka Shaolin Hand Lock)
The Deadly Angels
August 28, 1981
Queen Hustler
Chinatown Kid

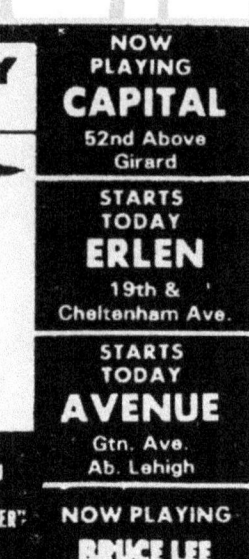

September 4, 1981
Kill or be Killed
The 5 Deadly Venoms
September 11, 1981
Challenge of the Ninja (aka Heroes of the East)
The Revenge of the Patriots (aka The Ming Patriots)
September 18, 1981
Fists of the Double K (aka Fist to Fist)
SuperManChu (aka The Stormy Sun)
September 25, 1981
Challenge of the Masters
The Kid with the Golden Arm
October 2, 1981
Revenge of the Bushido Blade (aka The Last Reunion)
The Hong Kong Connection (aka Black Guide)
October 9, 1981
Bruce is Loose (aka Green Dragon Inn)
Street Gangs of Hong Kong (aka The Delinquent)
October 16, 1981
Kung Fu Mama (aka Queen of Fist)
Bronson Lee, Champion (aka The Karate)
October 23, 1981
The Unbeatable Dragon (aka Invincible Shaolin)
Kill or be Killed
October 30, 1981
5 Masters of Death (aka Five Shaolin Masters)
The Master Avengers
November 6, 1981
The Executioners of Death (aka Executioners from Shaolin)
The Thunder Kick
November 13, 1981
The Savage 5
The Flying Guillotine
November 20, 1981
The Master of Kung Fu (aka Death Kick)
Dynamo
November 27, 1981
Kill and Kill Again
The Three Avengers (aka The Lama Avenger)
December 4, 1981
Slaughter in San Francisco (aka Yellow Faced Tiger)
The Godfathers of Hong Kong (aka The Mandarin)
December 11, 1981
10 Tigers of Kwangtung
18 Fatal Strikes
December 18, 1981
Blood Fingers (aka Brutal Boxer)
Hands of Death (aka The King of Boxers)

December 25, 1981
The Ninja Strikes Back (aka Bruce Tuan's 7 Promises)
Mantis Fist Fighter (aka The Thundering Mantis)
January 1, 1982
Octagon Force (aka Yoga and the Kung Fu Girl)
Nunchaku Lee (aka Return of Red Tiger)
January 8, 1982
A Fist for a Fist (aka Triumph by Two Kung Fu Arts)
Crazy Fist Executioner (aka Crazy Couple)
January 15, 1982
7 Commandments of Kung Fu
Killing Game (aka Story in Temple Red Lily)
January 22, 1982
Assignment to Kill (aka The New South Hand Blows and North Kick Blows)
Mean Drunken Master (aka Iron-Bridge Kung Fu)
January 29, 1982
Any Which Way You Punch (aka Scorching Sun, Fierce Wind, Wild Fire)
Nunchaku Lee (aka Return of Red Tiger)
February 5, 1982
A Man Called Tiger
Challenge of the Masters
February 12, 1982
The International Assassin (aka A Queen's Ransom)
The Four Assassins (aka Marco Polo)
February 19, 1982
Master Killer (aka The 36th Chamber of Shaolin)
The 5 Deadly Venoms
February 26, 1982
Dirty Ho
Fortress in the Sun
March 5, 1982
The Unbeatable Dragon (aka Invincible Shaolin)
The Tattoo Connection
March 12, 1982
Bruce Lee: His Last Days, His Last Nights (aka I Love You, Bruce Lee)
Duel of the Iron Fist (aka The Duel)
March 19, 1982
The Tattooed Dragon
Street Gangs of Hong Kong (aka The Delinquent)
March 26, 1982
When Taekwondo Strikes (aka Sting of the Dragon Masters)
Chinatown Kid
April 2, 1982
The Deadly Angels
The Golden Triangle

April 9, 1982
Death Chamber (aka Shaolin Temple)
Handlock (aka Shaolin Hand Lock)
April 16, 1982
Stoner
5 Masters of Death (aka Five Shaolin Masters)
April 23, 1982
Manhunt
Dynamo

Postscript: The Center wasn't the only porno theater to switch to the action track to avoid raids and prosecution during the '80s. The aforementioned Apollo (1311 Market Street) – which had operated as the Family Theater for over 40 years, ironically enough – became the Apollo Action Theatre on December 30, 1985 with a triple bill of Fighting Mad, Fists of Fury and The Chinese Connection. This "triple treat," as the ads described it ("3 action films for one low price!"), was popular enough to stick around a second week, but the theater only followed their action policy for a month, running two more triple bills – Legend of the Dragon, Greatest Warrior of Shaolin and The Dragon vs. Needles of Death the week of January 10, 1986 and Black Shampoo, Terminal Island and The Street Fighter on January 17 – before returning to the porn grind by January 24 with "four sure fire features with the hottest stars in erotica today."

THE PLAYERS

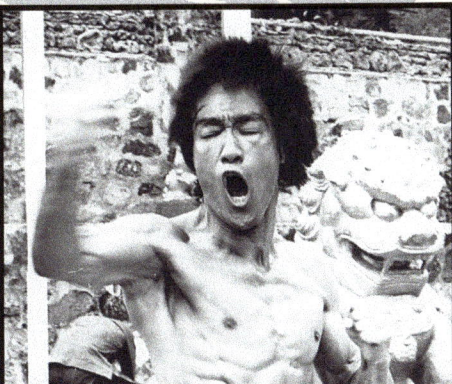

Bruce Lee - played the role of Lee, a martial artist who is recruited by a British intelligence agent to infiltrate an island fortress and take down a drug lord. Bruce Lee was a legendary martial artist and actor, widely considered to be one of the most influential figures in the history of martial arts cinema. Sadly, Lee passed away just weeks before the release of "Enter the Dragon" in 1973 at the age of 32.

John Saxon - played the role of Roper, a gambler who is also recruited to take down the drug lord. Saxon had a long and prolific career in film and television, appearing in over 200 roles throughout his career. He passed away in 2020 at the age of 83.

Jim Kelly - played the role of Williams, a martial artist and friend of Lee's who also joins the mission to take down the drug lord. Kelly had a successful career in martial arts and acting, appearing in several other martial arts films before his death in 2013 at the age of 67.

Robert Wall - played the role of O'Hara, a martial artist and friend of Roper's who also joins the mission. Wall had a successful career in both martial arts and acting, appearing in several other martial arts films throughout the 1970s and 1980s.

Shih Kien - played the role of Han, the villainous drug lord who the team is tasked with taking down. Shih Kien had a long and successful career in film and television, appearing in over 100 roles throughout his career. He passed away in 2009 at the age of 96.

Angela Mao - played the role of Su Lin, a martial artist who helps Lee infiltrate the island fortress. Mao had a successful career in martial arts and acting, appearing in several other martial arts films throughout the 1970s before retiring from acting in the early 1980s.

Betty Chung - played the role of Mei Ling, a woman who works for Han and helps the team infiltrate the island fortress. Chung had a relatively brief acting career, appearing in only a handful of films throughout the 1970s.

Roy Chiao - appeared in "Enter the Dragon" in a small role as a member of Han's security team. Chiao had a long and successful career in film and television, appearing in over 120 roles throughout his career

Geoffrey Weeks - played the role of Braithwaite, the British intelligence agent who recruits Lee and the others for the mission. Weeks had a relatively brief acting career, with "Enter the Dragon" being one of his most notable roles.

Bolo Yeung - played the role of Bolo, one of Han's top henchmen. Yeung had a successful career in martial artsand acting, appearing in many other martial arts films throughout the 1970s and 1980s.

Jackie Chan - Jackie Chan appeared in "Enter the Dragon" as a stuntman, performing several fight scenes and stunts in the film. At the time, Chan was still a relatively unknown actor and stuntman, but his work on "Enter the Dragon" helped to launch his career in the film industry.

Director Robert Clouse - Robert Clouse directed "Enter the Dragon," as well as several other martial arts films throughout his career. He passed away in 1997 at the age of 68.

THE BRUCE LEE COLUMN

THE FIRST BRUCE LEE UK CONVENTIONS
BY MICHAEL NESBITT

Looking back at the history of the Bruce Lee fandom in the UK, it's difficult to believe that the first Bruce Lee conventions only happened in 1979 and 1980, a time in which the Kung Fu boom had well and truly passed its peak. Even though Bruce Lee's stardom was on the decline, the conventions were a major success, and as Kung Fu Monthly's, Felix Dennis, Bruce Sawford and Pam Hadden began preparations for the first Bruce Lee UK convention in 1979, they weren't expecting to be embroiled in a rivalry to see who would dominate the convention scene.

19th May 1979 - 1st Kung Fu Monthly Bruce Lee Convention

The first-ever Bruce Lee UK Convention was to be held on Saturday, 19th May 1979 at the University Union Buildings, Malet Street, London. The Convention was to be held by Kung Fu Monthly in conjunction with The Bruce Lee Society. The doors opened at 10.30am, with it starting at 11.00am with an introduction of the day's events by Capital Radio's Tony Myatt, who was unexpectedly called away on important business, but luckily Rob Byrne was the man to step up and take his place. At 11.15am, there was a martial arts display by Anthony Oii and his team; this was followed up with a tribute to Bruce Lee. During the 12.00-1.00pm lunch break, a recorded Hong Kong interview of Bruce Lee was played. The uncut version of Way of the Dragon was shown on the big screen, with a live nunchaku demonstration straight afterwards, in which an original pair of nunchaku from the movie Fist of Fury was used. A number of short essays and competitions followed, including a question and answer session by Bruce Lee experts, which included, Fan Club President Pam Hadden, Capital Radio's Eddy Pumer, KFMs Bruce Sawford, Cathy Films Roy Byrne and the legendary Will Johnson who also came first in the essay competition. Then for the first time, the unseen Bruce Lee Screen Test was shown. But the best was left for last, a moving tribute by Bruce Lee's friend and student, actor James Coburn, was played to a packed house, there wasn't a dry eye among the fans, with many openly sobbing. The Kung Fu Monthly team expected around 400 fans to turn up, but on the day over 800 people walked through the doors, with many fans being turned away. The very first Bruce Lee UK Convention was a resounding success.

UINVERSITY of LONDON UNION BUILDING
MALET STREET LONDON WC1

19 MAY
10·30am to 5·00pm

ADMITS ONE
Nº

This portion to be retained.

BRITAIN'S FIRST BRUCE LEE CONVENTION 1979

THOUGH THE MASTER IS GONE HE WILL NOT BE FORGOTTEN

A SHORT HISTORY OF
KUNG~FU MONTHLY
AND
THE BRUCE LEE SOCIETY

The K.F.M. Editor-in-chief tells the story of success!

IN COMMEMORATION
The **Bruce Lee Society**
with
Kung-Fu Monthly
presents at the
University of London Union Building

BRITAIN'S FIRST BRUCE LEE CONVENTION 1979

THOUGH THE MASTER IS GONE HE WILL NOT BE FORGOTTEN
KUNG-FU MONTHLY
14 RATHBONE PLACE, LONDON W1P1DE

Delegate's Name

22nd Sept 1979 - 1st SIP Bruce Lee Worldwide Convention and Jamboree

Ashley Simmons had attended the first Bruce Lee Convention put on by Kung Fu Monthly, and was amazed at the turnout. As Ashley was not one for missing out on an opportunity, he decided to put on his own convention, and with the financial help of his father, he did just that on Saturday 22nd, September 1979. Ashley had formed S.I.P. (Simmons International Promotions), with their offices being at 28 Woodstock Road, Finsbury Park, London. The event itself took place at the Central Hall, Westminster, London, with advanced tickets only being £5 or £6.50 on the door. At the time Simmons didn't know that he wasn't able to show uncensored Bruce Lee movies which hadn't been passed by the film censors for viewing by the general public, and so to get around this problem, he used the Soho triple XXX loophole by screening them for "club members" only. This is the reason you got a blue membership card along with your yellow ticket for the convention. The blue card was a Bruce Lee Fan Club Membership Card, and thus Simmons was able to show the uncut movies to club members. But the highlight of the event was the special guests, which included the founder of the World of Bruce Lee Museum Norman Bourne, and Bruce Lee student, and star of Game of Death, Dan Inosanto, who was brought over from America specially to do a demonstration for the convention. Considering that Game of Death had been released just the year previous, this was a major achievement that guaranteed the success of the convention.

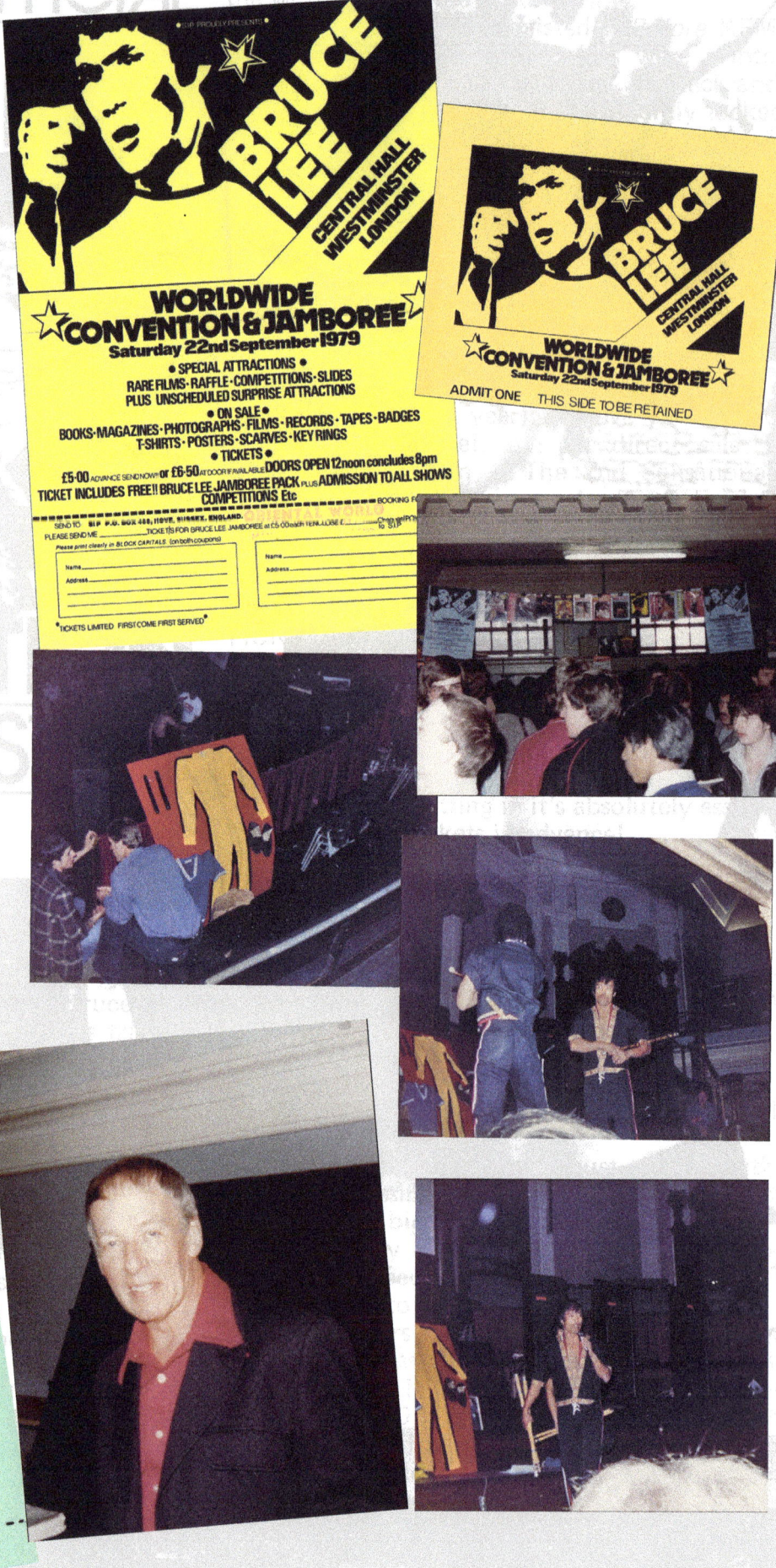

1st Dec 1979 – 1st Kung Fu Monthly Film Festival

The first-ever Bruce Lee Film Festival was put on jointly by Kung Fu Monthly and The Bruce Lee Society and was held on Saturday, 1st of December 1979 at the Gaumont State Theatre, Kilburn High Road, London. The head of the Kung Fu Monthly team, Felix Dennis, and the President of the Bruce Lee Society, Pam Hadden were in attendance to greet fans. The Film Festival started with an introduction from Capital Radios Eddy Pumer, who also played a special message to the fans from Bruce Lee's brother Robert Lee. Then there would be a showing of three Bruce Lee movies, The Big Boss, Fist of Fury and the Way of the Dragon. All were the original uncut Chinese 35mm prints with English subtitles. There was a 10-minute clip of one of Bruce Lee's early childhood movies shown, "My Son Ah Cheung", and a couple of stalls set-up that sold rare Bruce Lee memorabilia. But the highlight for many fans was a rare sound recording of Bruce Lee's own voice in both Cantonese and English, which had never been heard before. The Film Festival was an even bigger success than KFMs first convention, with over 1700 people showing up on the day.

14th June 1980 - 2nd SIP Bruce Lee Worldwide Convention

To say that the Kung Fu Monthly team weren't happy that Ashley Simmons had tried to muscle in on their territory was an understatement, and with many threats being passed back and forth, things got a little heated between the two parties. This didn't distract Ashley one bit; in fact, it spurred him on to put on an even bigger Convention than the first. He planned to wait until the Kung Fu Monthly team announced the date of their second Convention, and he would undercut them by putting his on a month before theirs, an underhanded trick, yes, but a successful one. The second Bruce Lee Worldwide Convention was held on Saturday, 14th June 1980, at the Central Hall, Westminster, London. The event began with a wonderful slideshow from Norman Bourne, showing photographs of his Bruce Lee Museum in California. Then two very special guests were brought up on stage, Bruce Lee's mother, Grace Lee, and his brother, Robert Lee. Robert even performed a song live on stage for all the guests, and for the first time in the UK, signed copies of his album, The Ballard of Bruce Lee, was available to buy from the memorabilia stalls in the foyer. The highlight of the event was a wonderful

demonstration of Nunchaku and Escrima Sticks put on by Bruce Lee's student and star of Game of Death Dan Inosanto. The second S.I.P. Convention was an even bigger success than the first one, but the underhanded tactics by Simmons and Co, left a sour taste in the mouths of many fans, including the Kung Fu Monthly team.

19th July 1980 - 2nd Kung Fu Monthly Bruce Lee Convention and Film Festival

Trying to fight off the success of SIP holding their Bruce Lee Convention before them, the KFM team decided to hold the convention and film festival together, hoping that it would generate more ticket sales. Advertised as being the only Official event recognised by the London offices of Golden Harvest, the convention took place on Saturday, July 19th, 1980 at the Gaumont State Theatre, Kilburn High Road, London. Guests who entered the theatre were greeted by a 12-foot by 8-foot blown-up image of Bruce, which took three hours to be put together. The day's proceedings kicked off by Eddy Pumer showing a slideshow of rare photographs of Bruce Lee from birth to death, with commentary from Capital Radio's Tony Myatt. Up next was an attempt by martial artist Ted Pollard to reconstruct the Chuck Norris/Bruce Lee fight from Way of the Dragon, followed by a special audio message from Chuck Norris played to the fans. The guests then got to watch Bruce Lee's childhood movie "My Son Ah Cheung". There was a Bruce Lee lookalike competition that took place and bundles of rare memorabilia were for sale at the Kung Fu Monthly stall. Then came the main event of the day, Robert Lee took to the stage for an interview conducted by Tony Myatt. Three 16mm films were shown throughout the day; the first being the short Enter the Dragon documentary, On-Location Hong Kong; then, The Bruce Lee Screen Test, and finally the new Game of Death 2 trailer. And to top it off, an uncut 35mm print of Game of Death was played to the appreciation of the crowd. To celebrate the convention, the Kung Fu Monthly team decided to release a 500 numbered copy reprint of the rare black and white Kung Fu Monthly Trade Dummy that was never released to the general public. Originally Felix Dennis had only made three copies of the trade dummy issue to send to prospective publishers in the hope they would publish the magazine. Even though the turnout wasn't as good as the previous conventions, the Convention was still considered a hit with the fans.

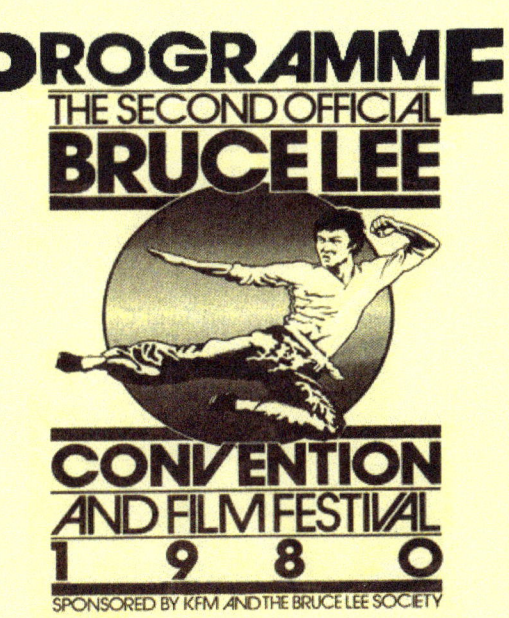

22nd August 1981 - 3rd Kung Fu Monthly Bruce Lee Convention

The third Bruce Lee Convention to be held by Kung Fu Monthly was to have taken place at the Rainbow Theatre, Finsbury Park, London. A full-page advert for the convention appeared in issue 61 of Kung Fu Monthly and teased Nunchaku and lookalike competitions, incredible Bruce Lee memorabilia, and Bruce Lee footage on the big screen. There was also going to be an auction to raise funds for a Bruce Lee Bust on behalf of the Bruce Lee Society Fan Club. However, fans started voicing their concerns about the convention to the President of the Bruce Lee Society Fan Club Pam Hadden, asking if the convention was going to take place, as many had bought tickets for the event, but had not heard anything back from Kung Fu Monthly. Being quite concerned, Pam made enquiries at the Kung Fu Monthly Head Office, only to be told that the convention was not going to take place. Incensed at the unprofessionalism of the Kung Fu Monthly team, and knowing that some fans were travelling from different countries for the event, and had already booked their flights and accommodation, Pam took it upon herself to contact each member of the fan club to let them know that the convention had been cancelled. This put a lot of pressure on Pam, who was ill at the time. The whole situation caused a lot of animosity between Pam's fan club, and Kung Fu Monthly that would unfortunately never heal.

All the Bruce Lee Conventions that took place in 1979 and 1980 were considered a success, even with the steady decline of Bruce Lee's popularity at the time. However, because of the lack of new Bruce Lee material being released, fans looked elsewhere for a new martial arts hero to follow, and they would soon find it with Asians new action hero, Jackie Chan. Even though Bruce Lee still had a large following of diehard fans, it wouldn't be until the late 1980s early 1990s that Bruce Lee Conventions and Film Festivals in the UK would once again take place, mainly thanks in part to The Bruce Lee Association and Chris Alexis' Tracking the Dragon Conventions.

(The 1980 KFM Convention Photos are ©Tony Lundberg. Special thanks go out to Tony for letting us use them in this article. All other Convention photos ©Michael Nesbitt.)

The Official Kung-Fu Monthly

BRUCE LEE SOCIETY

(Affiliated to America's World of Bruce Lee organisation)
Hon members: Grace Lee, Robert Lee, Danny Inosanto, Norman Borine, Eddy Leahy, Eddy Pumer

World President... Pam Hadden   Membership No.

Saturday,
8th August, 1981.

Dear

Yesterday (Friday 7th August) during a telephone call I made to Kung Fu Monthly to check when they would be sending out Convention tickets, I was informed that the Bruce Lee Convention scheduled for 22nd August was cancelled by them.

To say I was shocked is to put it mildly - no-one had discussed a possible cancellation with me nor given me to believe that this would be likely to happen. Indeed, K.F.M. had not been in contact with me about the format of the Convention for many weeks.

As you will know, I have nothing whatsoever to do with the sending out of tickets for the Convention, nor do I receive the money for this, and as a consequence therefore am unable to contact those people who have written in for tickets to K.F.M., other than yourself who I know (through your letters to me) will be attending - and I felt it my duty to write to you as soon as I possibly could to let you know what had happened. I would appreciate if you could contact anyone who was to travel with you to the Convention or that you know was going to attend, if you are able, to tell them what has happened.

I am contacting K.F.M. on Monday to request that they make some sort of announcement informing people of their cancellation, which is their responsibility.

My very sincerest apologies for any inconvenience caused to you - but I can assure you it was not of my doing and I knew NOTHING of this until yesterday; even some Members, on ringing K.F.M. about their tickets, knew of the cancellation four days before myself, yet I had not been contacted by K.F.M.

If you have any queries on the matter, please contact Felix Dennis who owns Bunch Books - the producers of K.F.M. magazine - at 14, Rathbone Place, or alternatively, telephone him on (London) 01- 631 1433.

Pam - PRESIDENT.
BRUCE LEE SOCIETY.

C/O 14, Rathbone Place, London W1P 1DE, England.

BOOK NOW FOR THE MARTIAL ARTS EVENT OF THE 1981!

THE 3RD OFFICIAL BRUCE LEE CONVENTION

HELD THIS YEAR AT THE RAINBOW THEATRE, FINSBURY PARK, LONDON
SATURDAY AUGUST 22ND

Stars, celebrities, rare films, competitions and, on sale, all sorts of valuable collector material — books, magazines, records, videos, and much, much more.

And special for this year, outstanding British martial artist and total devotee of Bruce the Master, Ted Pollard, will be demonstrating live on stage a typical Bruce Lee training session. He also promises to put on a full-on, JKD-style fight — which won't be scripted or rehearsed in any way!

PLUS — Enter our nunchaku competition (see rules below).
PLUS — A re-run of last years lookalike contest!
PLUS — an incredible display of genuine Bruce Lee memorabilia.
PLUS — the great Bruce Lee Auction (all funds raised to go towards the commissioning of a memorial Bruce Lee Bust for the Society).
PLUS, PLUS, PLUS. . . far more to be confirmed soon.

Meanwhile, don't get beaten by the "SOLD OUT" sign — BOOK NOW!!! The prices are as follows:

SINGLE TICKET (PRE-BOOKED BY SOCIETY MEMBER)	£7.00
SINGLE TICKET (PRE-BOOKED BY ANYONE ELSE)	£7.50
SINGLE TICKET (ON THE DOOR, IF AVAILABLE)	£9.00

And special offer for a short time only!!!

PACK OF 5 TICKETS (PRE BOOKED BY SOCIETY MEMBER)	£30.00
PACK OF 5 TICKETS (PRE-BOOKED BY ANYONE ELSE)	£32.50

Please send cheques/postal orders (made to KFM, please) to:
Convention Tickets, Kung-Fu Monthly, 14 Rathbone Place, London W1P 1DE.

Rules for the Nunchaku Competition

1. All entrants must be adept in the handling of nunchakus — the judges will have the right to stop any routine at any time and retire the competitor.
2. Each routine shall last between 20 and 30 seconds.
3. A nunchaku shall not be held in one hand for any longer than three seconds.
4. The judges will be looking for style, presentation and originality in their scoring.

Warning: Please remember that nunchakus, in the wrong hands, can be lethal to both the user, and those around him/her. If you are a novice, contact the martial arts clubs in your area for advice on proper instruction. Also, nunchakus are classified as a dangerous weapon. . . they should not be held — or carried openly — in any public place.

Entires for this event should be addressed to:

Convention Nunchaku Competition, Kung-Fu Monthly, 14 Rathbone Place, London W1P 1DE.
Please remember to give your name, address, age and a brief description of the experience you have of using nunchakus.

Mike Nesbitt's Memorabilia

USA PROMO COMIC

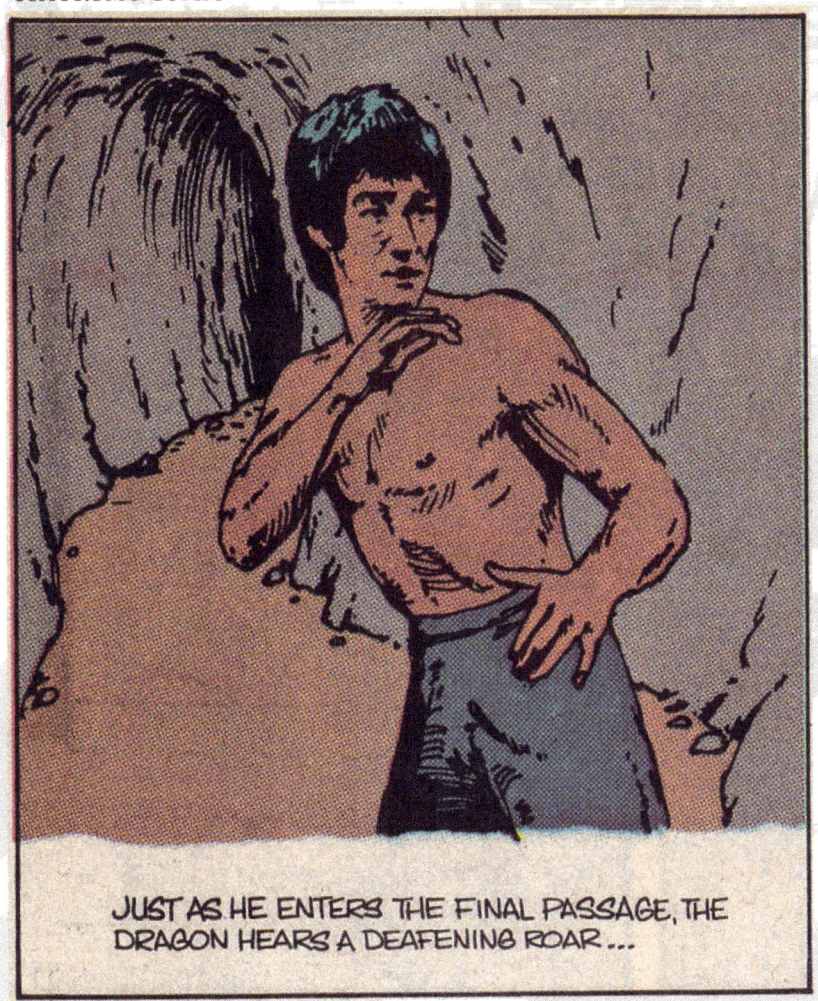

JUST AS HE ENTERS THE FINAL PASSAGE, THE DRAGON HEARS A DEAFENING ROAR...

CAN THE DRAGON AND HIS ALLIES RESCUE THE SISTER OF THE EVIL HAN'S MOST MERCILESS ENEMY IN TIME TO RESCUE THEM FROM A FATE WORSE THAN DEATH? SEE: ENTER THE DRAGON, THE ULTIMATE IN MARTIAL ARTS EXCITEMENT AND ADVENTURE, AND SEE FOR YOURSELF!

ON A MYSTERIOUS ISLAND FORTRESS IN THE SOUTH CHINA SEA, THE CRUEL HAN REIGNS OVER AN EMPIRE OF CRIME AND CORRUPTION. HE MUST BE STOPPED.

HAVING DEFEATED ALL OPPONENTS, THE DRAGON, THE MASTER OF MARTIAL ARTS, IS THE CHOSEN ONE TO INFILTRATE HAN'S HIDEOUT AS AN UNDERCOVER AGENT.

AFTER THE DRAGON AGREES TO UNDERTAKE THE DANGEROUS MISSION TO HAN'S DEADLY ISLAND, BRAITHWAITE TELLS HIM OF HAN'S VAST HEROIN PROCESSING OPERATION, THE INTERNATIONAL PROSTITUTION TRADE, AND HIS BRUTAL BODYGUARD, OHARRA.

THE DRAGON LEARNS THAT ON A TRIP TO HONG KONG, OHARRA HAD ATTACKED THE DRAGON'S SISTER, SU-LIN.

ALTHOUGH SU-LIN, A BLACK BELT KARATE EXPERT, FOUGHT WELL AGAINST HER ATTACKERS, SHE COMMITTED SUICIDE WHEN OHARRA SUBDUED HER. THE DRAGON LOOKS FORWARD TO AVENGING HER DEATH.

WHEN THEY ARRIVE ON HAN'S MYSTERIOUS ISLAND TO PARTICIPATE IN A MARTIAL ARTS TOURNAMENT, THE DRAGON AND HIS ALLIES, WILLIAMS AND ROPER, GET READY FOR THE TOUGH TASK OF EXPOSING THE CRIME LORD'S CORRUPT BUSINESS.

AFTER BEING SHOWN TO LUXURIOUS QUARTERS BY THE LOVELY TANIA, WILLIAMS SHOWS HIS SKILL BY BEATING PARSONS, THE AUSTRALIAN CONTESTANT.

JAPANESE CINEMA TICKETS

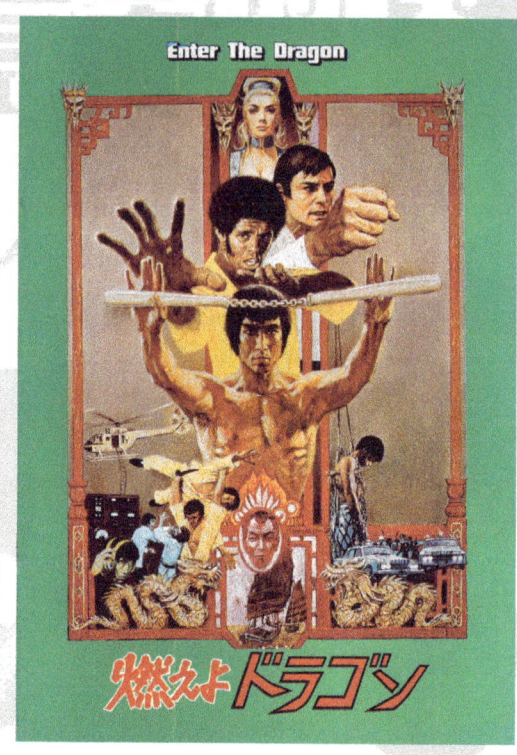

Enter The Dragon COMPETITION
500 PRIZES of oriental spice
toiletries for men
MUST BE WON!
in this FREE competition

100 FIRST PRIZES WORTH OVER £5 EACH

After Shave & Shower   After Shave & Shower & Dragon's Soap   Anti-Perspirant   Man Talc

HOW TO ENTER...

The Dragon on the left is the real and only 'Oriental Spice' Dragon. All the smaller dragons below contain one fault (see above). To win one of these super prizes mark a cross on the drawing you think matches the dragon at the top. Fill in your name and address and most important, finish the "limerick" at the bottom of the coupon — cut out and send to: "Enter The Dragon" Competition, Colorama Warner Distributors, 135 Wardour Street, London, W.1. If you don't want to damage the page behind, write all the details on a post-card with the number of the correct dragon, your name and address, and of course the completed Limerick. HAPPY DRAGON HUNTING!

150 SECOND PRIZES WORTH OVER £3 EACH

After Shave & Shower & Dragon's Soap

250 THIRD PRIZES WORTH OVER £2 EACH

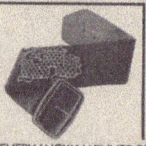  

After Shave & Shower Dragon's Head

EVERY LUCKY WINNER RECEIVES A FREE 'ORIENTAL SPICE' WRIST BAND

NAME ....
ADDRESS ....
....
TEL. NO ....

COMPLETE THE LAST LINE OF THIS LIMERICK
A film that you all must see Starring the fabulous Bruce Lee Who 'Oriental Spice' used If you want to real nice ....

RULES

The Dragon

'Enter The Dragon'
...Is Super Entertainment
First American Produced Martial Arts Spectacular
Bruce Lee Stars

Warner Bros. martial arts super-entertainment ENTER THE DRAGON, the first really big scale action to feature Karate and Kung-fu and filmed in America and Hong Kong, is to be screened in practically every cinema throughout the country starting early January.

The Picture has already scored fantastic box-office results in America, where it instantly topped the popularity of all other Karate movies. Many theatres have broken long-existing box-office records. In America and everywhere.

The Ancient Martial Arts Come to Life in 'Enter The Dragon'

In 'Enter The Dragon', Warner Bros.' international martial arts adventure film, three great actor-martial artists perform astonishing feats of strength and dexterity.

The three, Bruce Lee, who was Asia's top martial arts film star, John Saxon, American television and film star and karate expert; and Jim Kelly, 1971 International Middleweight Karate Champion, practice some of the variations of the ancient oriental arts of fighting self-defense. These are ancient disciplines which today are being practised by hundreds of thousands of Americans.

The martial arts developed over many centuries from several variation of Chinese boxing. Known under the general name 'Kung fu', Chinese boxing is probably the world's oldest sport, after boxing. It is certainly the world's oldest formal system of self-defense. The earliest references to it date from the fourteenth century before Christ.

During the ensuing centuries numerous variations of martial arts developed in the Orient. Different countries became identified with different styles: Chinese boxing (or Kung-fu); Korean (Tai Kwan Do); Japanese (Karate). The sudden surge of interest in these arts has confronted many Americans with an array of unfamiliar terms. This glossary is designed to clarify some of them.

KARATE, a highly respected discipline in Japan, means "empty hands". It is a style of fighting considered by practitioners to be an art form. Karate mainly involves the use of the hands, legs being used primarily for tripping. Participants are expected to hang up their honor.

JUDO, a sport derived from JU-JITSU. In Judo, everything goes - kicks, arm, jaws - but that is now. The rules of Judo, a highly respected sport in all of Asia, discourage major strikes. In Judo, submission is relegated to the category of back alley fighting.

TAI CHI CHUAN, is the Korean form of Karate which uses dynamic kicks even more than hand-jabs.

KENDO, a sport which finds its roots in the ancient techniques of Samurai sword-fighting. In Kendo the participants use bamboo sticks instead of swords and fight with means and padding to match the same way that fencers do.

NAPKIDO, a form of Karate which calls for grappling and choking. It was used in the Warner Bros. feature, 'Billy Jack'.

BRUCE LEE - The legendary Kung-fu star, delivers his opponent a devastating blow in a scene from the exciting 'Enter The Dragon'.

'Enter The Dragon' is a must

TWO leading American movie-makers, China's most popular action star and a popular American film and television star have come together in Hong Kong, bringing a fresh look to those roaring successful films about the martial arts.

The American producers are Fred Weintraub and Paul M. Heller. The stars are Bruce Lee and John Saxon. The explosive power of today's martial arts is 'Enter The Dragon'. Warner Bros. Pan-vision release which stars Lee and John Saxon and introduces Jim Kelly, and which will be released all over the country early in January.

The martial arts of Asia are man-ly sort of a field of combat. They form a giant society in which many different styles co-exist. They include Karate, Hapkido, Kung-Fu and Judo.

Recently, serious dramas tied to the martial arts have become enormously popular around the world. 'Enter The Dragon' marks the first time that a major American film company has come to Hong Kong, birthplace of martial arts movies, to make an international martial arts film. The bouts are engaged by prominent Westerners and Asian stars who stars of the United States, Europe and Orient.

JOHN SAXON - stars in this international adventure.

JIM KELLY American Karate champion

Jim Kelly, a handsome young black youth whose chief profession up to now has been karate fighter and teacher, co-starring with Bruce Lee in 'Enter The Dragon' will be publicly shaped as the typical Shakespearan Theater. As a complete progression of engagement coincided with casting of the screening of the mother Prince T.V. and Radio, in addition to several jet plane creatures of the martial arts.

Martial Arts Expert

With the intention of making the launch of 'Enter The Dragon' one of the most exciting movie panels, Warner Bros. has secured the services of one of the world's top martial arts practitioners. J. H. Barry, who has recently staged fights for the typical Shakespearan Theater. As a complete progression of engagement coincided with casting of the screening of the mother Prince T.V. and Radio, in addition to several jet plane creatures of the martial arts.

STOP PRESS!

JIM KELLY - lands a fight-finishing blow in this scene from 'Enter The Dragon'.

燃えよドラゴン

Enter The Dragon

■解説

映画史上最強のアクション・スター、ブルース・リーが、世界の映画界に驚異のデビューを飾った彼自身の最高傑作である。しかも彼の主演作5本(未完成フィルムを含む)の中で唯一のアメリカ映画。この映画を見ずしてブルース・リーは語れない。

ご承知のように日本では、彼の最後の作品となるこの「燃えよドラゴン」が一番最初に公開されて、史上空前の大ヒットを記録し、当時無名だったブルース・リーが一躍世界のトップ・スターとなり、強烈なそのイメージで、50年代のジェームス・ディーンに匹敵する70年代の永遠のスターとなった。

また、ブルース・リーをはじめ世界的にその名を知られる大スターとなったのはこの「燃えよドラゴン」によってだが、悲運にも彼は全世界に先駆けるアメリカでの公開の一月前、7月20日、その爆発的な大ヒットを知らずに、この世を去っている。それまでのブルース・リー同様、永遠に色あせることのない新鮮さを保ち、何度見ても満足できるものとなっている。

共演は「許されざる者」「シノーラ」のジョン・サクソン。そして「黒帯ドラゴン」のジム・ケリー、「女必殺拳」のアンジェラ・マオ・イン等が見事なアクションでもりあげている。製作はフレッド・ワイントロープとポール・ヘラーの名コンビ。監督は巨匠ロバート・クローズ。「ブリット」「ダーティハリー」などの名匠ラロ・シフリンの音楽も爆発的ヒットを記録した傑作である。

(上映時間——1時間40分)

〈スタッフ〉

- 監督……ロバート・クローズ
- 脚本……マイケル・オーリン
- 音楽……ラロ・シフリン

〈キャスト〉

- リー……ブルース・リー
- ローパー……ジョン・サクソン
- タニア……アーナ・カプリ
- ウィリアムス……ジム・ケリー
- オハラ……ボブ・ウォール
- ハン……シー・キエン
- スー・リン……アンジェラ・マオ・イン

■ストーリー

少林寺拳法の達人リー(ブルース・リー)は、ホンコンの郊外で国際情報機構のブレイスウェイト(ジェフリー・ウィークス)に会い、その要請で、ある孤島で、リーの兄弟子ハン(シー・キエン)が催す、命がけの武術試合に参加する事になった。少林寺道場を破門されたハンは、いまは、多くの武道の達人たちを手下にして、麻薬と売春のボスになっていた。孤島がその本拠である。リーの使命はそこで情報を収集する事にあった。

三年前、リーの妹スー・リン(アンジェラ・マオ・イン)は、ハンの一味オハラ(ボブ・ウォール)とその手下に襲われた。スー・リンも合気道の達人だったが、ついに逃げ場を失い、自殺した。ハンの武術大会には、外国から、ローパー(ジョン・サクソン)、ウイリアムス(ジム・ケリー)、などの達人たちが参加した。

一同は島の女主人タニア(アーナ・カプリ)の出迎えを受け、ハンの宴会に招かれた。リーの味方である情報員のメイ・リン(ベティ・チュン)という美女も、すでにその島に潜入していた。

その晚、何も知らずに、ウイリアムスが散歩に出たのをしりリーは島の中を探り、地下の洞窟にある巨大なアヘン工場を発見した。そこには大勢の捕虜が監禁されていた。

翌日の試合で、ハンの用心棒ボロ(ヤン・スエ)は、四人の守衛を次々に殺した。地下工場に潜入したスパイがした罰である。

続いてリーとオハラの試合。白人のオハラもカラテの達人だったが、妹の仇への復讐に燃えるリーに、あえなく殺されてしまった。怒ったハンは、自分で彼に試合をいどみ、ウイリアムスをスパイだと思い込んだハンは、鋼鉄の義手でなぐり殺した。その晚、またも地下工場に潜入したリーは無線でブレイスウェイトに、すべてを報告したが、その直後に捕えられた。

翌日の試合で、ローパーは仲間に入るのを断った上え、心棒ボロを殺した。怒ったハンは、リーとローパーを殺せと全員に命じたが、ローパーはリーと協力して次々に襲いかかる男たちをなぎ倒していった。しかもメイ・リンが解放した捕虜たちも加わって、試合場は大乱闘となった。鏡の中の迷路に逃げこんだハンとリーの秘術を尽くした決闘が続いた——息づまる緊張と手に汗にぎる激闘の末、ついにハンは倒された。

[燃えよドラゴン] 復活宣言！

凄い！強い！カッコいい！究極の衝撃！眩暈のような鮮烈！熱狂的興奮！怒涛の感動！格闘技映画のバイブル！アクション映画の金字塔！…。もちろん、いかなる賛辞も、どんな感嘆も、この映画の圧倒的な魅力を表現し尽くすことなど出来ない。これは、**ブルース・リー映画の最高峰**というだけでなく、間違いなく**映画百年の歴史上最も重要な作品**の1本であると同時に、単なる映画などでもなく、文武や宗教、哲学に至るまで、人間の叡智と可能性のすべてを包括する、**世界の、いや、宇宙の中心そのもの**なのである。ついにスクリーンに蘇るこの映画を見ることは、いまを生きる人間の**義務であり使命**である。とにかく、劇場に駆け付けよ！そして、**考えるな、感じるんだ！**奇跡と真実がそこにあるハズだ。

―――― 江戸木 純（映画評論家）

- お帰りなさいブルース・リー先生。「燃えよドラゴン」は永遠に不滅です。―――― 関根 勤（タレント）
- お手製のヌンチャクを頭にブチ当てて流れ出る涙をものともせず、キメのポーズをとってオタケビを上げた少年の日の僕が、また蘇る。―――― 永瀬正敏（役者）
- ブルース・リー映画ではやっぱりダントツの面白さでしょう。ヘア・スタイル、イカしてます。人間じゃない、ウルトラマンとかそういう、架空ものの、ほんとのヒーローですな。―――― ウルフルズ・トータス松本（ミュージシャン）
- 何度見てもこの映画だけは目玉が飛び出してしまいます！カッコ良過ぎ!!―――― みうらじゅん（イラストレーターなど）
- 「考えるな、感じるんだ！」この言葉は今も僕の座右の銘だ！―――― 田口トモロヲ（俳優・ブロンソンズ）
- 「燃えよドラゴン」は熱き魂の教科書。いかに予算をかけたアクション映画も、この映画の魂にはかなわない!!―――― 浜岡賢次（漫画家）
- ヒーローが復活するのは当然です。―――― ロンドンブーツ1号2号・田村 亮（お笑いタレント）
- 映画史上、最も「ファンカデリック（This is FUNKADELIC!!!）」な映画。―――― 北村信彦（HYSTERIC GLAMOUR）
- ブルース・リーは全ての男の憧れだ。僕らも中2の時ヌンチャクを作った。―――― ハロルド作石（漫画家）
- ブルース・リーの華麗な脚蹴りは横長のスコープ大画面いっぱいに躍動する。ぜひ映画館で見て欲しい。―――― 日野康一（映画評論家）
- この映画を観る前と観た後では確実に何かが変わる。―――― スチャダラパー・アニ（ラッパー）
- 「燃えよドラゴン」は、究極の武道家リー先生の魂の映画である！―――― 中村頼永（ジークンドー日本代表者）
- 昔、俺の村にはブルース・リーが10人いた。…今では俺1人になった。―――― 江頭2：50（お笑い芸人）
- 僕は今でも「彼ならどうするか」を考えて常に行動している。―――― コンタキンテ（お笑い芸人）
- ブルース・リーの考え方は驚くほど今日のラップ アーティストに似ている。彼は、才能とポリシーを持った、単なる俳優を超えた存在だった。彼はアーティストだったのだ。―――― ビースティ・ボーイズ（ラップ・グループ）グランド・ロイヤル・マガジンより
- 「燃えよドラゴン」は聖典…いや映画自体がもはや「神」の領域にある。―――― 大槻ケンヂ（ミュージシャン）
- 敵を殺す瞬間のブルース・リーの目つき。もう一回大きいスクリーンで見たいです。―――― 蔡 瀾（ゴールデン・ハーベスト副総裁・製作総指揮）
- ついにあの男が帰って来る！そう思うだけで全身の血が白熱する！―――― 梶 研吾（劇画作家）
- 彼（リー）の凄さは言葉では説明できない。「考えるな！感じるんだ！」そうです「考えるな！観るんだ！」なのです。―――― 唐沢寿明（俳優）

- 格闘技映画に関して、優れた批評家である日本の方々に、ブルースの作品が高く評価されることは、非常に光栄なことです。彼は、卓越した格闘家であり、才能豊かなフィルムメーカーであり、また人生における哲学者でもある、超人的なひとでした。ブルースを愛してくれて本当に有難う。―――― リンダ・リー・キャドウェル（ブルース・リー夫人）

（敬称略・順不同）

1973年／アメリカ映画／シネマスコープ／カラー／上映時間：1時間40分／サントラ盤CD：WEAジャパン／提供：ワーナー・ブラザース映画／配給：日本ヘラルド映画

8/2(土)より〈復活〉ロードショー！　シネセゾン渋谷

■特別鑑賞券1500円・絶賛発売中
特製オリジナル・ポスター付（劇場窓口のみ）

渋谷道玄坂ザ・プライム6F　TEL☎03(3770)1721
10:20　12:30　2:40　4:50　7:00
※10:20の回は8月中の連日および土・日・祝のみ上映

「超人ブルース・リー伝説展」
- 会期／8月22日(金)〜9月上旬
- 会場／吉祥寺パルコ 7F 特設会場
- お問いあわせ　吉祥寺パルコ代表 0422(21)8111　入場料：400円

THE FIRST AMERICAN PRODUCED MARTIAL ARTS SPECTACULAR!
WITH THE LEGENDARY BRUCE LEE

Enter The Dragon

USA PRESS BOOK

PRESSBOOK
INTERNATIONAL EDITION

From Warner Bros
A Warner Communications Company

 Celebrating Warner Bros. 50th Anniversary

COLUMBIA-FILM
WERBERATSCHLAG

06SP 43
ニュー・パーシー・フェイスの不滅の名演
NEW GOLD DISC
燃えよドラゴン
ENTER THE DRAGON
ツァラトゥストラはかく語りき
(2001年宇宙の旅)
2001 (Also Sprach Zarathustra)
パーシー・フェイス・オーケストラ
PERCY FAITH AND HIS ORCHESTRA
CBS SONY
¥600
06SP 43
A

ベリー・ベスト映画音楽シリーズ 20
本命盤
燃えよドラゴン ドラゴン怒りの鉄拳のテーマ
FMS-1020
STEREO
¥600
ロベール・ベルナール・オーケストラ

★7周忌追悼記念企画★
怪鳥音入り!
ブルース・リー自身が語った
「私の武道哲学」
MY WAY OF KUNG-FU
by BRUCE LEE

ドラゴン・パワー(ブルース・リーに捧ぐ)
演奏/ブルース・リーとJKDバンド
SATRIL
ブルース・リーの肉声入り
燃えよドラゴンより

DRAGON POWER
A Tribute To Bruce Lee
special limited edition
JKD BAND
featuring the voice of Bruce Lee

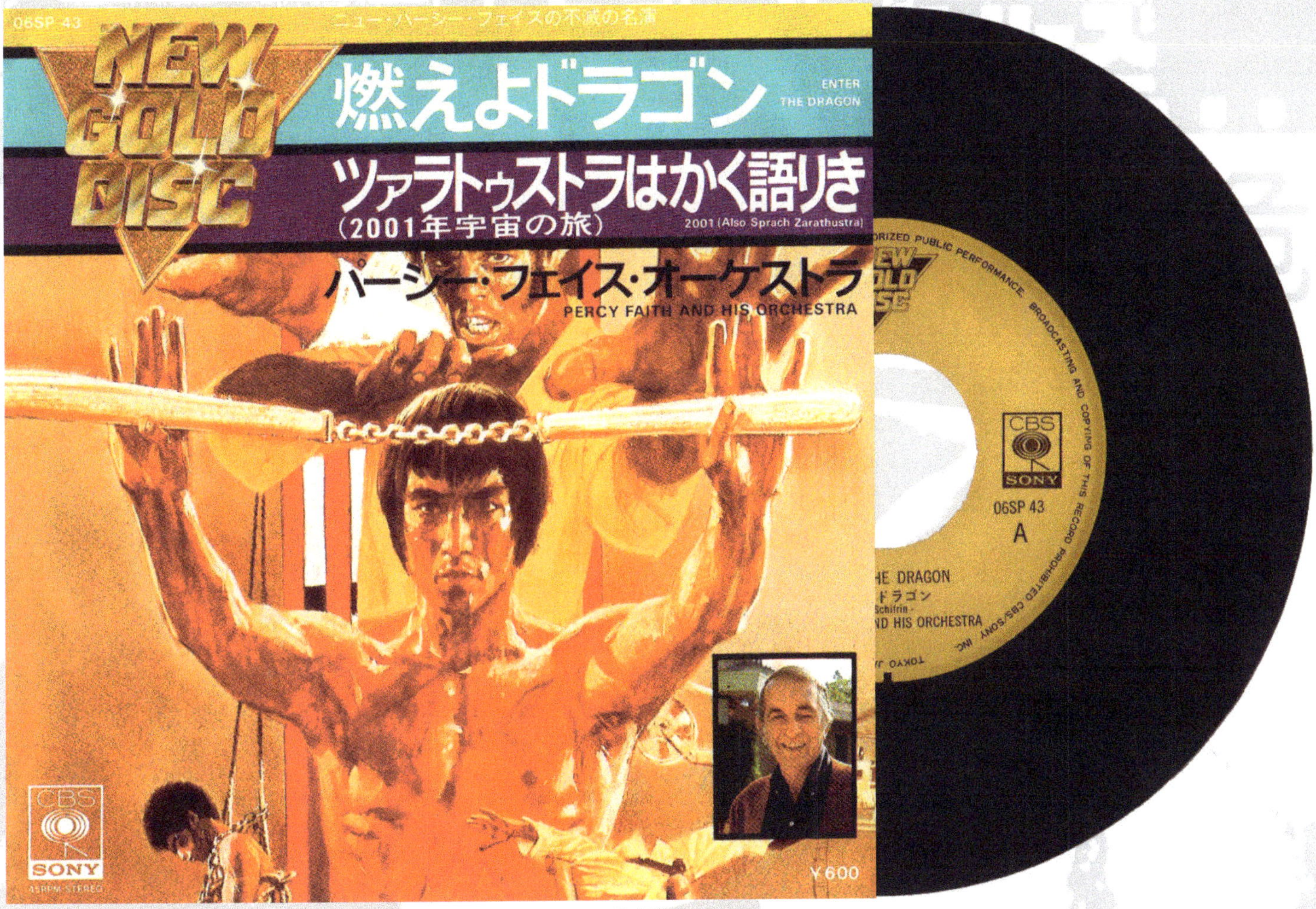

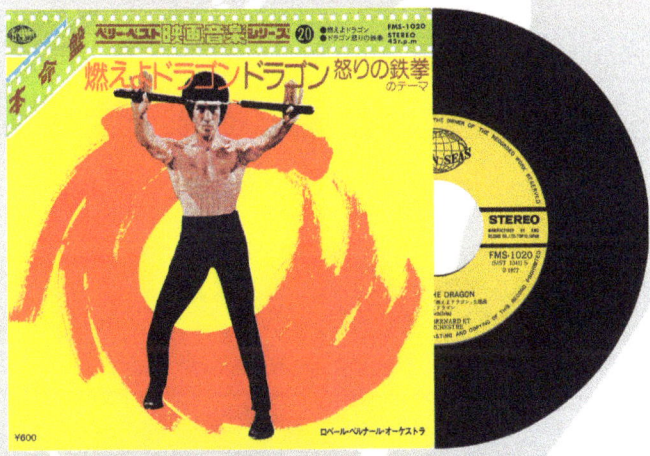

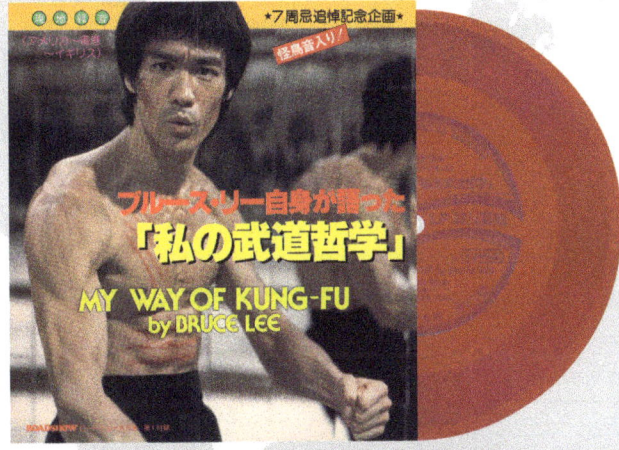

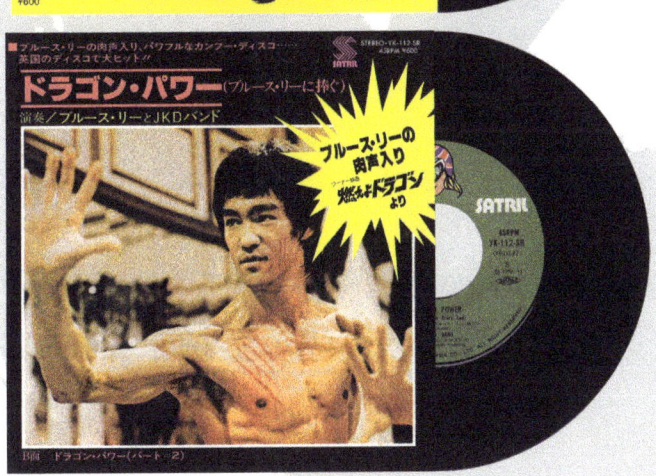

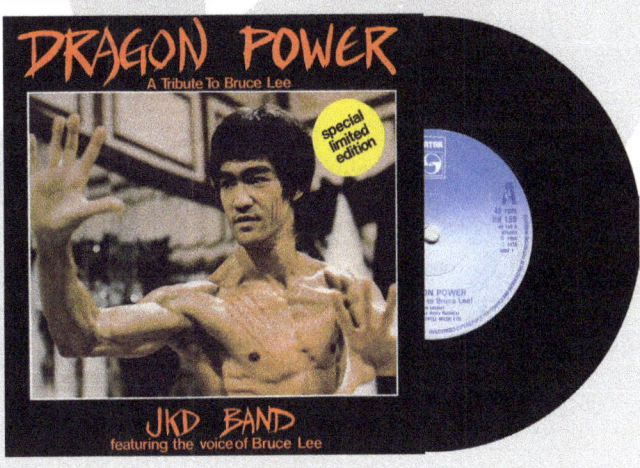

ACTION MOVIE THEMES
LPs

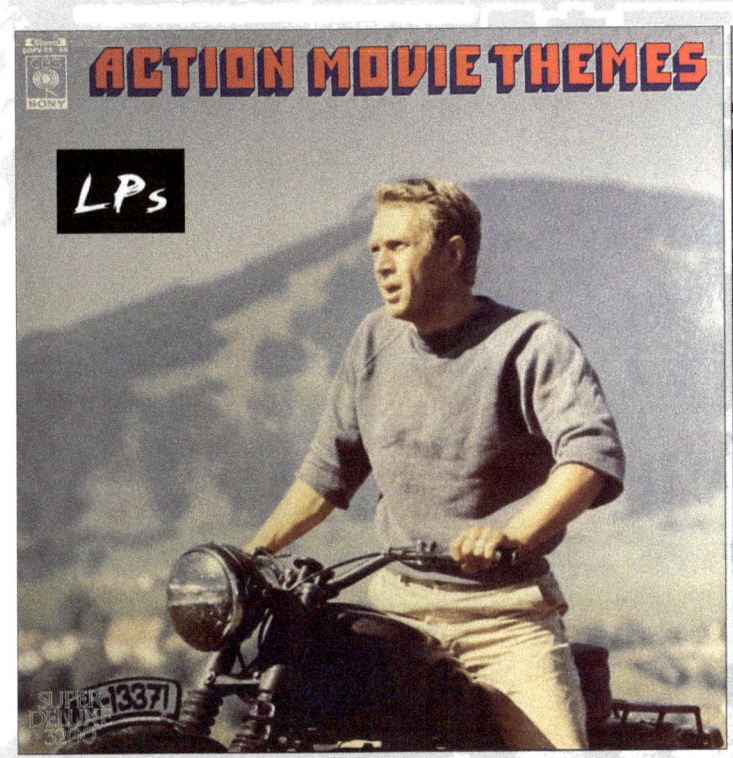

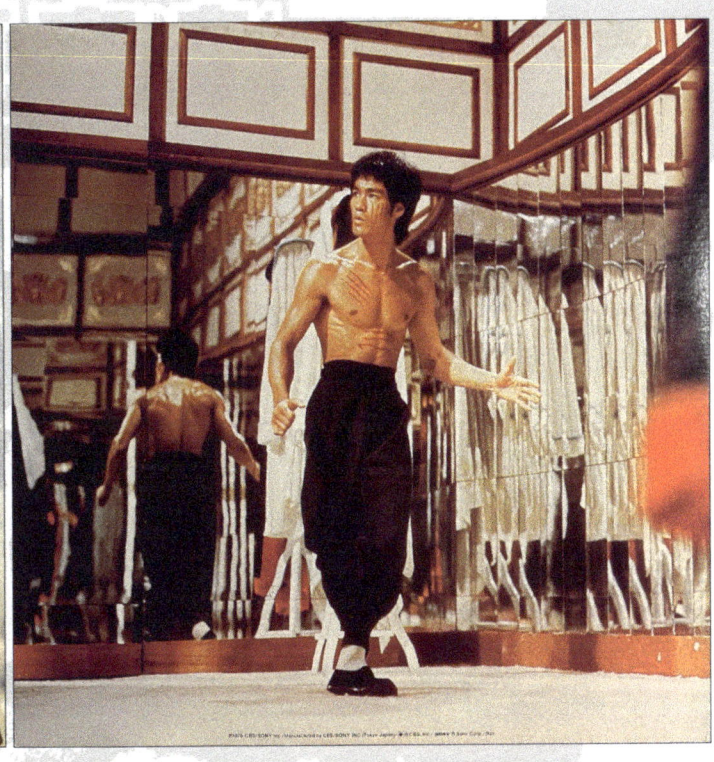

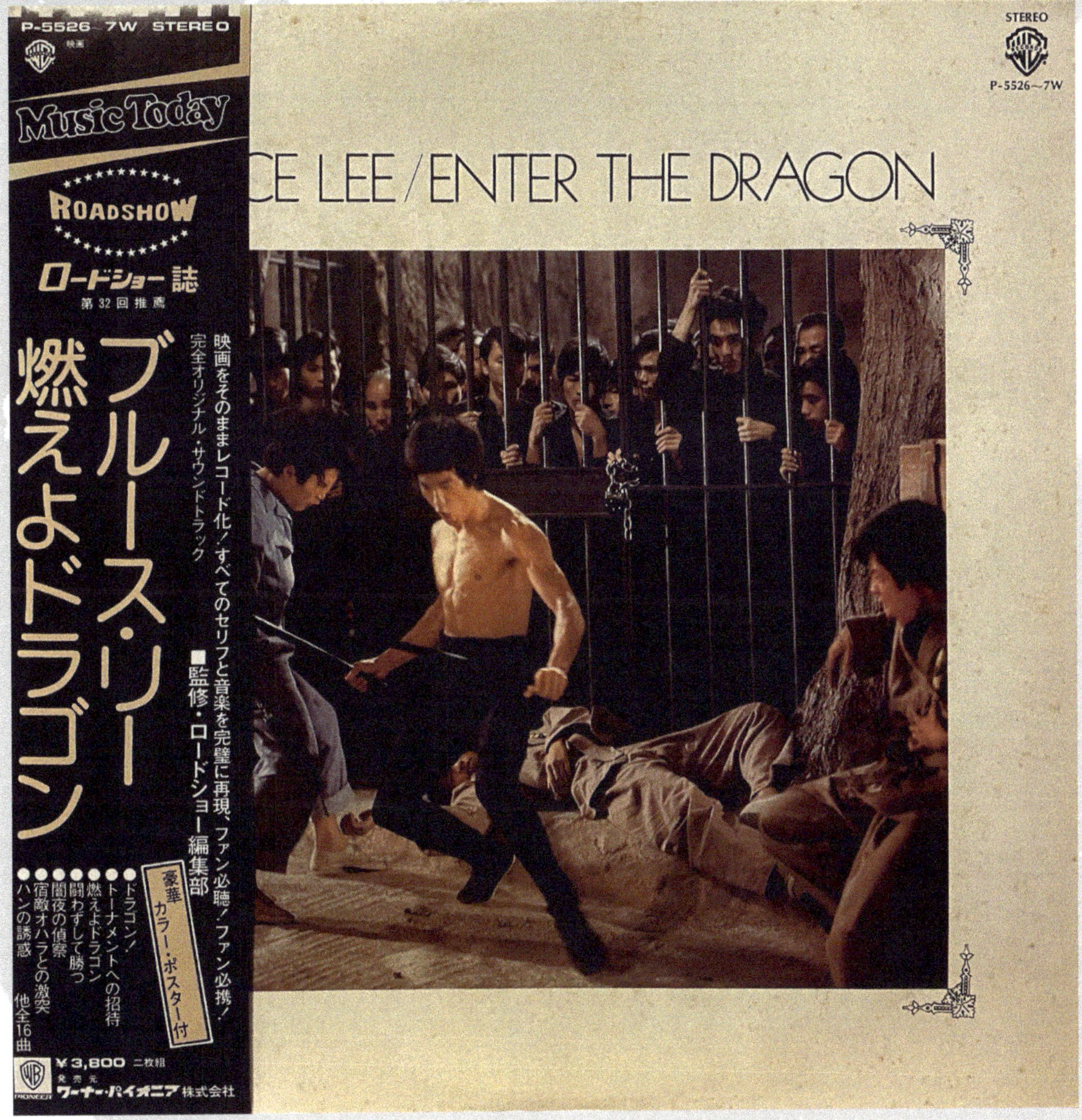
P-5526~7W STEREO
Music Today
ROADSHOW
ロードショー誌
第32回推薦
ブルース・リー
燃えよドラゴン
映画をそのままレコード化！すべてのセリフと音楽を完璧に再現、ファン必聴！ファン必携！
完全オリジナル・サウンドトラック
■監修・ロードショー編集部
豪華カラー・ポスター付
●ドラゴン！
●トーナメントへの招待
●燃えよドラゴン
●闘わずして勝つ
●闇夜の偵察
●宿敵オハラとの激突
●ハンの誘惑
他全16曲
¥3,800 二枚組
発売元
ワーナー・パイオニア株式会社
STEREO
P-5526~7W
CE LEE / ENTER THE DRAGON

あのブルース・リーの
"燃えよドラゴン"、
アラン・ドロンの
"地下室のメロディー"、
そして"ブリット"から
話題の"ジョーズ"まで
傑作のテーマがこの一枚に

燃えよドラゴン
アクション・サスペンス映画傑作集

燃えよドラゴン
007 黄金銃を持つ男
大地震
エアポート
リスボン特急'75
ブリット
ジョーズ
愛のテーマ〜ゴッドファーザー
ジョーズ
007/ダイヤモンドは永遠に
シシリアン
地下室のメロディー
ロシアより愛をこめて

〈演奏〉ミシェル・クレマン楽団
モーリス・ルクレール楽団 ほか

ENTER THE DRAGON

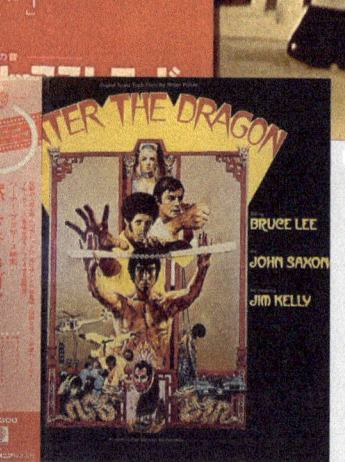

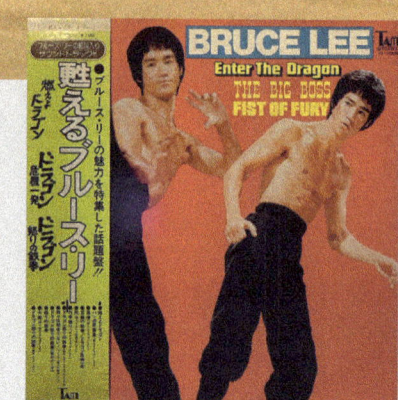

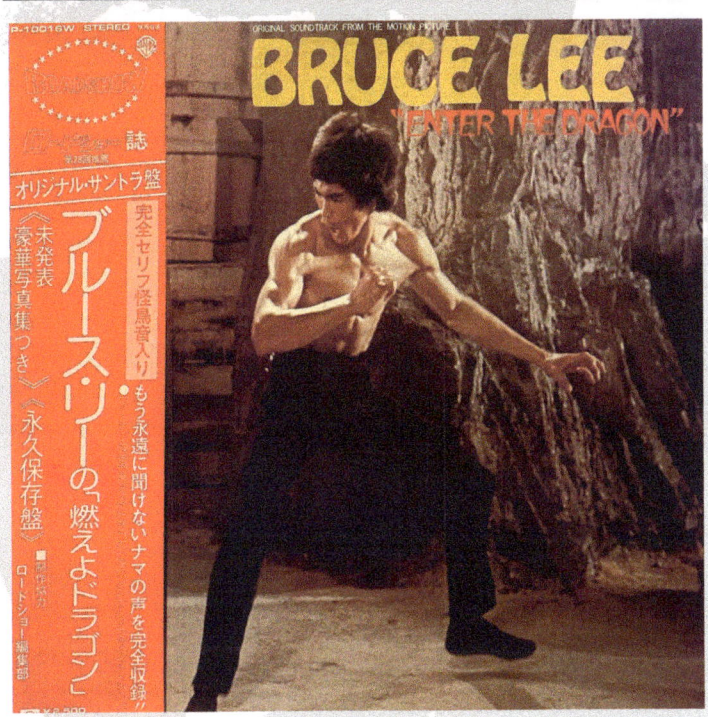

SIGNED BOOKS

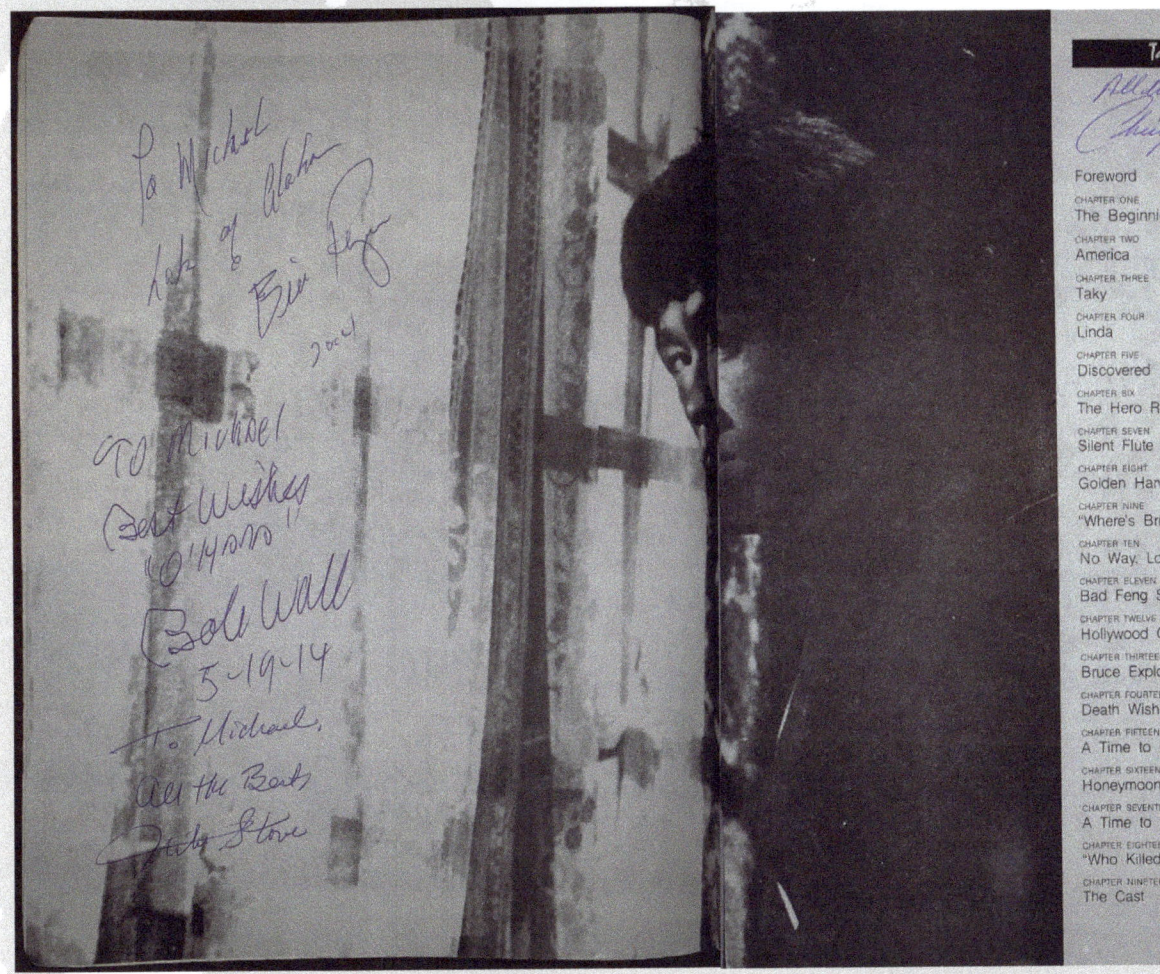

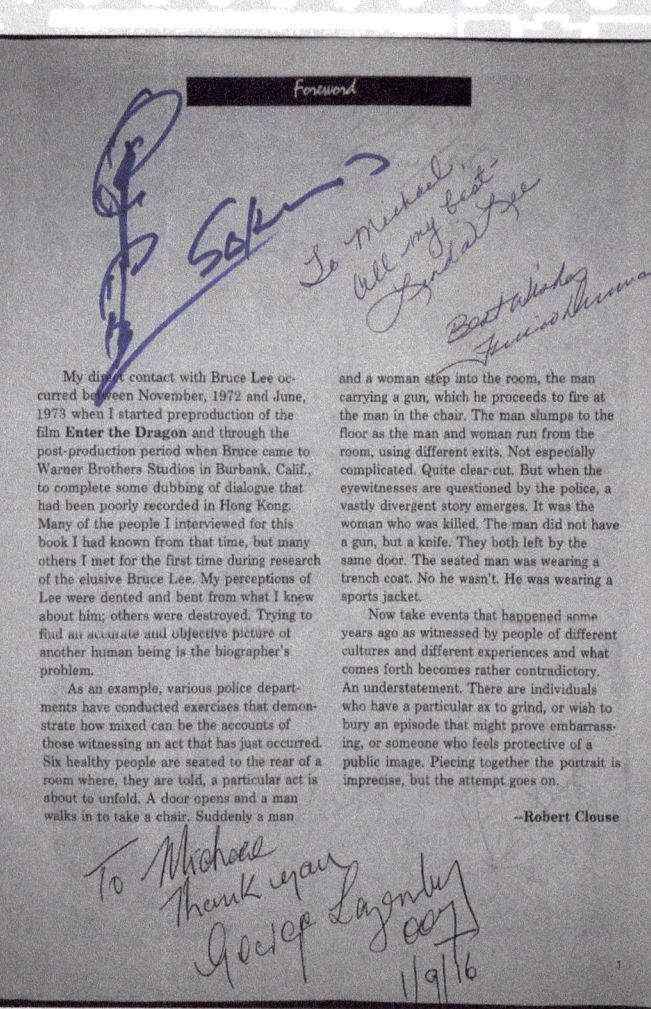
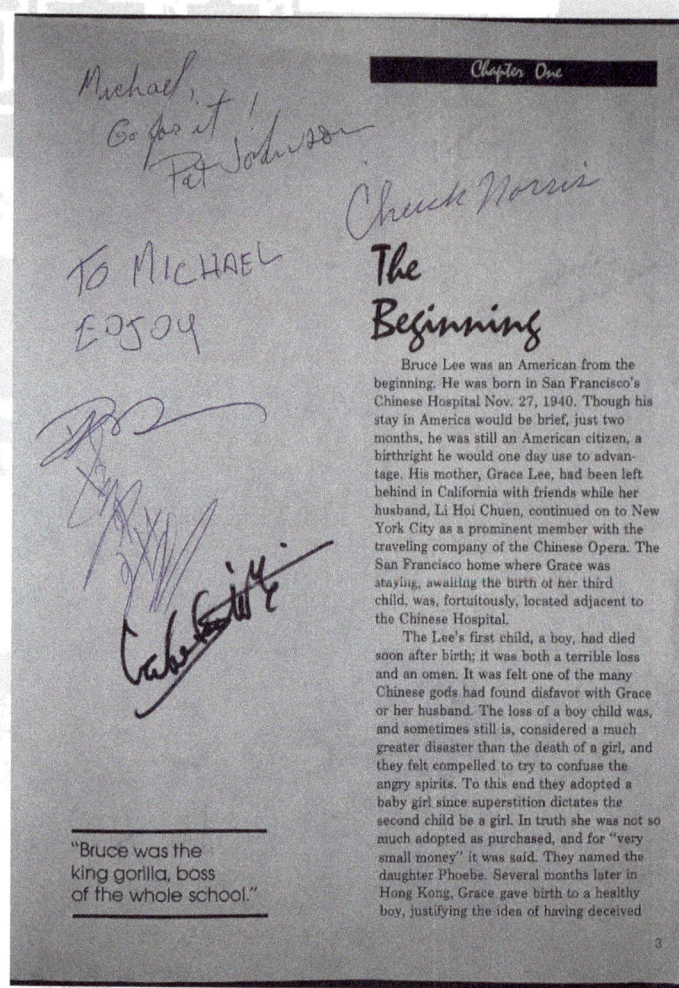

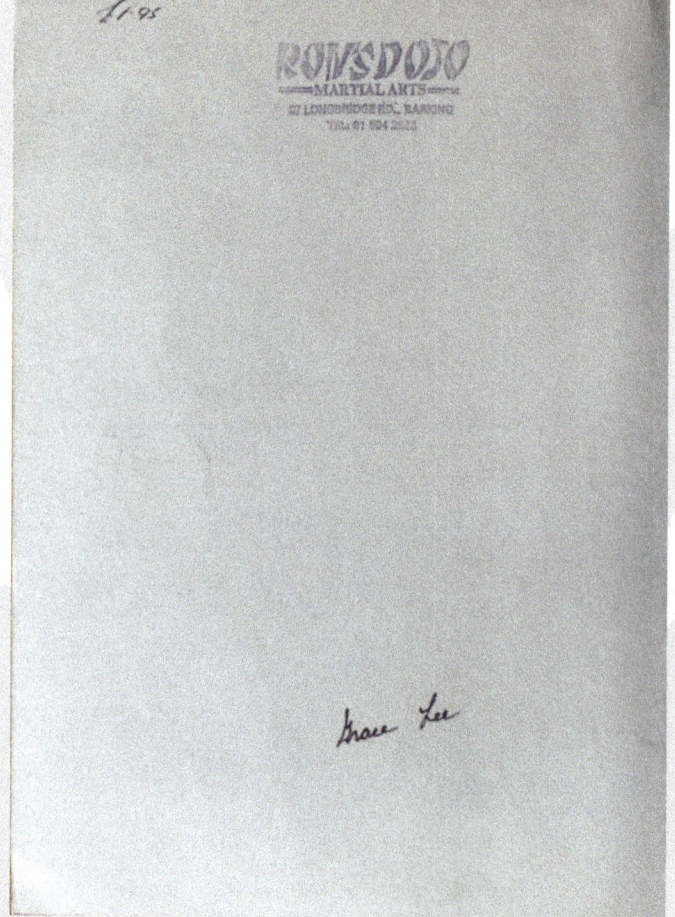

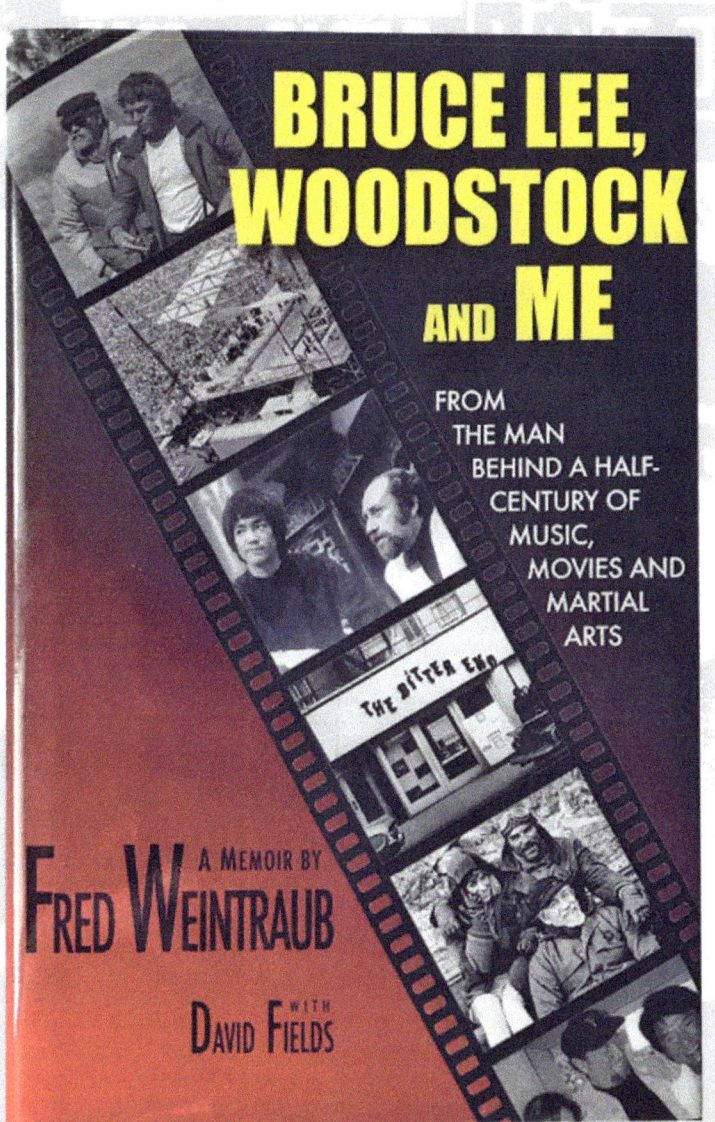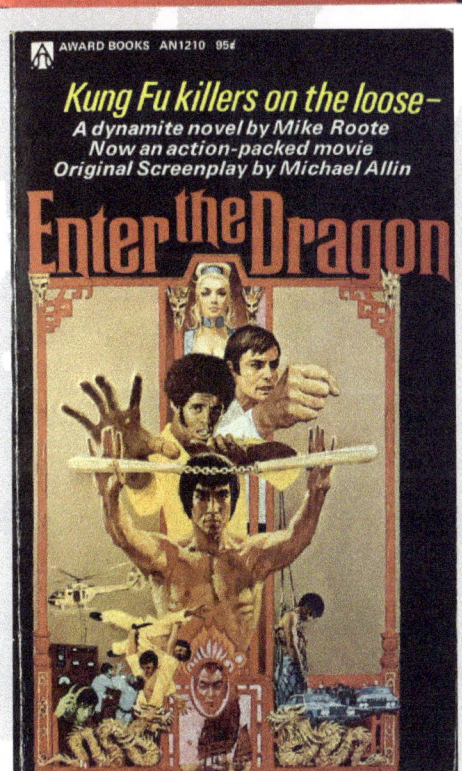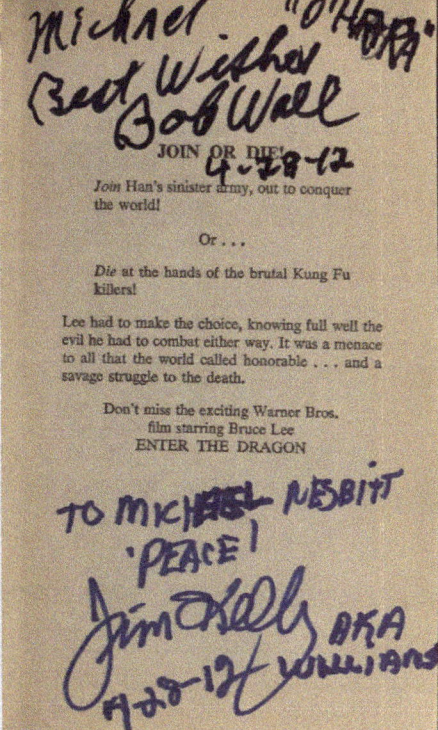

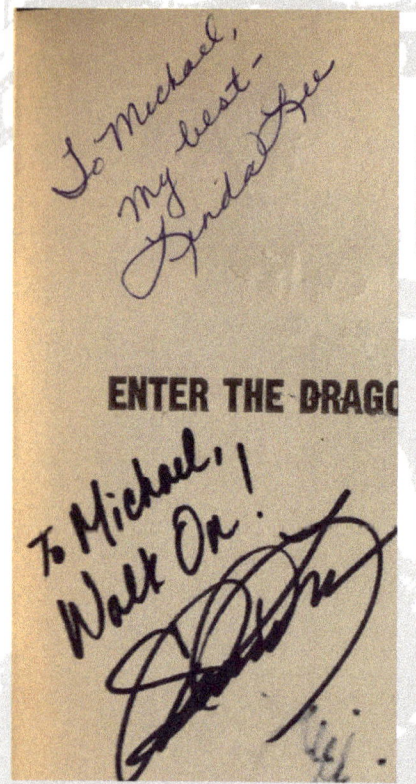
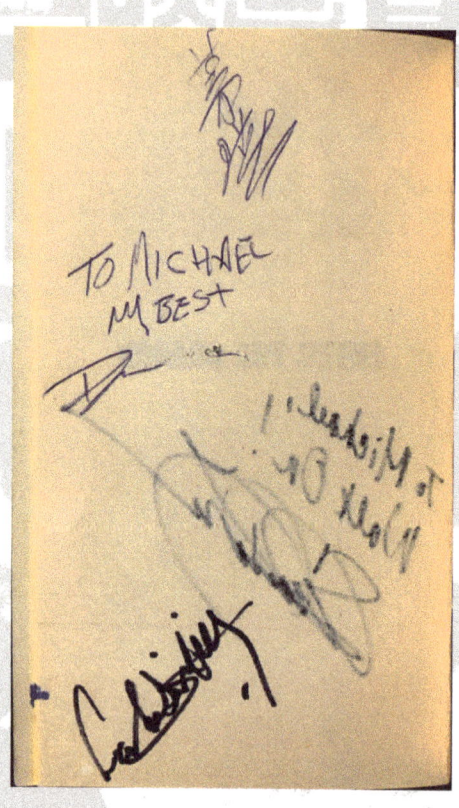

SIGNED PHOTOS

To. Michael
Best Wishes

To. Michael
Best Wishes
John Saxon
2-10-13

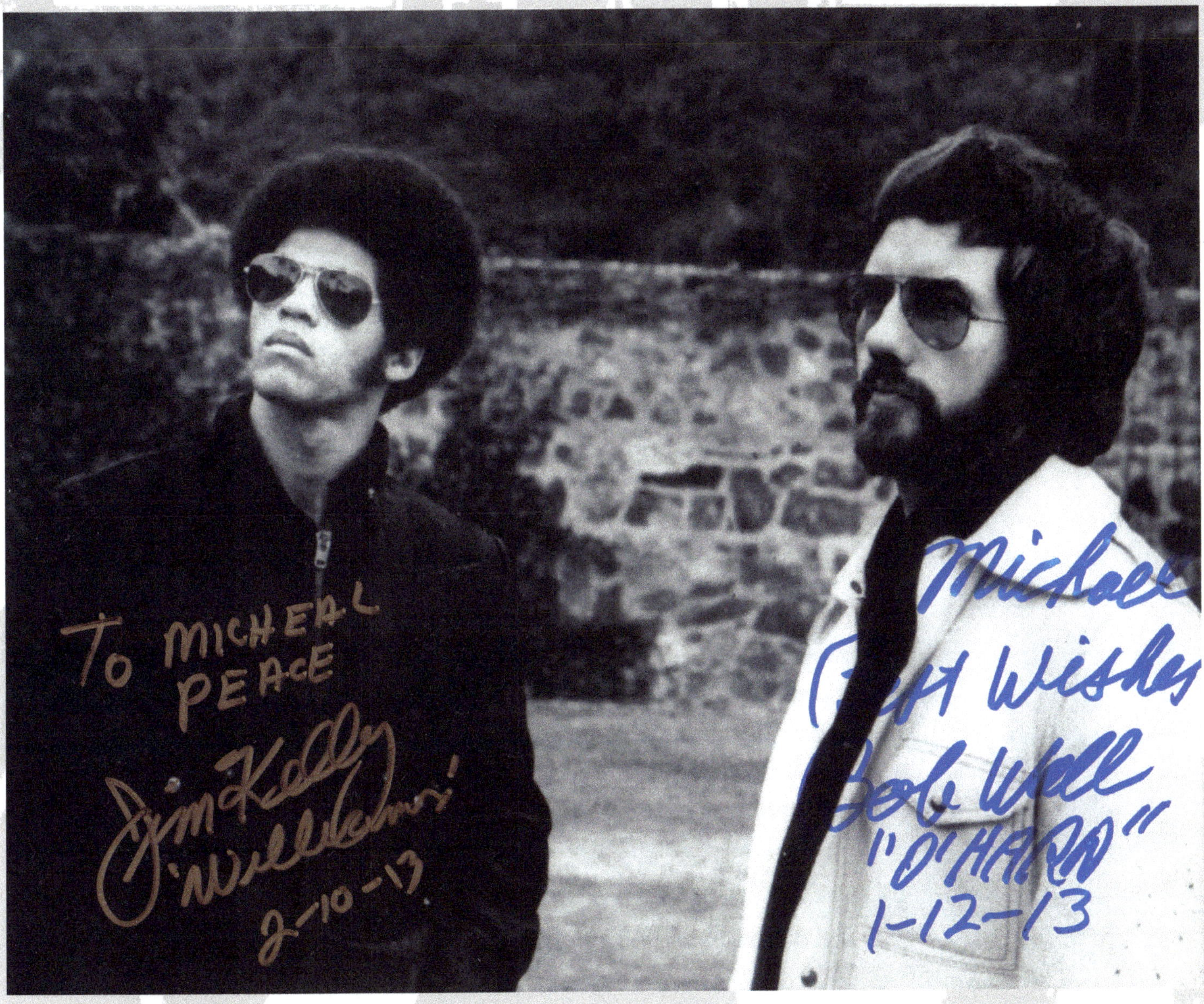

To MICHEAL
PEACE
Jim Kelly
"Williams"
2-10-13
Michael
Best Wishes
Bob Wall
"O'HARA"
1-12-13

To:
Michael
Best Wishes
"Roper"
John Saxon
TO MICHEAL
PEACE
Jim Kelly
Williams

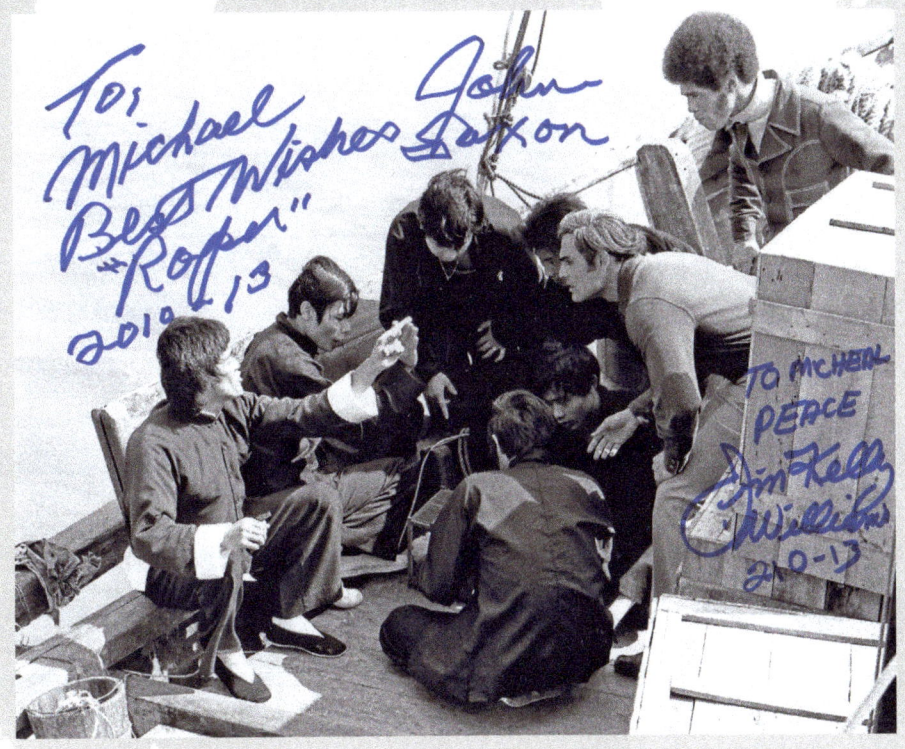

Robert Clouse
The Genius behind the Success of "Enter the Dragon"

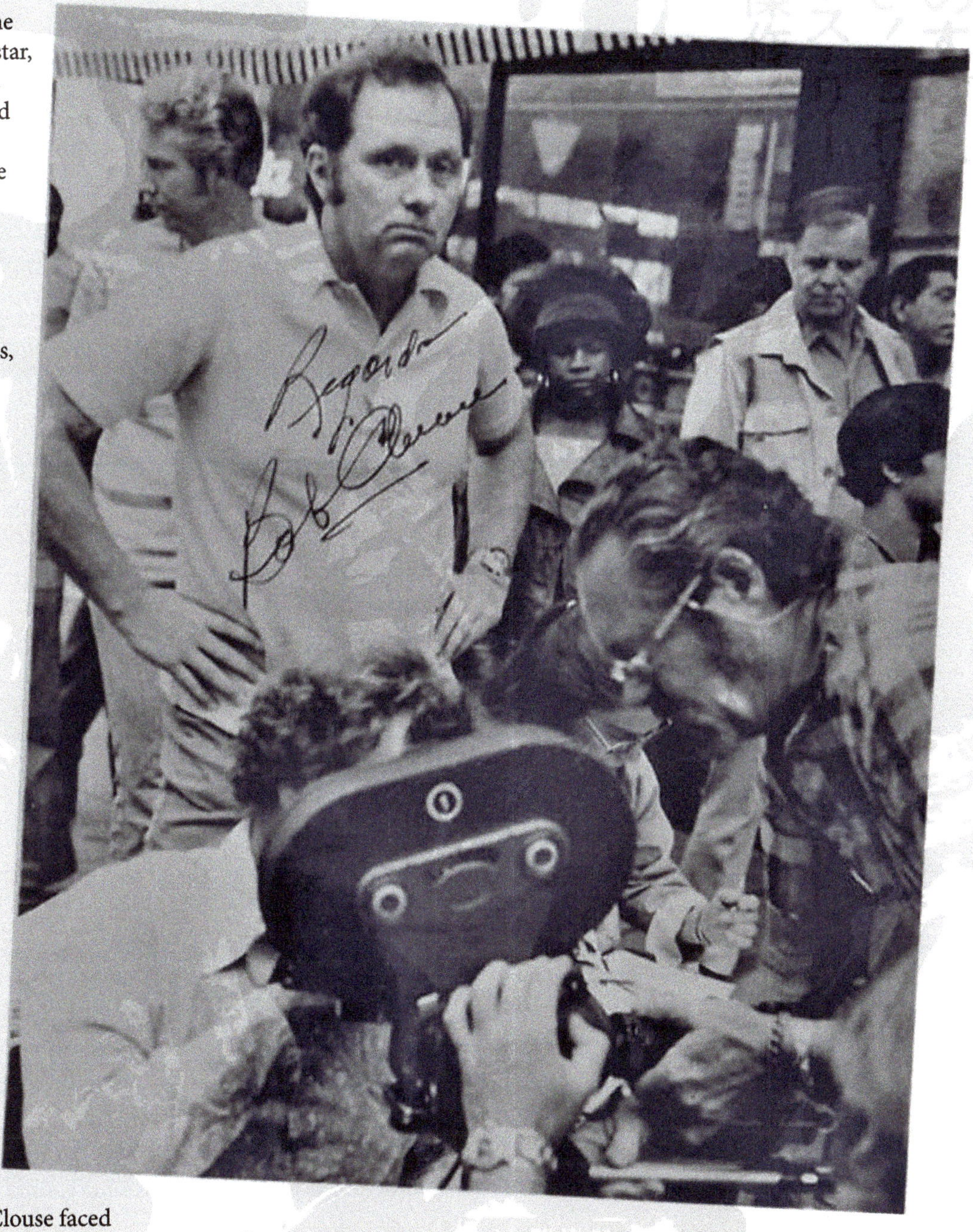

When most people think of the classic martial arts film "Enter the Dragon," they likely think of its star, Bruce Lee. But while Lee's iconic performance undoubtedly helped to make the film the success it was, there was another key figure behind the scenes who was just as instrumental in bringing the movie to life: its director, Robert Clouse.

Born in 1928 in the United States, Clouse began his career in the film industry as a writer and director for television, working on a number of popular shows throughout the 1960s and 1970s. But it wasn't until he began working on martial arts films that his career truly took off. And it was with "Enter the Dragon" that he cemented his status as a master of the genre.

At the time that "Enter the Dragon" was being made, martial arts films were still a relatively new phenomenon in the West. Bruce Lee had burst onto the scene just a few years earlier with his breakout film "The Big Boss," and his popularity had helped to spark a renewed interest in martial arts cinema. But the genre was still very much in its infancy, and it was up to Clouse to help bring it to a wider audience.

One of the key challenges that Clouse faced when making "Enter the Dragon" was the fact that the film was being made on a relatively small budget. While Warner Bros. had agreed to produce the film, they were still somewhat skeptical about its potential success, and as a result, they weren't willing to invest a lot of money in it. This meant that Clouse had to get creative when it came to filming the movie's many action sequences, often relying on practical effects and clever camera work to create the illusion of more elaborate fight scenes. But despite these budgetary constraints, Clouse managed to create a film that was both visually stunning and highly engaging. Working closely with Bruce Lee, he was able to craft a movie that showcased Lee's incredible martial arts skills while also telling a compelling story about a group of fighters who are recruited to take down a ruthless drug lord. And thanks to Clouse's

Rehearsing the fight between Saxon and Leung Sze (Bolo)

skilled direction, the film was a huge success both commercially and critically, grossing over $90 million worldwide and earning rave reviews for its action sequences and performances.

So what was it about Clouse's direction that made "Enter the Dragon" such a hit? For one thing, he was able to create a film that was highly accessible to Western audiences, despite its Hong Kong roots. He did this by blending elements of traditional martial arts cinema with more familiar Hollywood-style action scenes, creating a movie that felt both fresh and familiar at the same time.

But perhaps even more important was Clouse's ability to work closely with his actors and choreographers to create fight scenes that were both realistic and visually stunning. He understood the importance of using a variety of camera angles and editing techniques to create a sense of tension and excitement during these scenes, and he was able to bring out the best in his cast members, many of whom were still relatively inexperienced at the time.

Ultimately, it was Clouse's vision and leadership that helped to make "Enter the Dragon" the classic martial arts film that it is today. While Bruce Lee's performance was undoubtedly a huge part of the movie's success, it was Clouse who helped to bring that performance to life on the big screen, and who helped to make "Enter the Dragon" the iconic film that it remains to this day.

Setting up shot on tournament field.

Bruce, Saxon and myself in the banquet set.

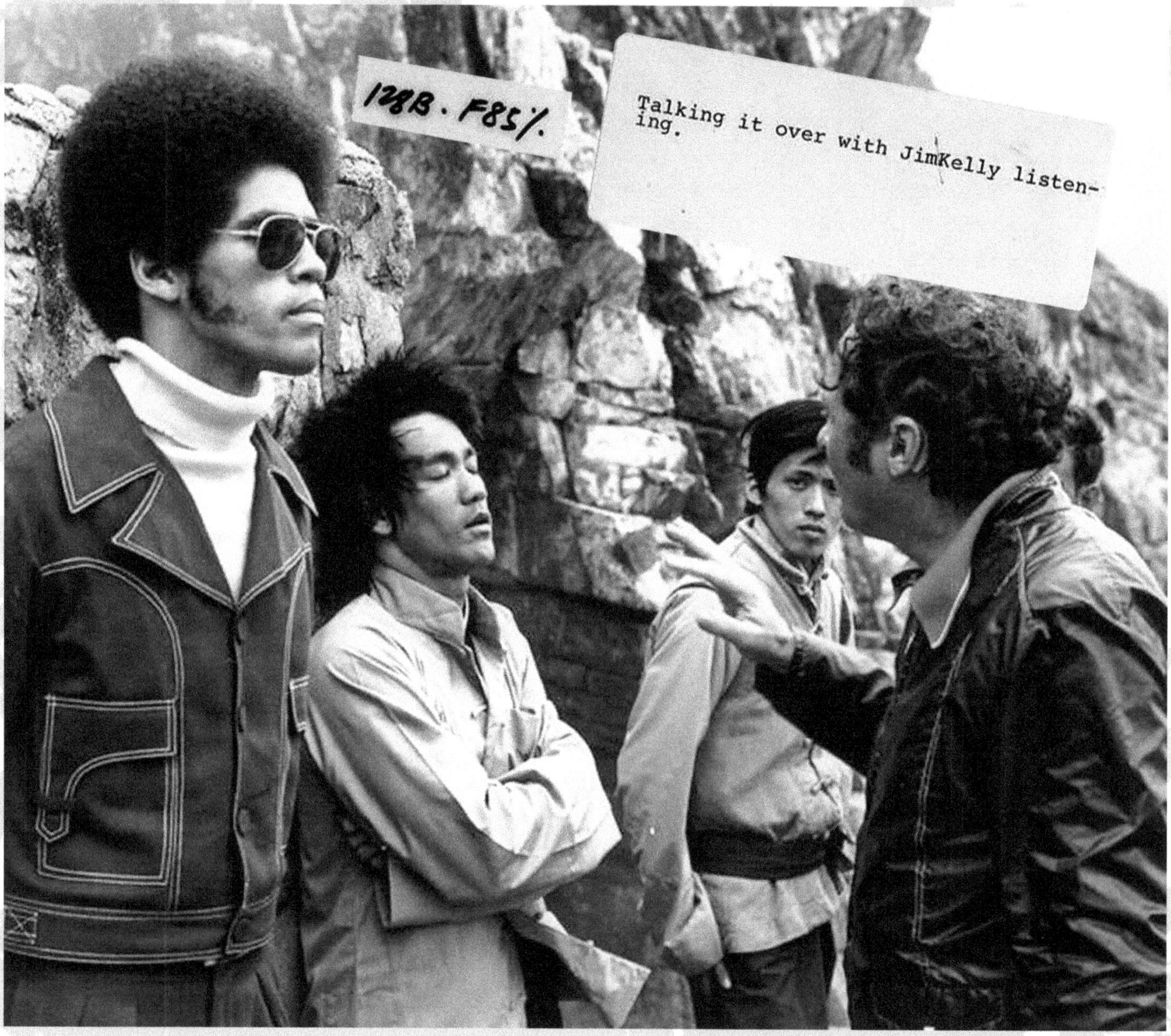

128B. F85%.

Talking it over with JimKelly listening.

200%.

At this point Bolo(Lueng Sze) was winning.

FANATICAL DRAGON PRESENTS
5 FINGERS OF DISCS

Where else could I turn my attention to in this Enter the Dragon special issue than to look at a few of the many releases of Bruce Lee's arguably most famous movie that have made their way onto Bluray these past few years. Enter The Dragon remains very much a special movie for me personally, as my own love of Bruce Lee, of Hong Kong, it's Cinematic history and indeed of martial arts movies in general all started with seeing
Enter the Dragon on UK TV so, so many years ago.
It is ultimately, my favourite Bruce Lee movie (though arguably not his best film) but you do always remember your first love with rose tinted glasses!
So let's follow the finger pointing to the moon making sure not to miss all the Heavenly Glory that the various E.T.D Bluray releases contain and how much they vary…
Don't think….Feeeeeeel.

1) **Bruce Lee at Golden Harvest**
   Arrow Video
   UK Only Release
   4K/UHD and Bluray Editions Available.
   ETA - July 17th 2023

 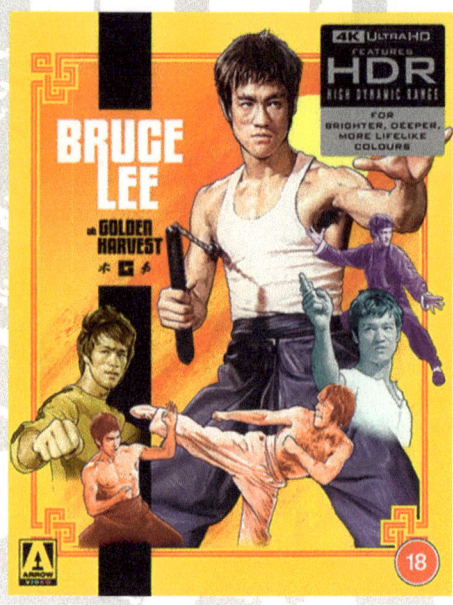

Just as we were going to print with this issue, Arrow Video dropped a massive bombshell and unveiled their forthcoming UK Only 'Bruce Lee at Golden Harvest' Boxset details, and God Damn is it impressive. This 10 disc set will contain a mix of 4K UHD Discs and Blurays (But also comes in a Region B Locked Bluray only edition too, with largely the same extras) There is refreshingly very little overlap with previous releases apart from when it comes to Enter The Dragon itself, as Warner Brothers are still intending to release their own standalone 50th Anniversary edition of that later in the year, so only provided Arrow with their old 40th Anniversary Bluray (see elsewhere in this article for the breakdown of its extras)

Now given that this set has basically set the HK movie loving side of the internet on fire today I'd be remiss if I didn't cover the massive list of new and exclusive content Arrow has commissioned for the Boxset. Here's just what has been announced so far (more extras are to be confirmed later this month, maybe even by the time you have this magazine in your hands!)

• Brand new 4K restorations of The Big Boss, Fist of Fury, The Way of the Dragon and Game of Death and brand new 2K restoration of Game of Death II
• 4K (2160p) UHD Blu-ray presentations in Dolby Vision (HDR10 compatible) of The Big Boss, The Big Boss: The Mandarin Cut, Fist of Fury, The Way of the Dragon and Game of Death
• High Definition (1080p) Blu-ray presentations of the Hong Kong cut of Game of Death, Game of Death II, Bruce Lee: The Man & The Legend and Bruce Lee: The Legend
• Newly restored original Mandarin, English and Cantonese mono audio
• Newly translated optional English subtitles, plus subtitles for the deaf and hard-of-hearing on the English dubs
• Multiple alternate cuts on most films, including the extended Mandarin Cut on The Big Boss, English export cuts of The Big Boss and Fist of Fury, the Japanese cut of The Way of the Dragon and Hong Kong cuts of Game of Death and Game of Death II (aka Tower of Death)
• Brand new feature commentaries by David Desser, Jonathan Clements, Frank Djeng & Michael Worth, Brandon Bentley and Mike Leeder
• Return to Thailand, a new documentary by Matt Routledge on the original locations for The Big Boss
• Newly uncovered deleted scenes from The Big Boss, plus a video essay by Bentley about scenes still missing such as the 'saw-in-the-head' kill
• Legend of the Dragon, a brand new 80-minute overview of Lee's career by film critic and historian Tony Rayns
• Two new documentaries on Lee's fighting and working methods, featuring interviews with Golden Harvest producer Andre Morgan, martial arts experts Michael Worth, John Kreng, Andy Cheng, Frank Djeng and David Yeung, film historian Courtney Joyner and others
• Brand new interviews with actors Malisa Longo and Colleen Camp, plus hours of archive interviews with Lee's former co-stars, colleagues and friends, including Nora Miao, Dan Inosanto, Bob Wall, Yuen Wah and many others
• The Final Game of Death, a brand new feature-length video essay by Arrow Films on Lee's original vision for The Game of Death, featuring a new 2K restoration of the footage directed by Lee in 1972
• 40th Anniversary Special Edition Blu-ray of Enter the Dragon, with archive extras including The Curse of the Dragon, In His Own Words, Backyard Workout and more
• Archive featurettes including The Hong Kong Connection, Bruce Lee Remembered, Legacy of the Dragon, Dragon Rising and The Grandmaster & The Dragon
• Comprehensive trailer and image galleries for each film
• Limited edition packaging featuring newly commissioned artwork by Tony Stella
• 200-page hardbound book featuring new writing by Walter Chaw, Henry Blyth, Andrew Staton, Dylan Cheung, David West and James Flower
• Twenty-four lobby card reproductions
• Ten glossy photos of Lee in action
• Reversible poster with vintage poster artwork
•and much, much more!!!

The set is already available for pre-order own Arrow's own website as well as Zavvi, Amazon etc, however Arrow's own website offers an exclusive alternate cover option only available there which will doubtless sell out fairly quickly. Most of the responses I've seen online so far are all drooling over the Game of Death, yellow suit inspired colour palette of the alternate set.. Pretty damn impressive all in all, Arrow Video have really been leaning hard into East Asian Cinema of late with their incredible work on their Two Shawscope Boxsets and countless Japanese Cinema releases. It will be very interesting to see how the other labels rise to the challenge and hopefully up their game with their own releases over the course of the year. Rest assured you can keep up to date with the latest news here in the pages of your beloved Eastern Heroes magazine and by following me over on Youtube for more regular updates! With that slice of excitement covered, let's take a look at the best of the rest of the versions of Enter The Dragon out there currently….

2) The Bruce Lee - His Greatest Hits
Criterion Collection
Region A Blu-ray
Available now.

I've mentioned this release a few times now over the course of our various special issues dedicated to the Little Dragon, and with very good reason, it's easily the best American release to date and offers the only source (currently) for the original (shorter) US theatrical release of Enter The Dragon presented restored in 2K on Bluray. The set is also fairly unique in actually including Enter the Dragon at all! Most of the previous Bruce Lee boxsets from Shout Factory, Hong Kong Legends, Kam and Ronson etc were never able to include Enter The Dragon due to Warner Brothers holding onto the rights for it like a fat kid holds onto cake. Thankfully the power and deep pockets of Janus Films (Criterion's parent company) and the prestige of the Criterion Collection itself allowed them to negotiate to include the movie within the set. Most of the key extras from the Warner Brothers standalone releases are ported over here including the Audio commentary track by producer Paul M. Heller and most of the main documentaries alongside a raft of extras created by Criterion themselves that you won't find elsewhere. The most notable extra being the above mentioned Theatrical Cut of the film remastered in 2K! But you also get the Bruce Lee Biographer Matthew Polly interviewed on Enter the Dragon" which runs for about 10minutes. The original Warner Brothers making of Enter The Dragon titled "Blood and Steel" made in 2004 which runs for about 30mins.
As well as the old "Bruce Lee: In His Own Words" featurette from 1998 (19:21)
A 2003 Interview with Linda Lee Cadwell (16:24), An Interview with Tung Wai (in Cantonese with optional English subtitles) (3:20) as well as all the usual Promotional Materials featured on Warner's own releases. The Original Warners Electronic Press Kit (7:40), Theatrical Trailers (9:15). TV Spots (5:40 as well as the rarer Radio Spots (0:58) too.

In addition Criterion have also provided the following other exclusive extras..
"Risk and Reward" interview with producer Andre Morgan (16:11)
"Bruceploitation" interview with author Grady Hendrix (10:21)
Bruceploitation Promos for "Call Me Dragon", "Black Samurai", "Rage of the Dragon", "Dragon on Fire", "Bruce and the Iron Finger", "Golden Dragon Silver Snake" and "Goodbye Bruce Lee: (His Last Game of Death" radio spot) (13:13),
"Match the Lips" interviews with voice performers Michael Kaye (the English-speaking voice of Lee's Chen Zhen in Fist of Fury) and Vaughan Savidge (11:54)
And lastly, the lengthly "The Grandmaster and the Dragon" documentary (54:41)
Criterion's Bruce Lee His Greatest Hits set was until this very month largely

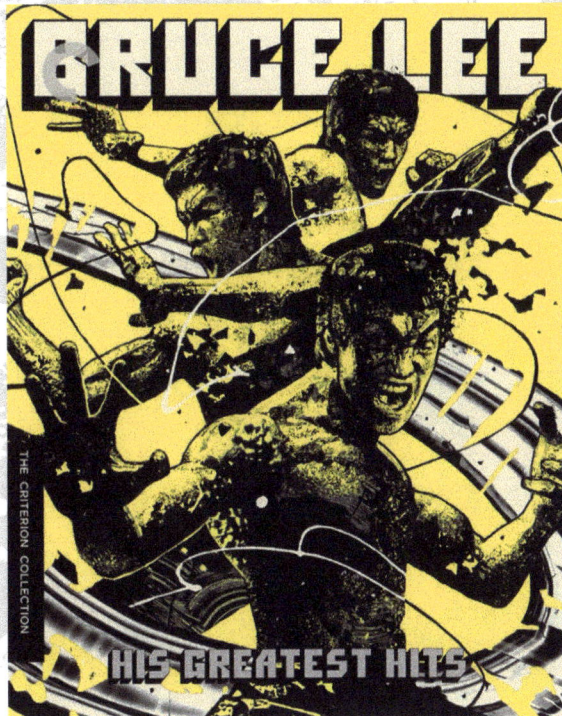

considered THE definitive Bruce Lee boxset on Bluray. However Arrow Video's forthcoming 4K UHD boxset covered above represents a true challenge to this king's throne, and looks like it'll take the crown as being the best Bruce Lee Boxset released onto Bluray and indeed, onto 4K UHD Disc.
It is worth noting however, that all the other movies on the Criterion Boxset set are just as stacked as Enter The Dragon in terms of extras. This was actually the main release I originally purchased a multi region Bluray player just to be able to access (alongside Criterion's incredible Police Story 1+2 set) It's still an absolutely essential!
Take a look at the list of other extras for the other four films on the Criterion set…
• 4K digital restorations of The Big Boss, Fist of Fury, The Way of the Dragon, and Game of Death, with uncompressed original monaural soundtracks
• New 2K digital restoration of the rarely seen 99-minute 1973 theatrical version of Enter the Dragon, with uncompressed original monaural soundtrack
• New 2K digital restoration of the 102-minute "special-edition" version of Enter the Dragon, with alternate 5.1 surround DTS-HD Master Audio soundtrack
• Alternate soundtracks for the films, including original English-dubbed tracks
• Six audio commentaries: on The Big Boss by Bruce Lee expert Brandon Bentley; on The Big Boss, Fist of Fury, The Way of the Dragon, and Game of Death by Hong Kong–film expert Mike Leeder; and on the special-edition version of Enter the Dragon by producer Paul Heller
• High-definition presentation of the 1981 film Game of Death II
• Game of Death Redux, a new presentation of Lee's original Game of Death footage, produced by Alan Canvan
• New interviews on all five films with Lee biographer Matthew Polly
• New interview with producer Andre Morgan about Golden Harvest, the company behind Hong Kong's top martial-arts stars, including Lee
• New program about English-language dubbing, featuring performers Michael Kaye (the English-speaking voice of Lee's Chen Zhen in Fist of Fury) and Vaughan Savidge
• New interview with author Grady Hendrix about the "Bruceploitation" subgenre that followed Lee's death, and a selection of Bruceploitation trailers
• Blood and Steel, a 2004 documentary about the making of Enter the Dragon
• Multiple programs and documentaries about Lee's life and philosophies, including Bruce Lee: The Man and the Legend (1973) and Bruce Lee: In His Own Words (1998)
• Interviews with Linda Lee Cadwell, Lee's widow, and many of Lee's collaborators and admirers, including actors Jon T. Benn, Riki Hashimoto, Nora Miao, Robert Wall, Yuen Wah, and Simon Yam and directors Clarence Fok, Sammo Hung, and Wong Jing
• Promotional materials
• New English subtitle translations and subtitles for the deaf and hard of hearing
• PLUS: An essay by critic Jeff Chang

3) Bruce Lee - The Master Collection
Mediumrare
Region B Blu-Ray
Available now.

The other notable set that managed to negotiate and include Enter The Dragon hails from right here in the UK and it's the Mediumrare Bruce Lee the Master Collection set.

This draws mostly from the old Hong Kong Legends boxset and adds in Mike Leeder's commentary tracks for Bruce's HK movies from the now OOP Shout Factory boxset (which incidentally are also on the Criterion set)

The extra features on here for Enter the Dragon are also pulled straight from Warner's own standalone releases and will start to become very familiar as you read through this article! Once again we get the Audio commentary with producer Paul M. Heller and screenwriter Michael Allin (to my knowledge, the only official commentary track created for the film so far) You also get the newest Warner's mini docs:"No Way As Way", "Wing Chun" and "Return to Han's Island" that you can only find on the Warner's 40th Anniversary and HMV Exclusive Bluray releases outside of this set as well as the more standard, "Curse of the Dragon" documentary, The "Blood and Steel" making of documentary, Linda Lee Cadwell Interviews, Bruce Lee"In His Own Words" featurette And the 1973 Archive Enter The Dragon Featurette as well as the "Backyard Workout with Bruce" short and the usual Theatrical Trailers and TV spots found on almost every release.

As with the Criterion Set you obviously also get ALL Bruce's HK movies too and all housed together in one box. It's pretty good all in all (The Criterion set is miles, miles better and the upcoming Arrow Boxset will beat this set into oblivion faster than Bruce takes down a Japanese Dojo.) It is worth noting though that the Mediumrare set ports over all the extras from the excellent Hong Kong Legends Bruce Lee 30th Anniversary DVD Boxset.

4) Enter The Dragon
HMV Exclusive / Warner Brothers
Region B - Bluray

In recent years, Warner's have mostly just focused on packaging and printed materials to differentiate their various Bluray and DVD releases. The selection of extras on

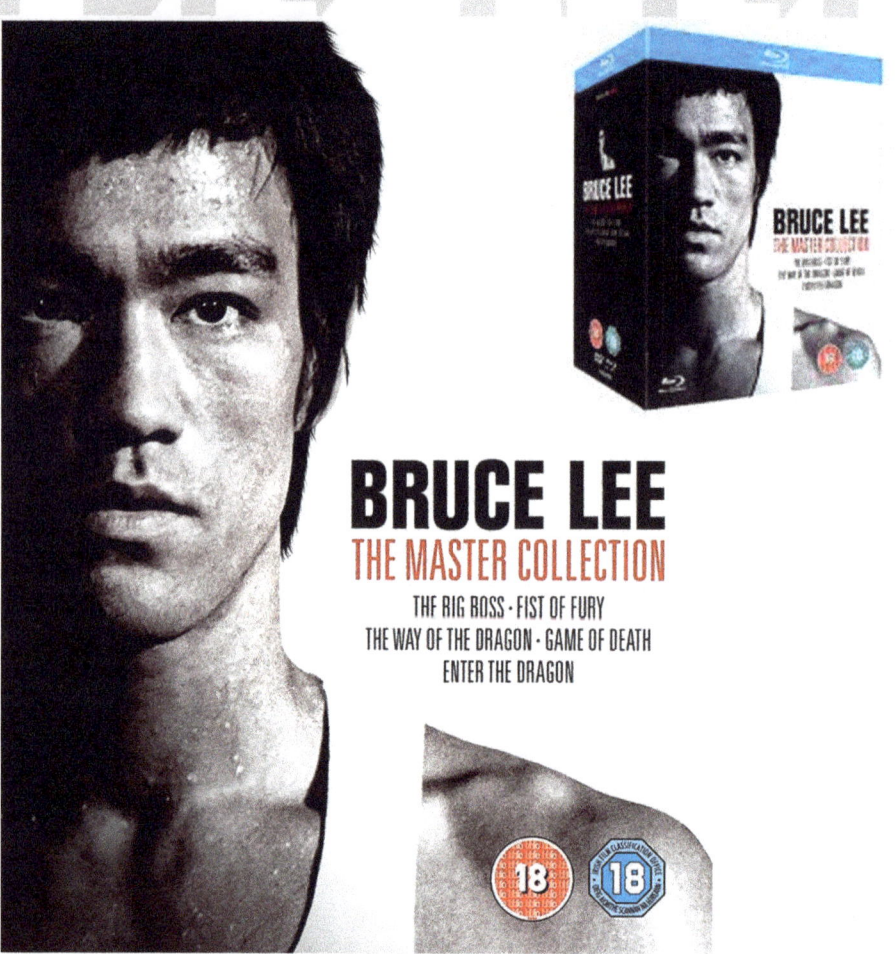

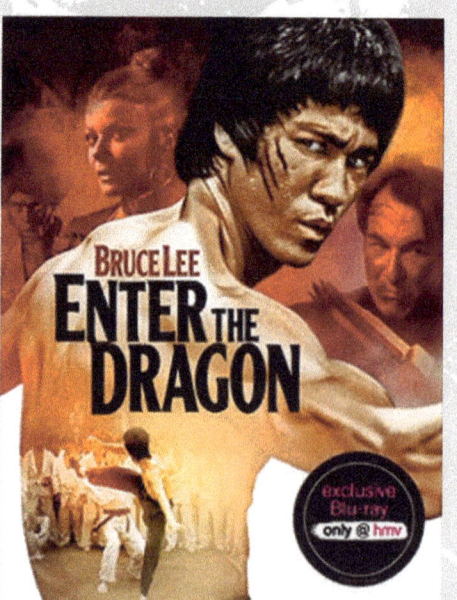

this set remains entirely unchanged from the 40th Anniversary Bluray from 2013 (listed in full further below on the original Steelbook / Keep case Warner's Bluray release) but this HMV Exclusive is easily the nicest of the Official Warner's releases to date. Coming in a full slip case with spot glossing on the pretty cool illustrated image of Bruce on the cover, and bundling in a reprint of the original theatrical poster, A photo booklet, 4 x photo postcards and a rather random but still quite cool, embroidered patch that you won't find elsewhere. This sold out pretty quickly but is still quite easy to find on the second hand market, expect to pay close to its original RRP of £25 if you're in the UK.

5) Enter The Dragon
   40th Anniversary Special Edition
   Warner Brothers
   Region B - Bluray

If you're not fussed about the packaging and prints in the above HMV edition, a cheaper alternative is the 40th Anniversary Bluray from 2013 that Warner's put out. It did originally come with a slipcase, as well as some nice reproduction lobby cards. On disc extras are almost identical to Warner's previous outings (are you noticing a slightly lazy theme emerging with WB's releases ??) But does add in three new mini documentaries, totalling about 50 mins of new content, These are titled:
"No Way As Way" (HD, 26:28) , "Wing Chun" (HD, 20:02) and
"Return to Han's Island" (HD, 10:28)

6) Enter The Dragon
   Bruce Lee Legendary Collection
   Hong Kong Release
   Kam & Ronson - HK

The Kam and Ronson HK edition is largely bare bones in terms of on disc extras, offering just a photo gallery and the unedited opening sequence but it does have radically different artwork than you'll see anywhere else, and is available as a standalone release or also as a part of their now long out of print, 'Bruce Lee Legendary Collection' boxset.
This will cost you a small fortune on the secondhand market and is, in my opinion anyways, one purely for the 'gotta catch em all' super collectors. Just get the Criterion set instead. you can buy it AND a multi region player for less than this boxset sells for secondhand.

7) Enter The Dragon
   Steelbook Bluray / Regular Keep Case
   Warner Brothers
   Region Free

This is essentially just an upgrade to HD/1080p from the old WB Special Edition DVD release but made available in either a somewhat limited edition, ultra minimalist Steelbook or in a regular keep case (with the same artwork as the old Special Edition DVD)
The extras you'll find on here are almost identical to the old S.E DVD,
If you don't really care about packaging or printed extras of the other later Warner's releases listed above, this is your cheapest option, and still absolutely holds up in terms of its on disc content. you get the Audio Commentary with producer Paul M. Heller and screenwriter Michael Allin as well as a pretty extensive list of extras:

• The "Blood and Steel: The Making of Enter the Dragon" featurette (30:12)
• "Bruce Lee: In His Own Words" featurette (19:20)
• "Linda Lee Cadwell Interview Gallery"
• Lair of the Dragon: - "Original 1973 Enter The Dragon Featurette" (7:38)
• "Backyard Workout with Bruce Lee" (1:52)
• "Curse of the Dragon" (1993) documentary (87:27)
• The disc is rounded out with 4 different Trailers and 7 Tv Spots…
• Trailers:
• "Mysterious Island" (3:34)
• "Champion of Champions" (1:11)
• "Deadly 3" (1:38)
• "Island Fortress" (2:54)

TV Spots:
• "Roper, Williams and Lee" (0:32)
• "Deadly 3" (1:01)
• "The Island of Han" (1:02)
• "Review Spot" (1:01)
• "Champion of Champions" (1:02)
• "The Fury Is Back" (0:32)
• "The Crown Prince of Combat" (0:31)
This is still available from Amazon UK for about £7 at the time of going to print.

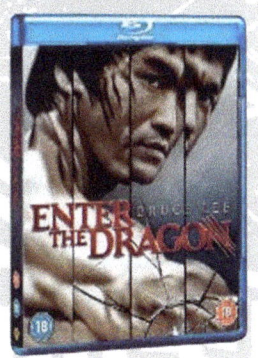

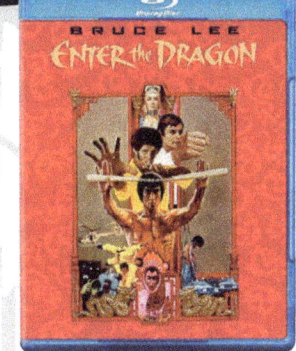

8) In other news….

Shout Factory, mentioned in passing this issue for their old out of print Bruce Lee Boxset
have decided to jump onto the Shaw Brothers on Bluray Money Train that 88 Films and Arrow Video have been riding these past few years and announced
two Shaw Brothers boxsets, the first, is a 5 movie, 5 discs Brace Archer Boxset (released this month but only as a US and Canadian Website exclusive) The second is due in June of this year and will contain 11 movies on 11 discs, all from the late 60's era of Shaw's Back Catalogue and all mostly Wu Xia films. You can find full details and breakdowns of these sets already, (and unboxings and reviews of both sets in due course) over on my Youtube Channel where I post regular news, reviews and Bluray unboxing videos every few days.

Written by
Johnny 'The Fanatical Dragon' Burnett
www.youtube.com/thefanaticaldragon

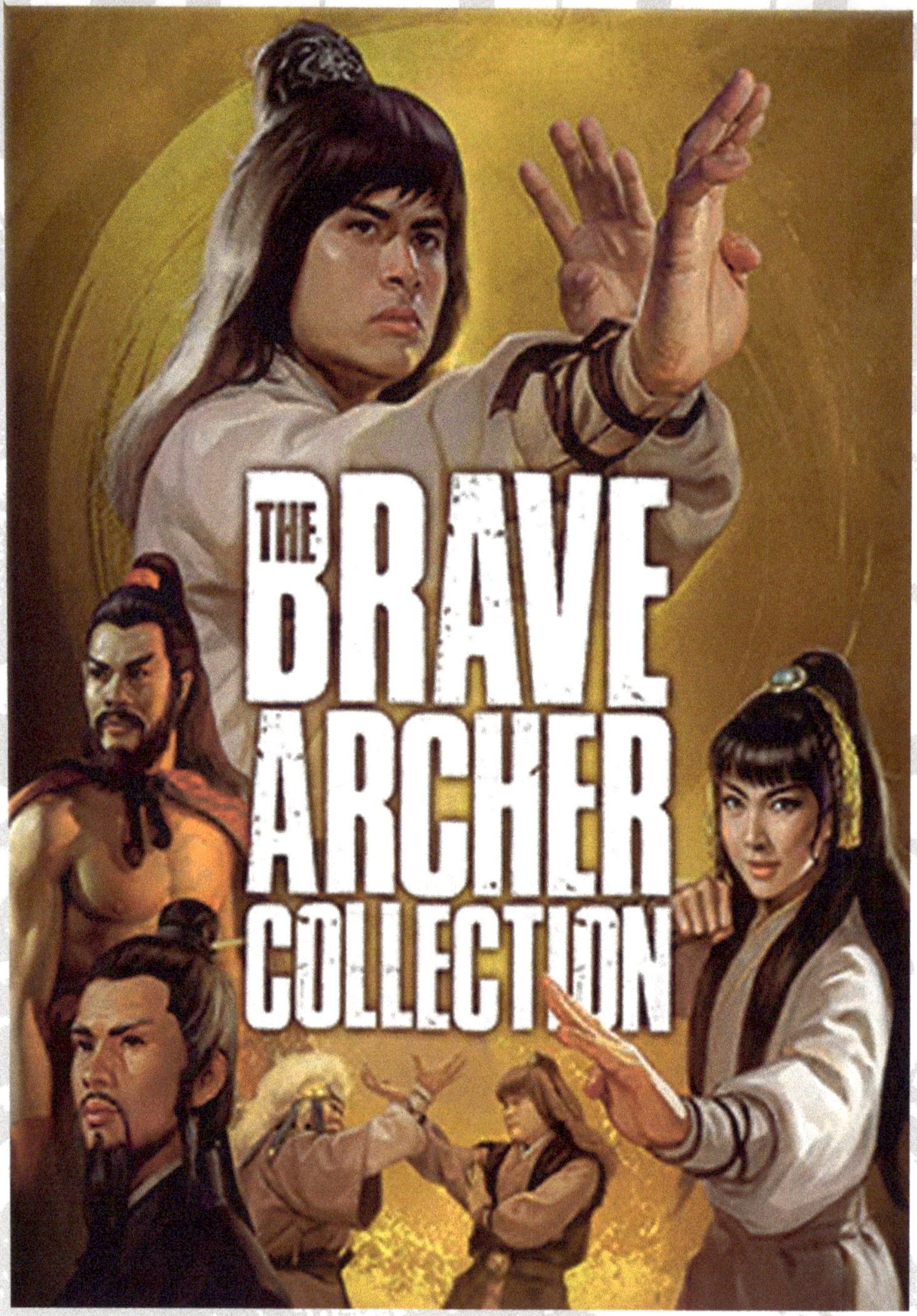

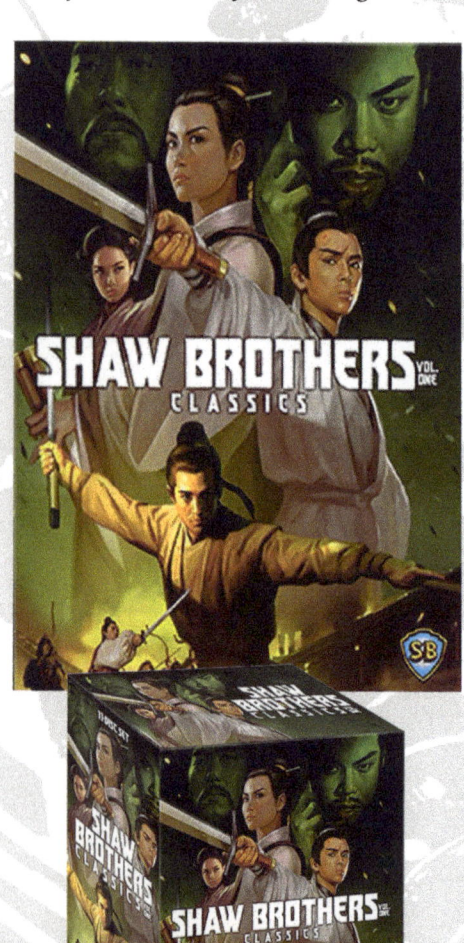

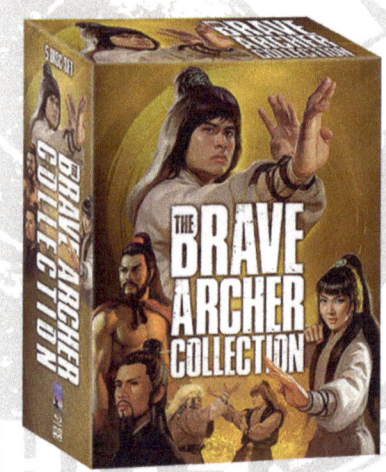

Enter The Dragon
THOMAS GROSS MEMORABILIA

Egypt Release

Argentina 1st & 2nd release

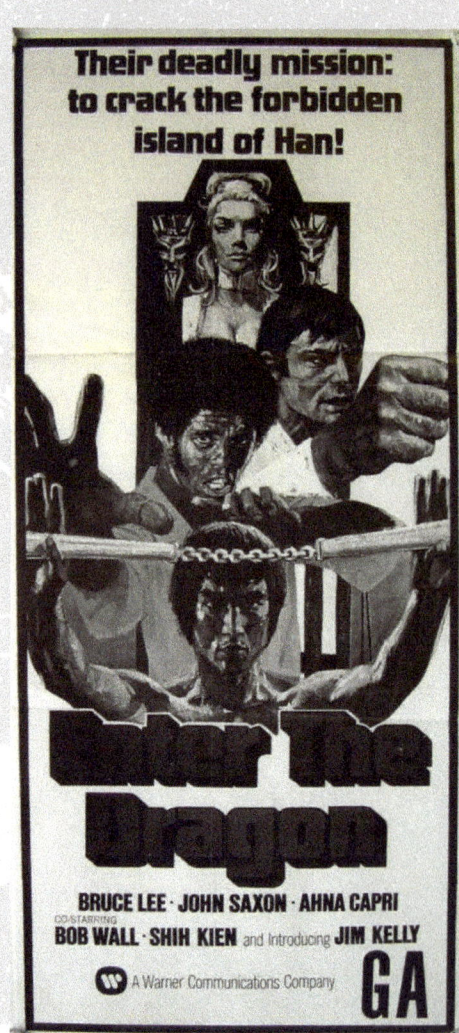
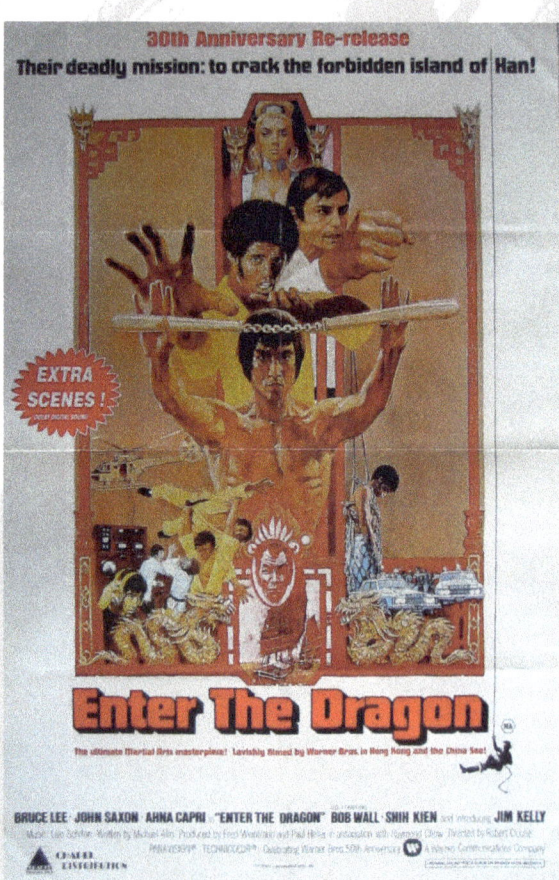

Australian Releases

Austrian Release

Belgian Release

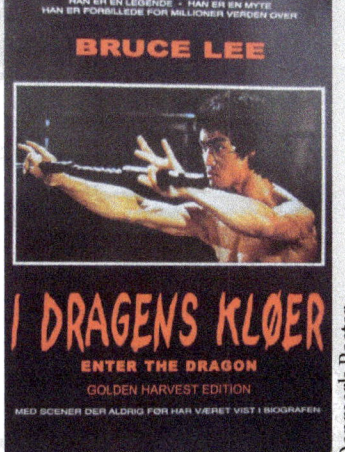

Denmark Poster

Denmark Poster

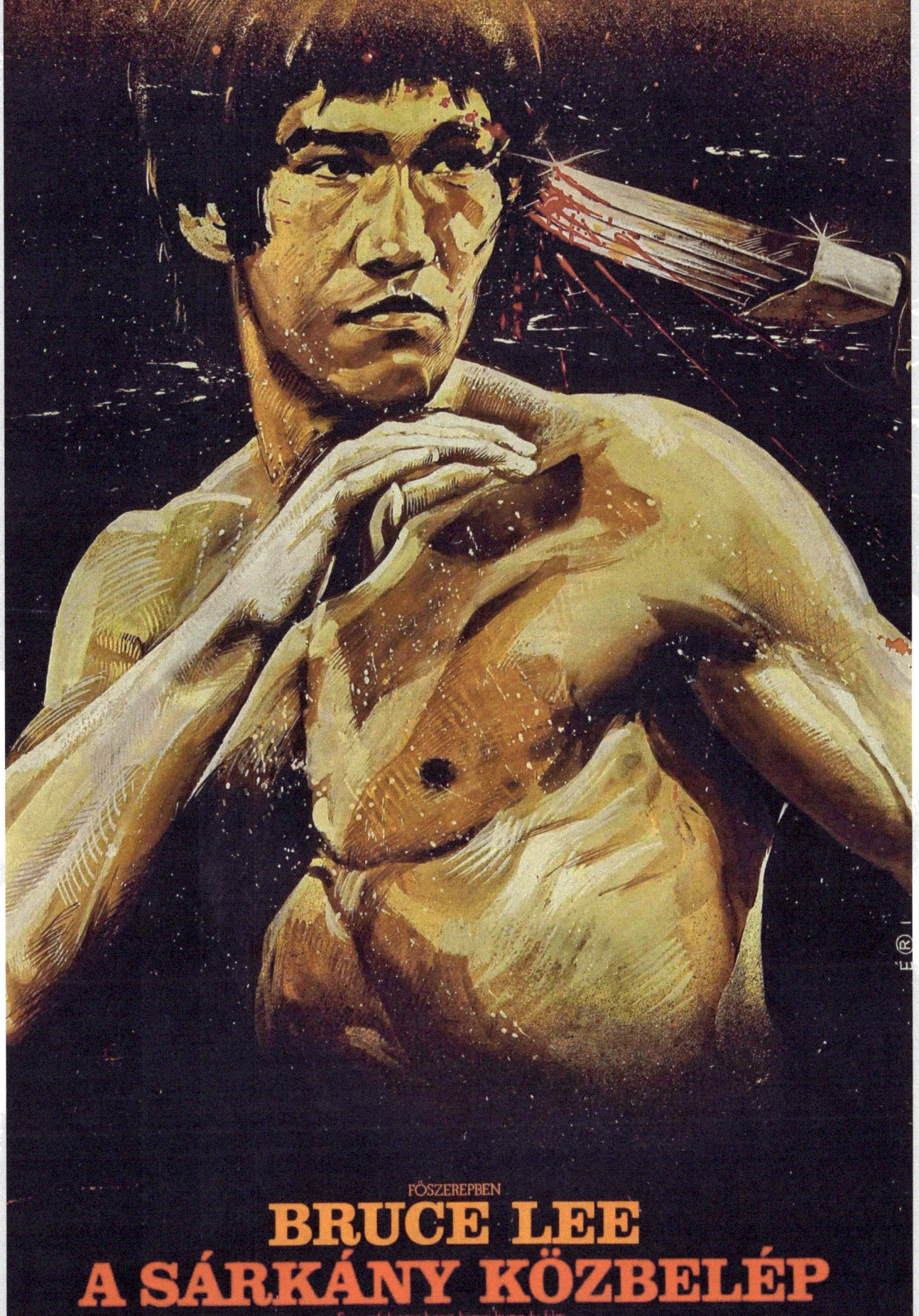

French poster

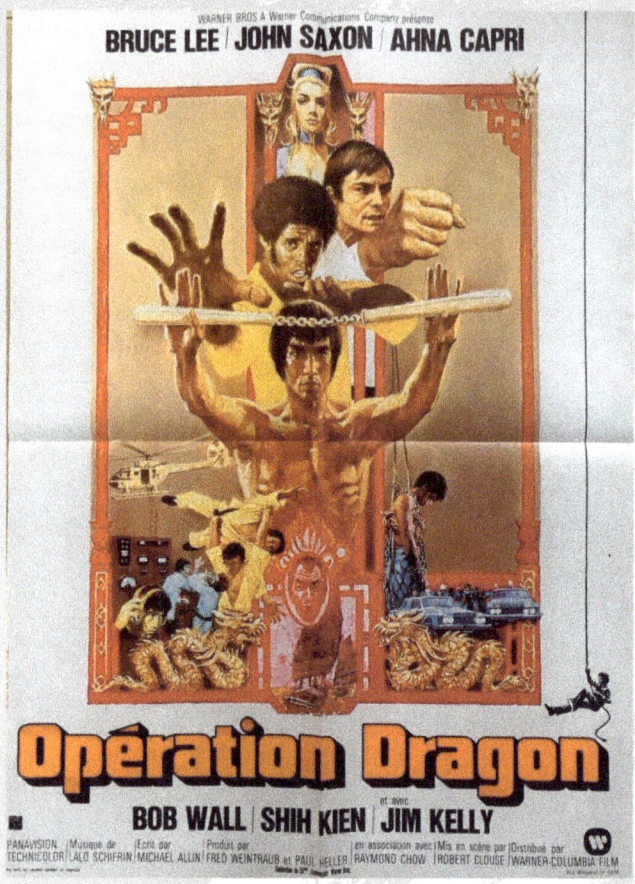

German Poster

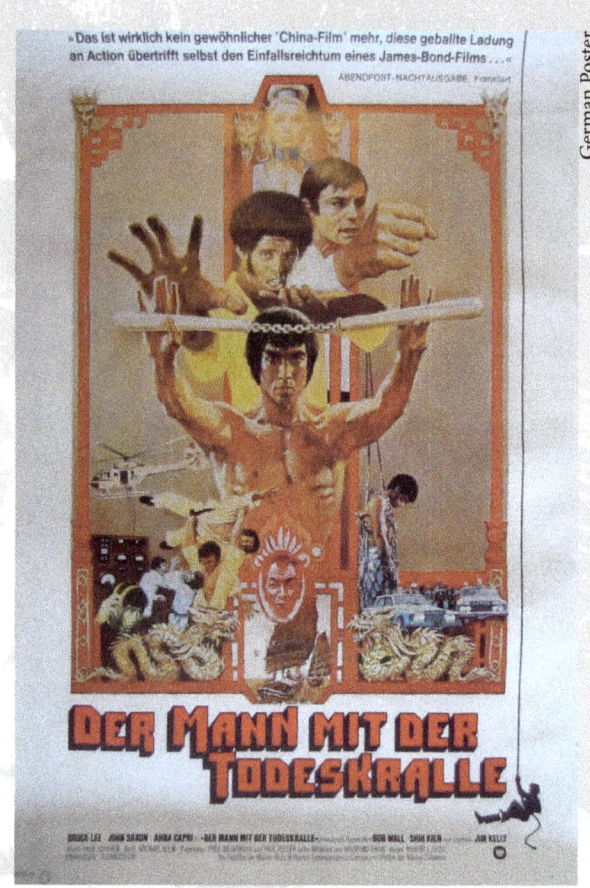

German Poster

German Poster

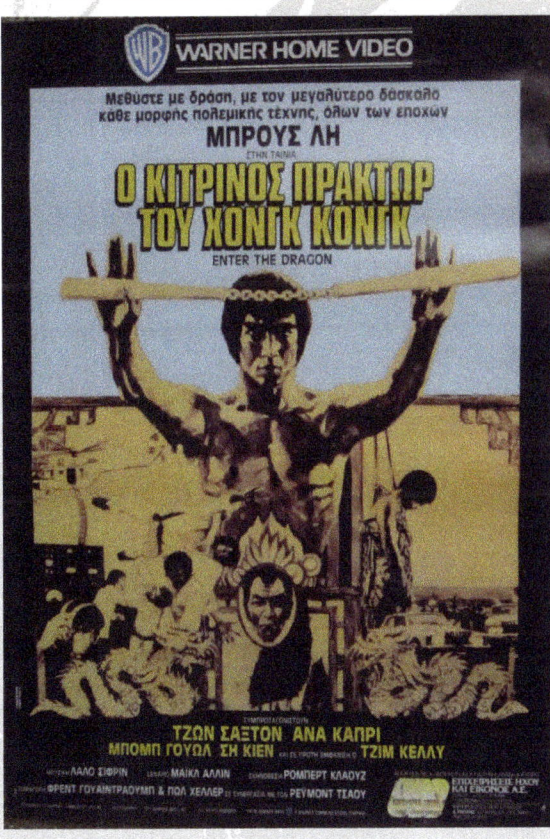

Hong Kong Poster

Indian Poster

Israel Poster

Italian Poster

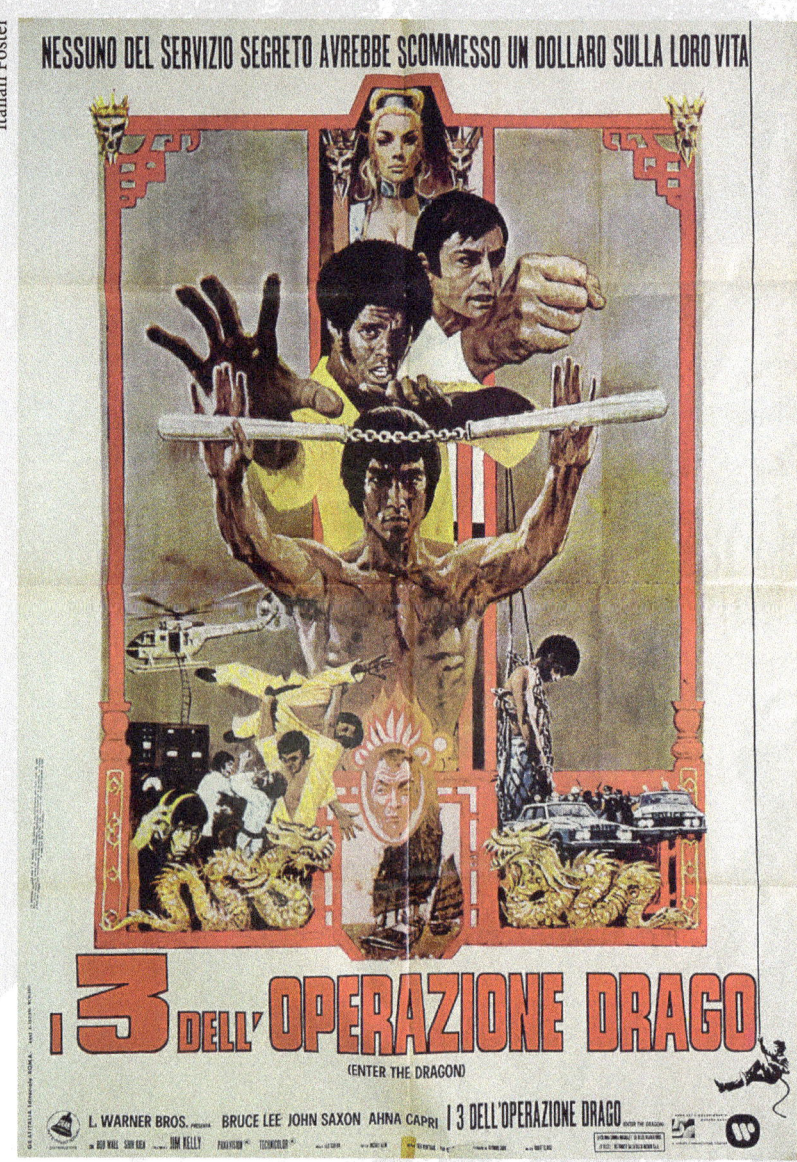

Italian Poster

Japanese Posters

Korean Poster

Lebanese Poster

Lebanese Poster

Netherlands Poster

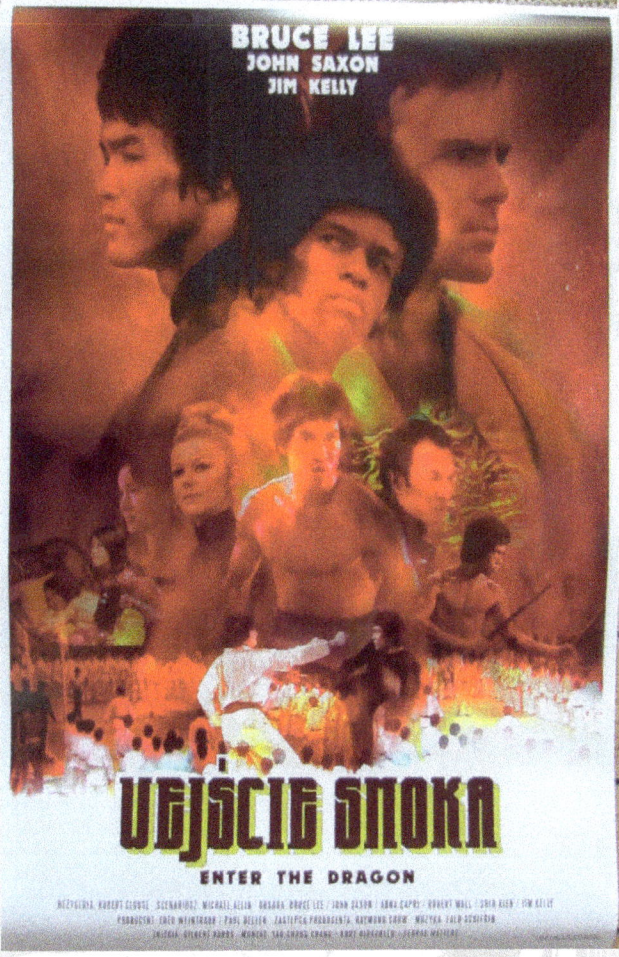
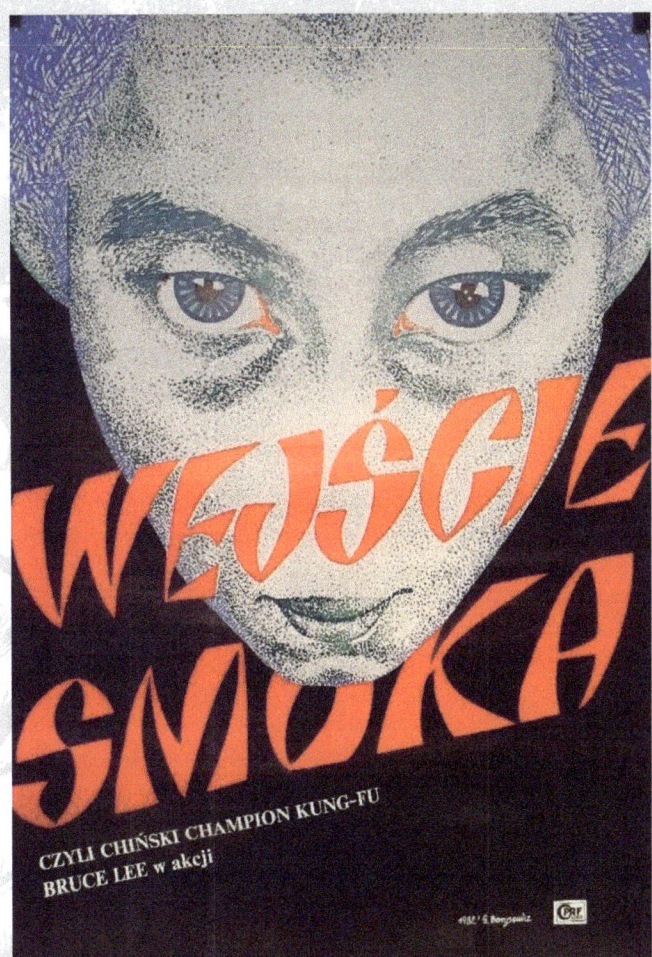

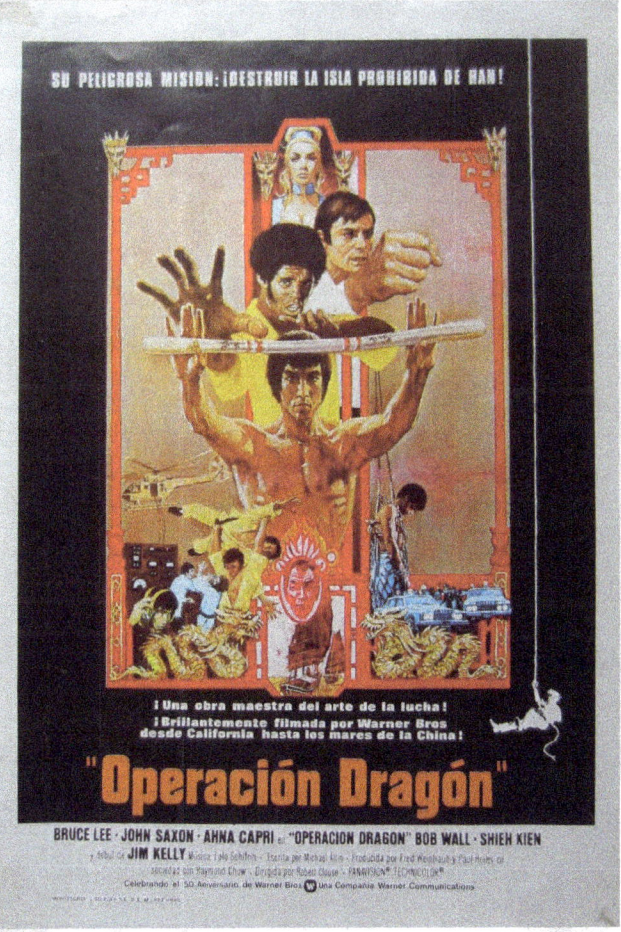

Taiwan Poster

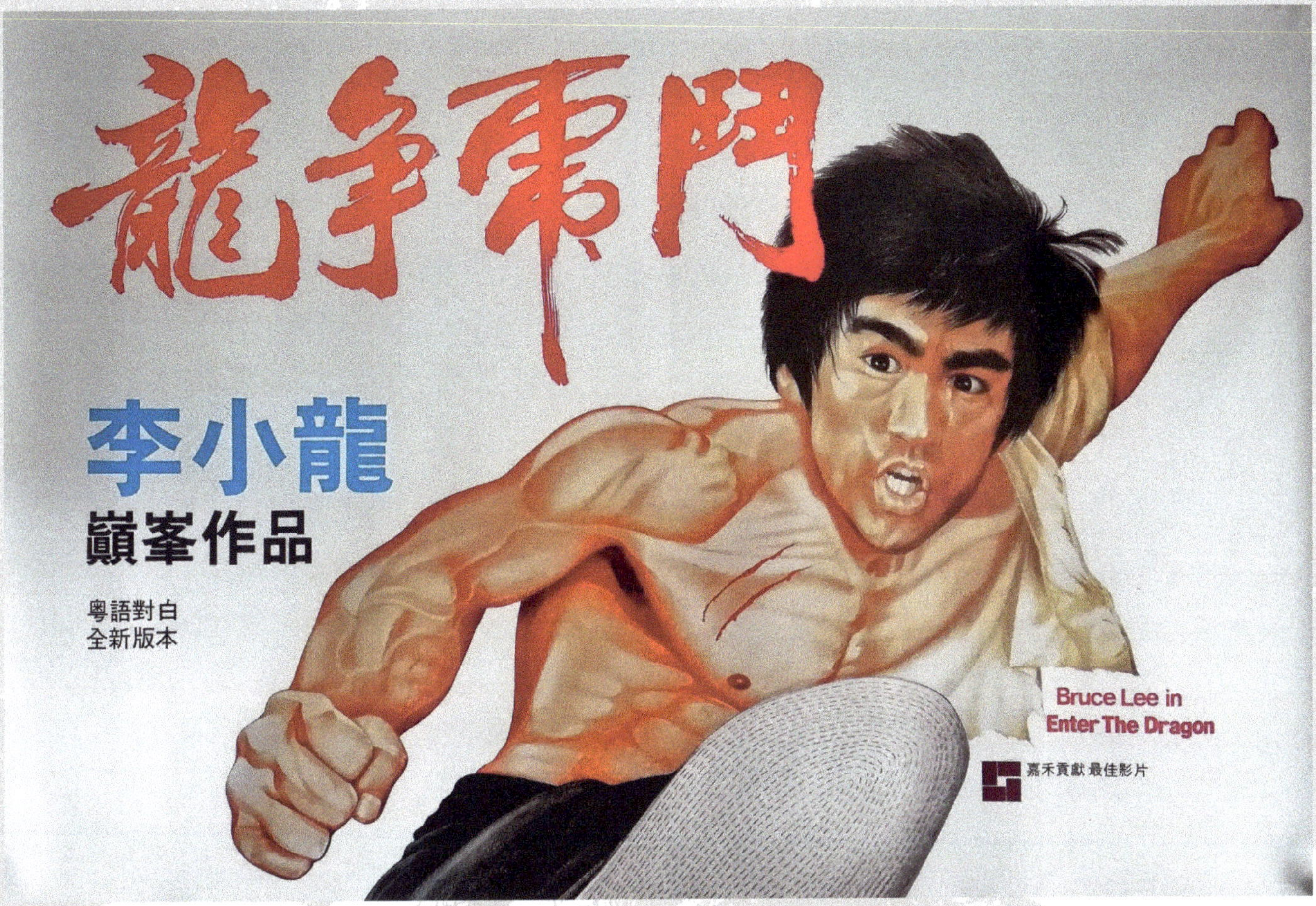

Tailand Poster

UK Quad Poster

UK Promo Poster (First Release)

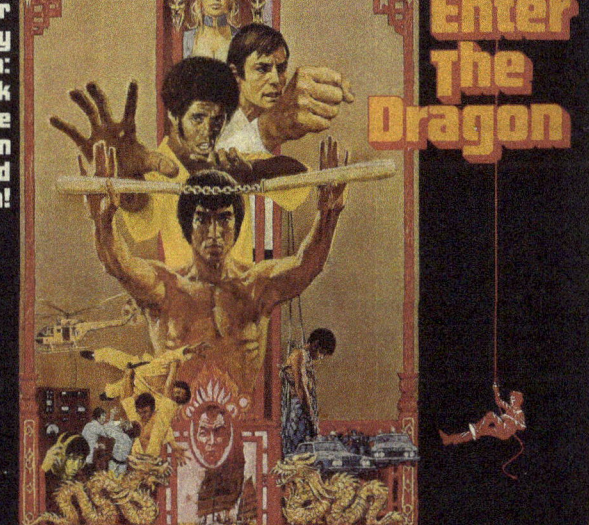

USA Super size Poster

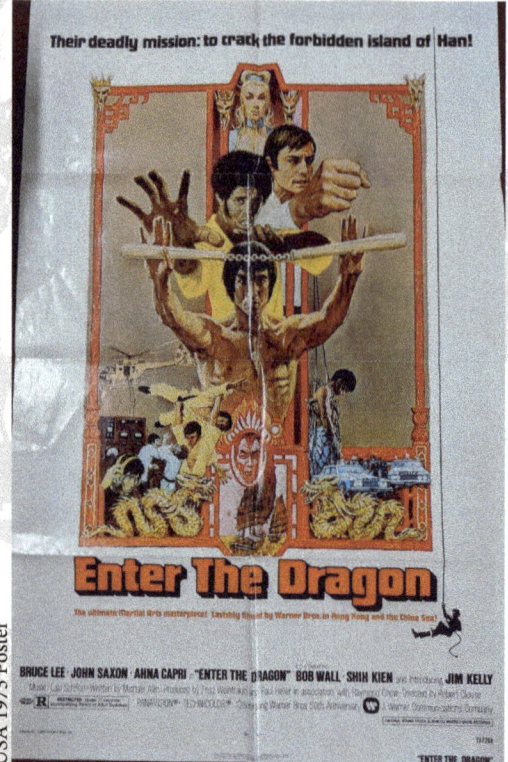

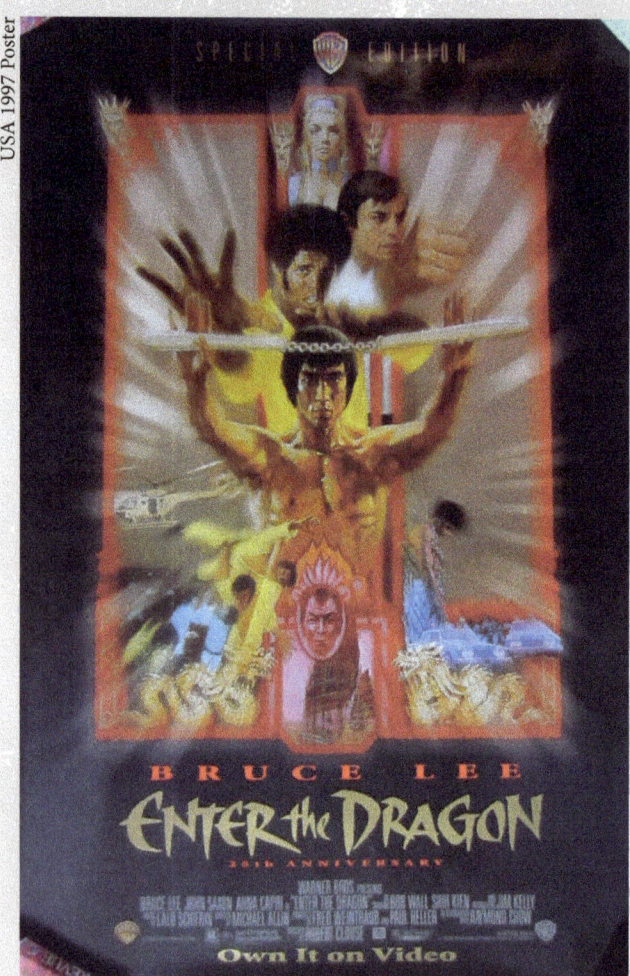
USA 1997 Poster

USA 1997 Poster

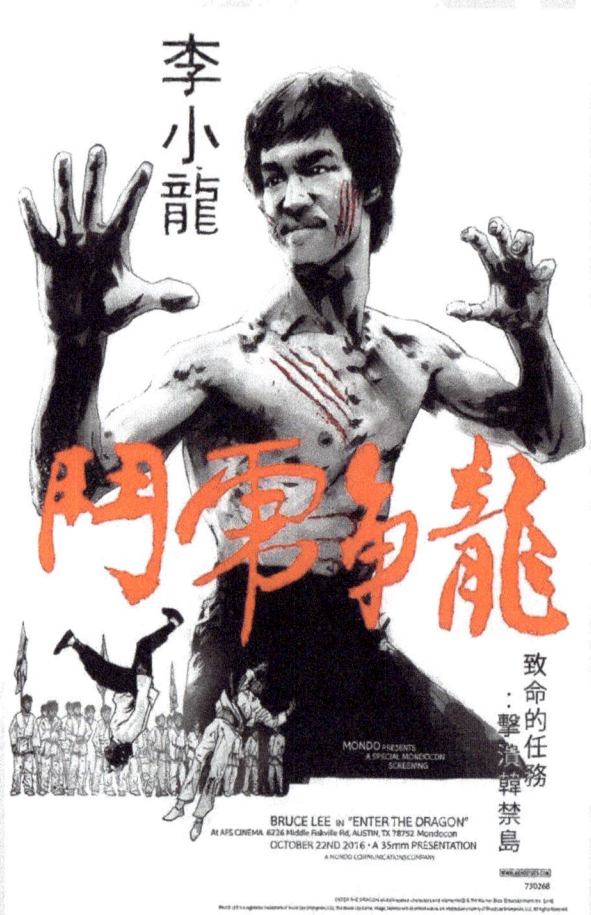
USA Monococon - Texas 2016

USA Spanish International Poster

Yugoslavian Poster

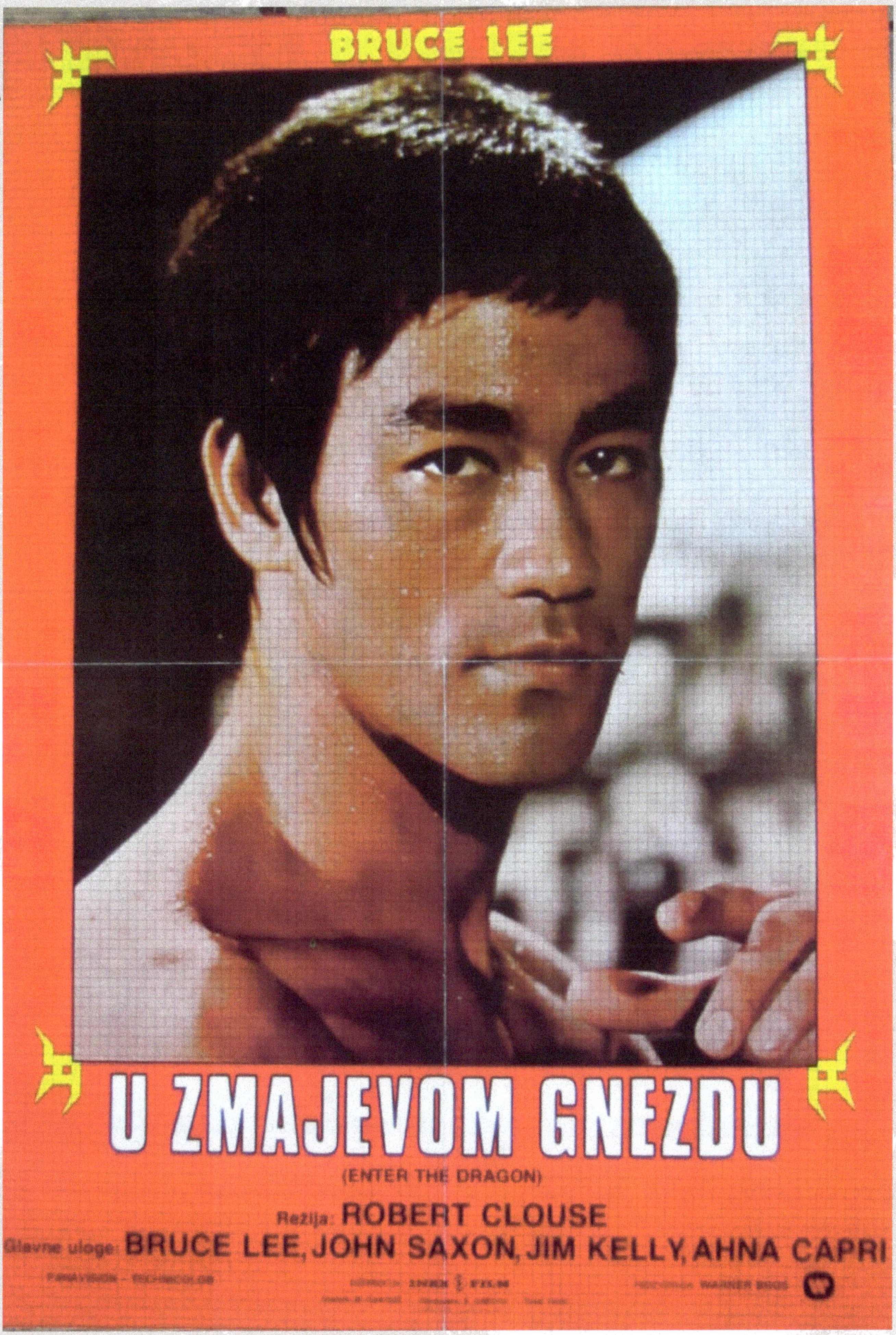
BRUCE LEE
U ZMAJEVOM GNEZDU
(ENTER THE DRAGON)
Režija: ROBERT CLOUSE
Glavne uloge: BRUCE LEE, JOHN SAXON, JIM KELLY, AHNA CAPRI

Magazine Adverts

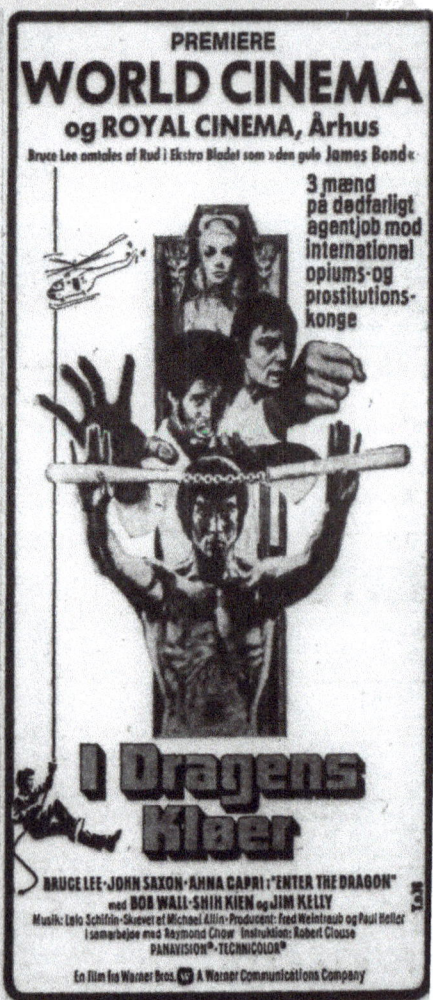

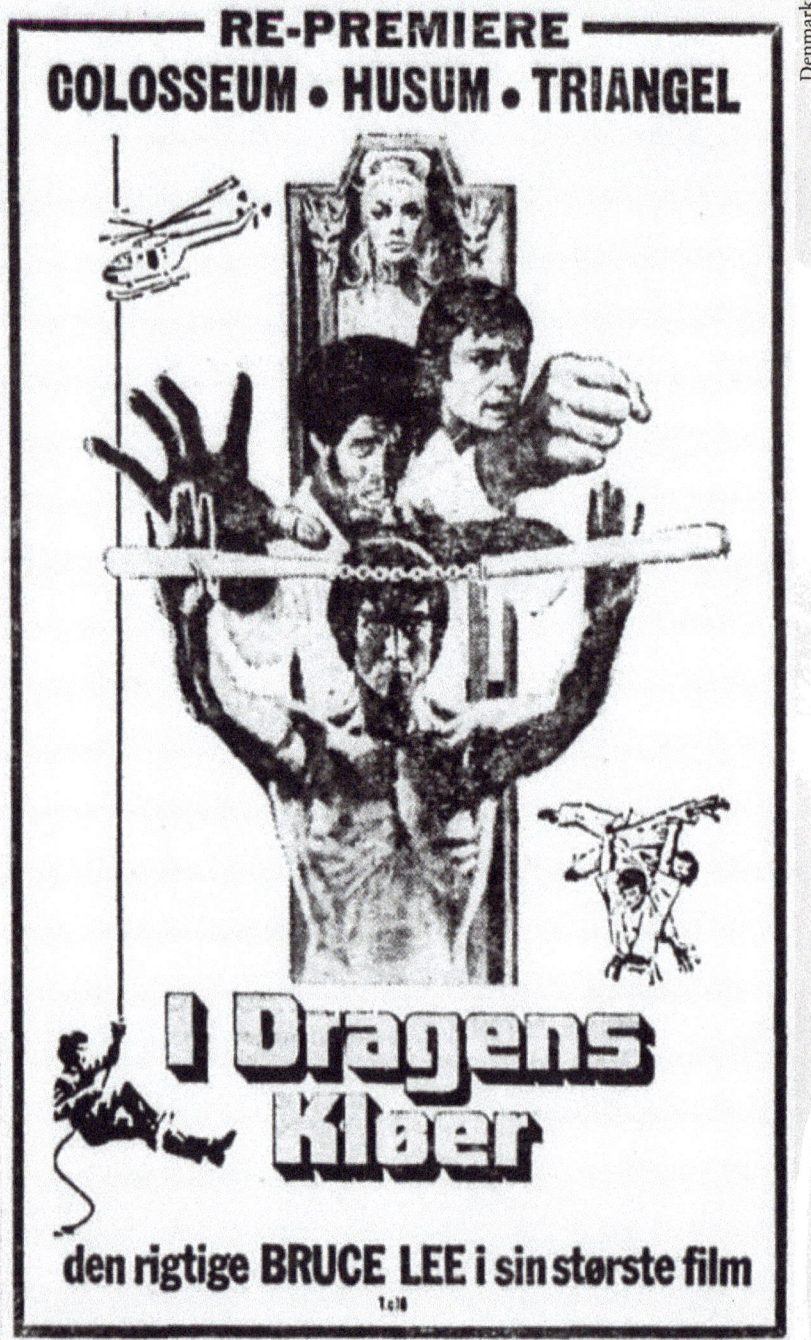

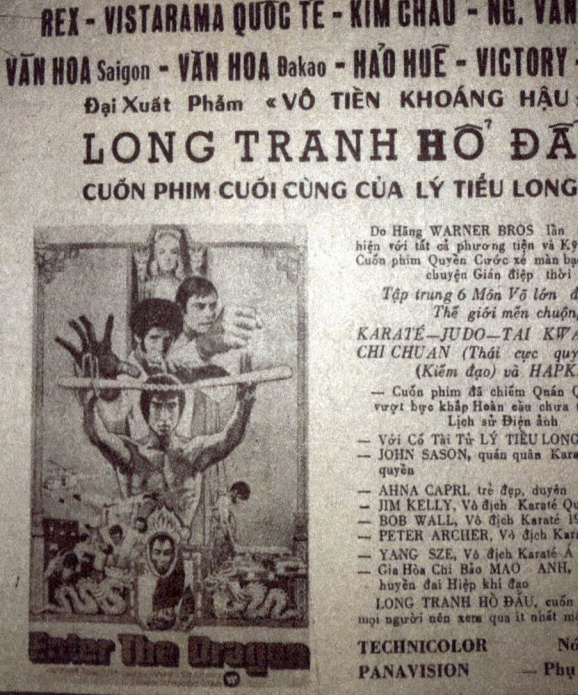

Warner Bros. is Proud to Announce Trade Screening Sneak Previews of One of its Major Productions — the Ultimate in Martial Arts Excitement and Adventure.

Enter The Dragon

BRUCE LEE · JOHN SAXON · AHNA CAPRI in "ENTER THE DRAGON"
Co-Starring **BOB WALL · SHIH KIEN** and Introducing **JIM KELLY**
Music: Lalo Schifrin · Written by Michael Allin · Produced by Fred Weintraub and Paul Heller in association with Raymond Chow · Directed by Robert Clouse · PANAVISION® · TECHNICOLOR®

TRADE SCREENING SNEAK PREVIEWS – SAT. AUG. 4

ATLANTA Fox	8:00 PM	MEMPHIS Malco	8:00 PM
BOSTON Savoy	8:30 PM	MILWAUKEE Palace	8:00 PM
CHARLOTTE Tryon Mall	10:00 PM	MINNEAPOLIS Cine #4, St. Paul	8:00 PM
CHICAGO United Artists	8:00 PM	NEW ORLEANS Saenger	8:00 PM
CINCINNATI Grand	8:30 PM	NEW YORK Loews State 2 Fri Aug 3	8:30 PM
CLEVELAND Center Mayfield	9:00 PM	OKLAHOMA Sheppard #1	8:00 PM
DALLAS Medallion	8:00 PM	PHILADELPHIA Milgram	8:30 PM
DENVER Centre	8:00 PM	PORTLAND Broadway #2	8:30 PM
DES MOINES Galaxy	8:00 PM	SALT LAKE Utah	8:00 PM
DETROIT Madison	8:00 PM	SAN FRANCISCO Warfield	8:30 PM
JACKSONVILLE Florida	8:00 PM	SEATTLE U.A. 70	8:45 PM
KANSAS CITY Metro #4	9:00 PM	ST. LOUIS Loews State	8:00 PM
LOS ANGELES Pantages Hollywood Jul 27	8:30 PM	WASHINGTON Town #2	8:00 PM

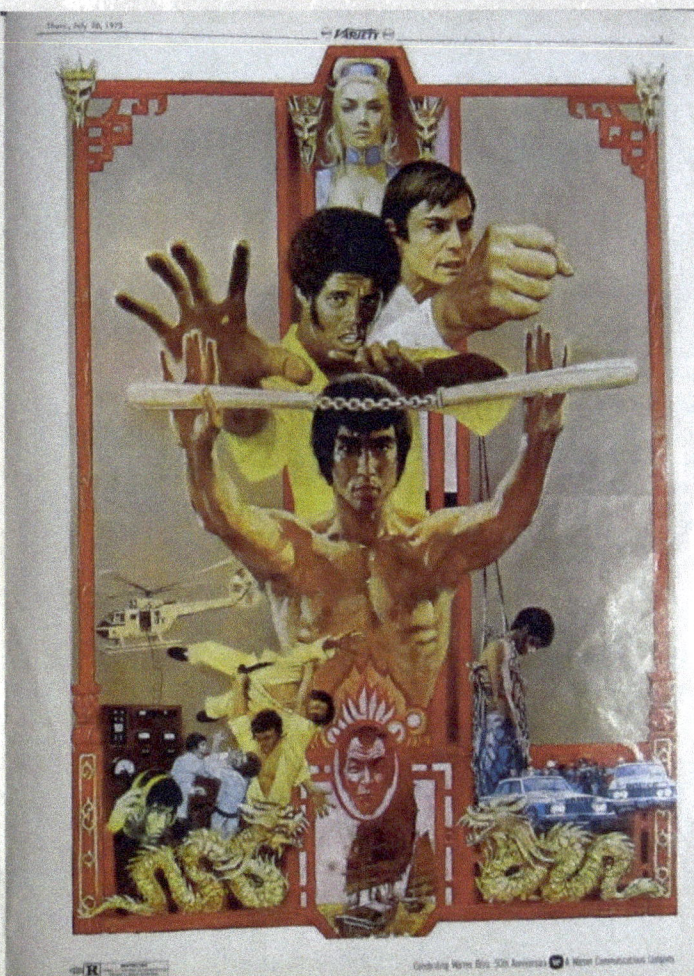

Enter The Dragon ENTERS THE RECORD BOOKS!

$35,122 Grand Theatre, Cincinnati — First week house record.

$134,513 State Lake, Chicago — First week house record.

$82,554 Chinese, Los Angeles — First week non-holiday house record.

$20,051 Pinehaven Cinema I Theatre, Charleston, S.C. — First week house record.

Their deadly mission: to crack the forbidden island of Han!

Enter The Dragon

The ultimate in adventure and excitement!
Lavishly filmed by Warner Bros. from California to the China Seas!

Lobby Cards

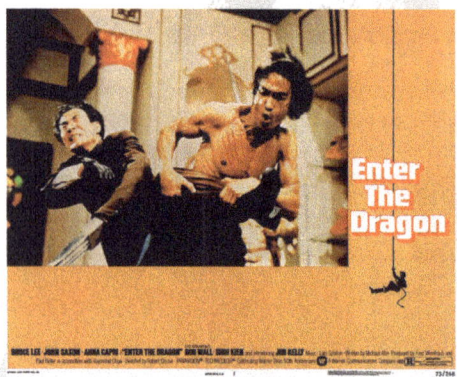

USA Lobby Cards

French Lobby Cards

Hong Kong Lobby Cards

Yugoslavian Lobby Cards

Brazilian Lobby Cards

Page: 124

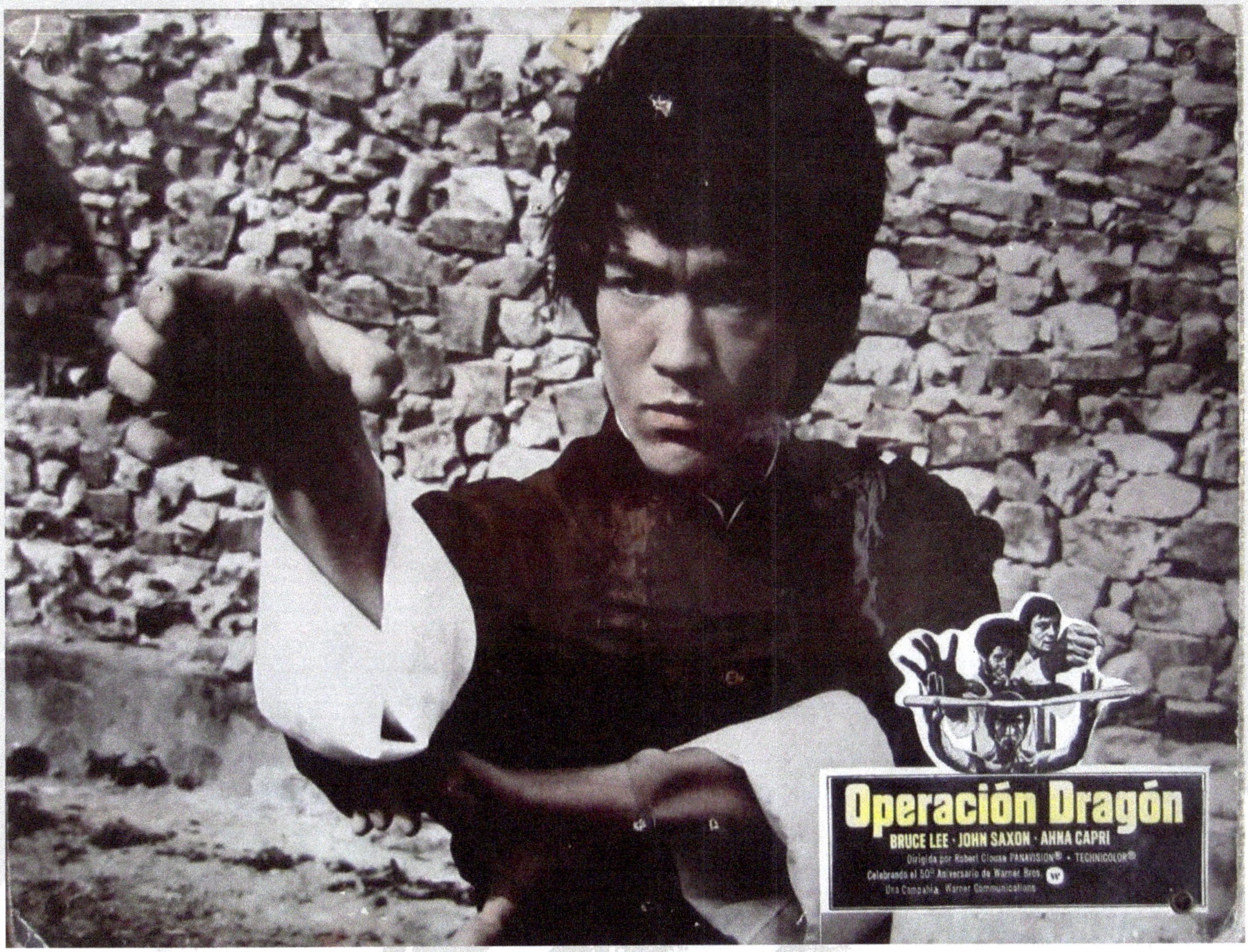
Operación Dragón
BRUCE LEE · JOHN SAXON · AHNA CAPRI
Dirigida por Robert Clouse PANAVISION® · TECHNICOLOR®
Celebrando el 50° Aniversario de Warner Bros.
Una Compañía Warner Communications

Operación Dragón
BRUCE LEE · JOHN SAXON · AHNA CAPRI

Operación Dragón
BRUCE LEE · JOHN SAXON · AHNA CAPRI

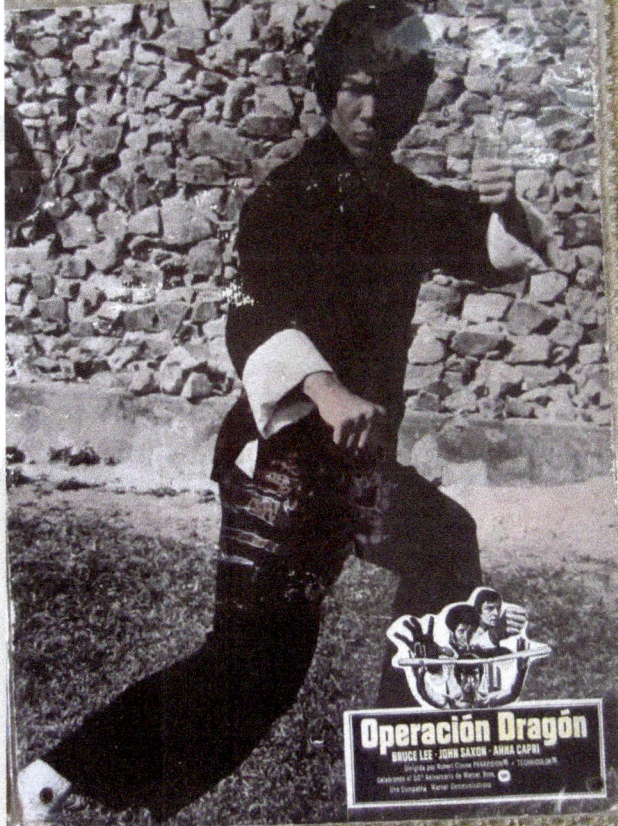

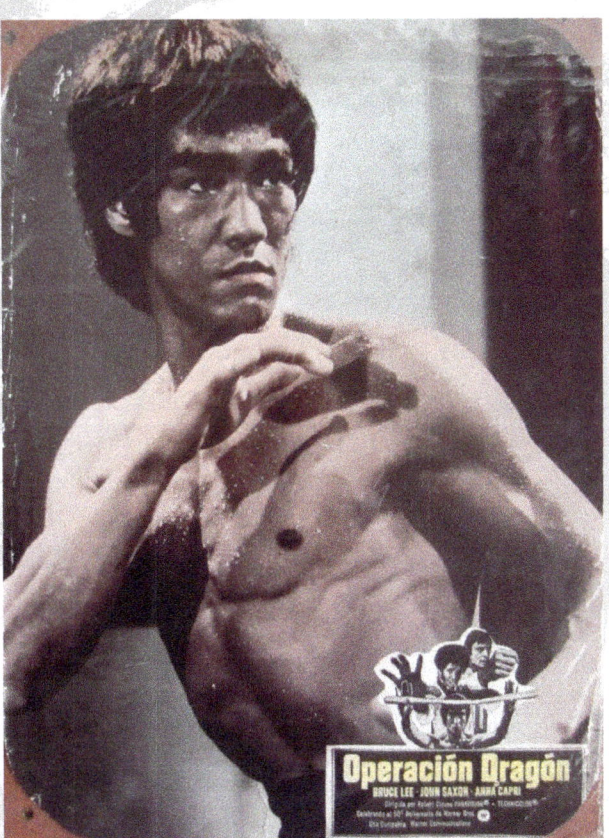

Various

WARNER HOME VIDEO
Bruce Lee
Der Mann mit der Todeskralle
gekürzte Fassung
MIT ORIGINAL-KINOTRAILER
WARNER HOME VIDEO

龍爭虎鬥

BRUCE LEE IN
龍爭虎鬥

BRUCE LEE IN
龍爭虎鬥

NEUES
Film-PROGRAMM
Nr. 6525
DER MANN MIT DER
TODESKRALLE

Enter The
Dragon
2023
MARTIAL ARTS SPECTACULAR!
WITH THE LEGENDARY
BRUCE LEE
50TH
ANNIVERSARY
PALACE NOVA
EASTEND
MAR 8

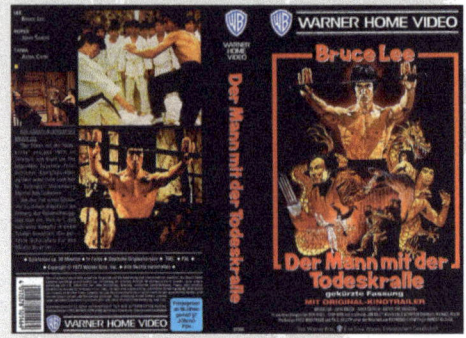

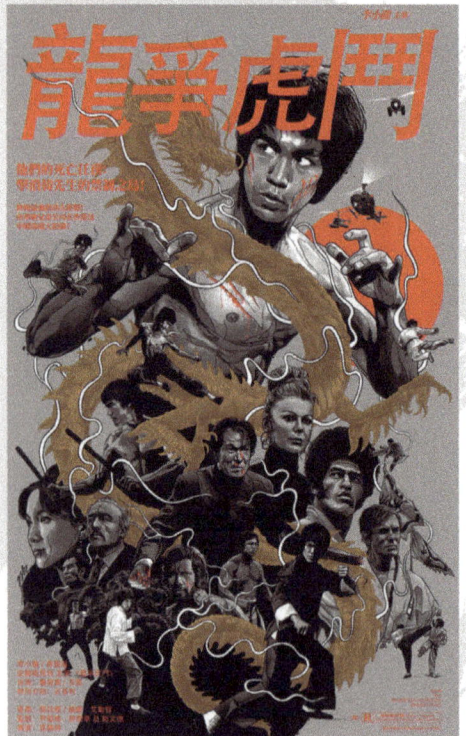

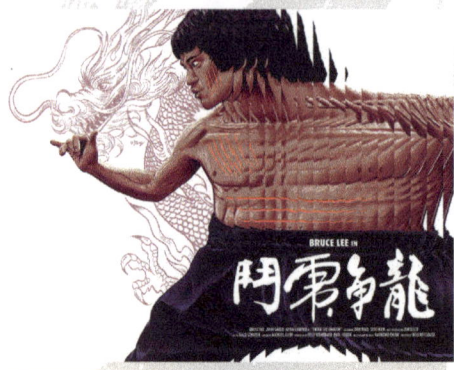

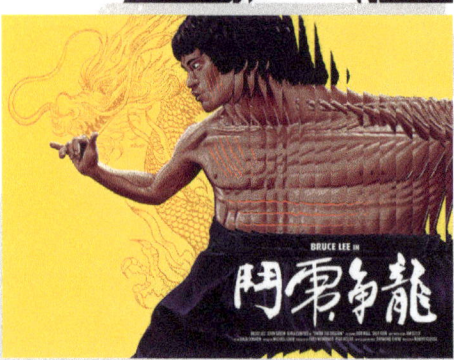

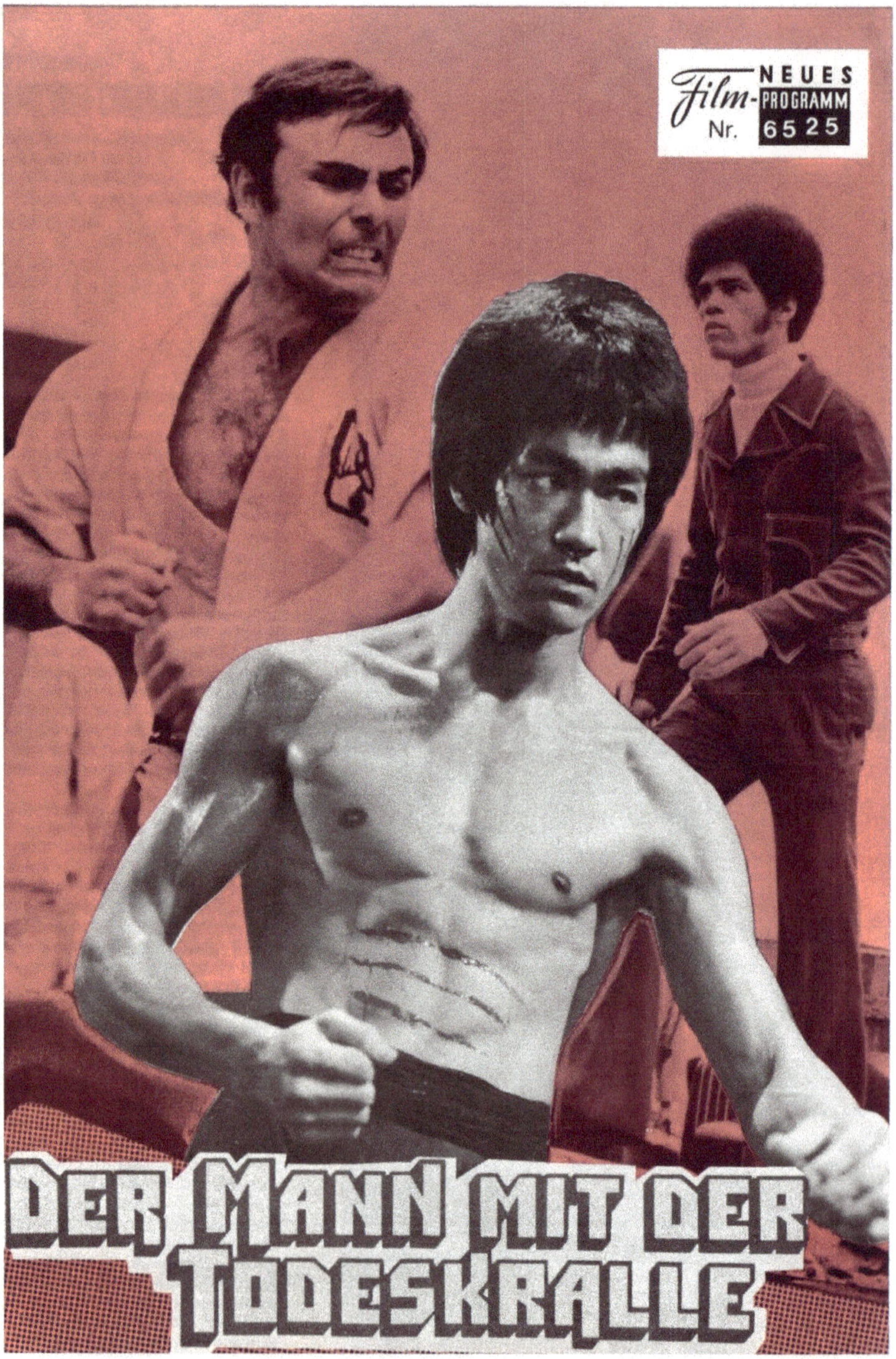

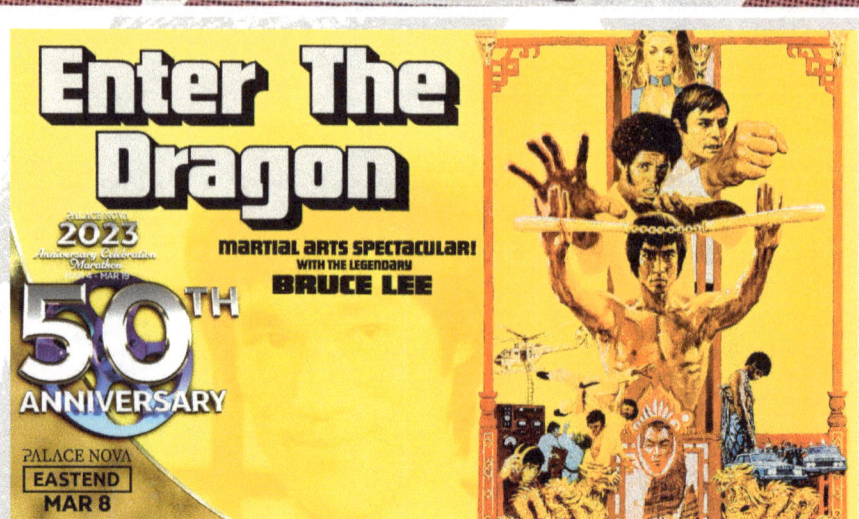

BRUCE LEE
JOHN SAXON
Enter The Dragon
AHNA CAPRI
JIM KELLY

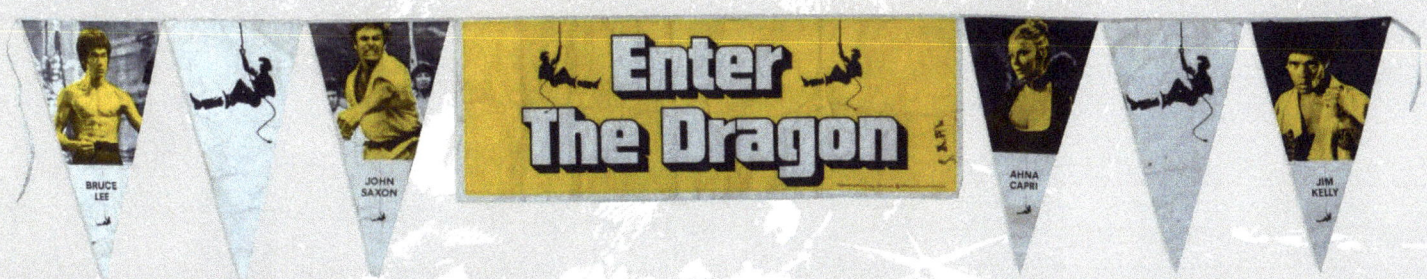

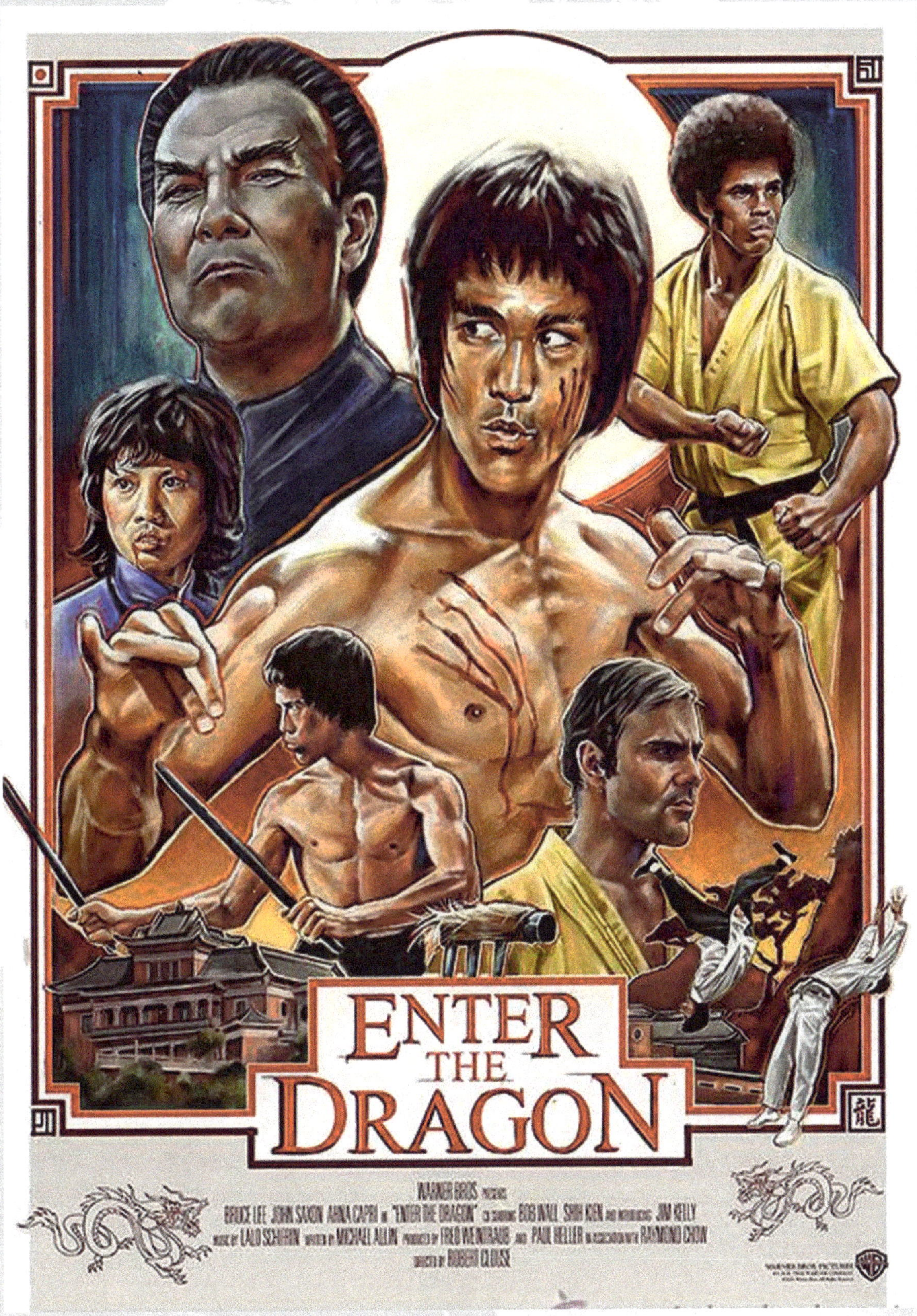
ENTER THE DRAGON
WARNER BROS
BRUCE LEE JOHN SAXON AHNA CAPRI "ENTER THE DRAGON" BOB WALL SHIH KIEN JIM KELLY
LALO SCHIFRIN MICHAEL ALLIN FRED WEINTRAUB PAUL HELLER RAYMOND CHOW
ROBERT CLOUSE

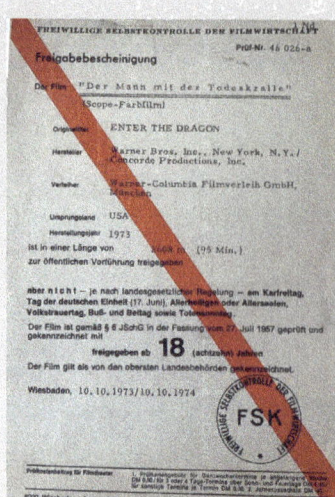
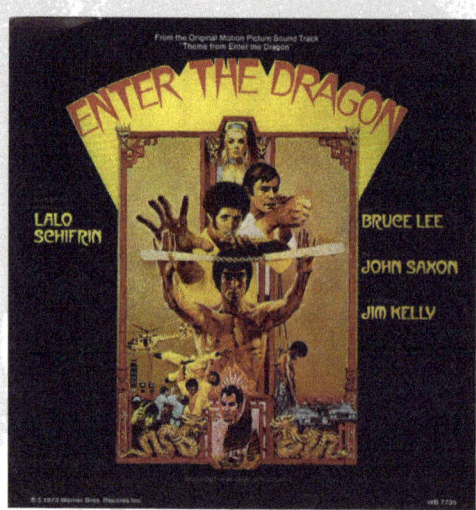
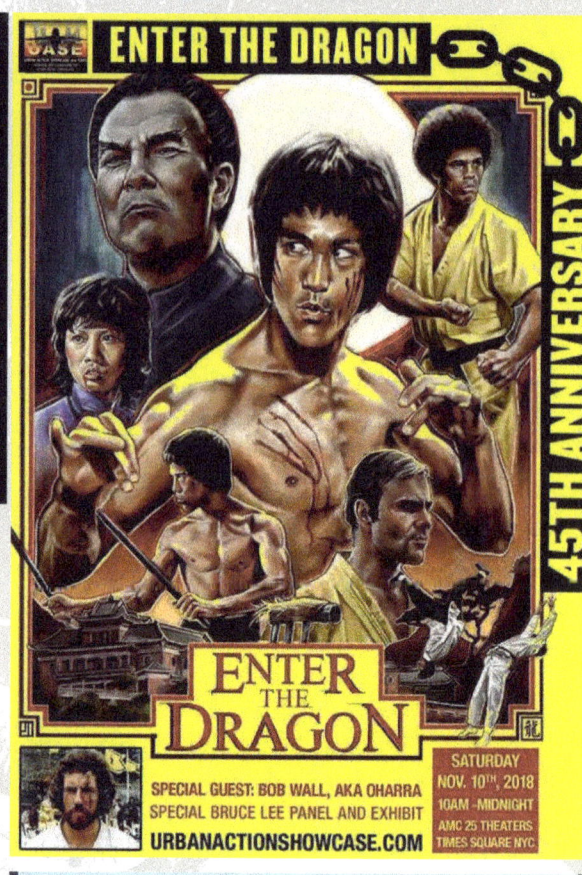
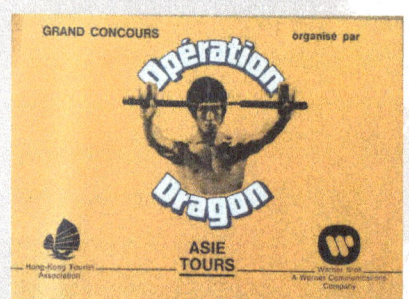

John Negron's Memorabilia

PHOTO'S, PROMOTIONAL & POSTERS

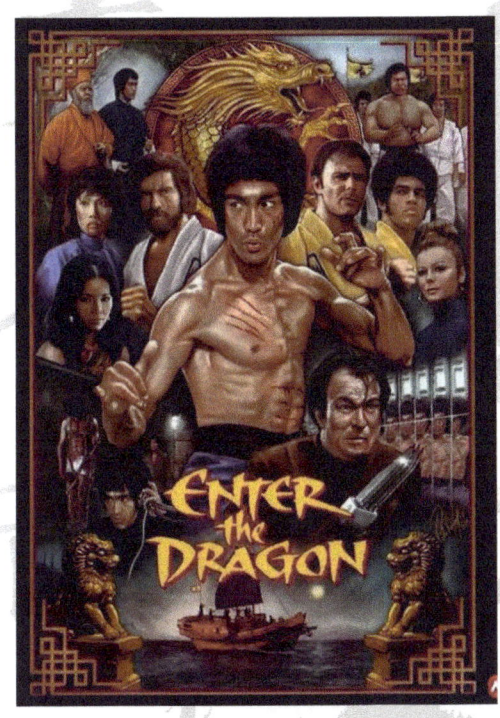

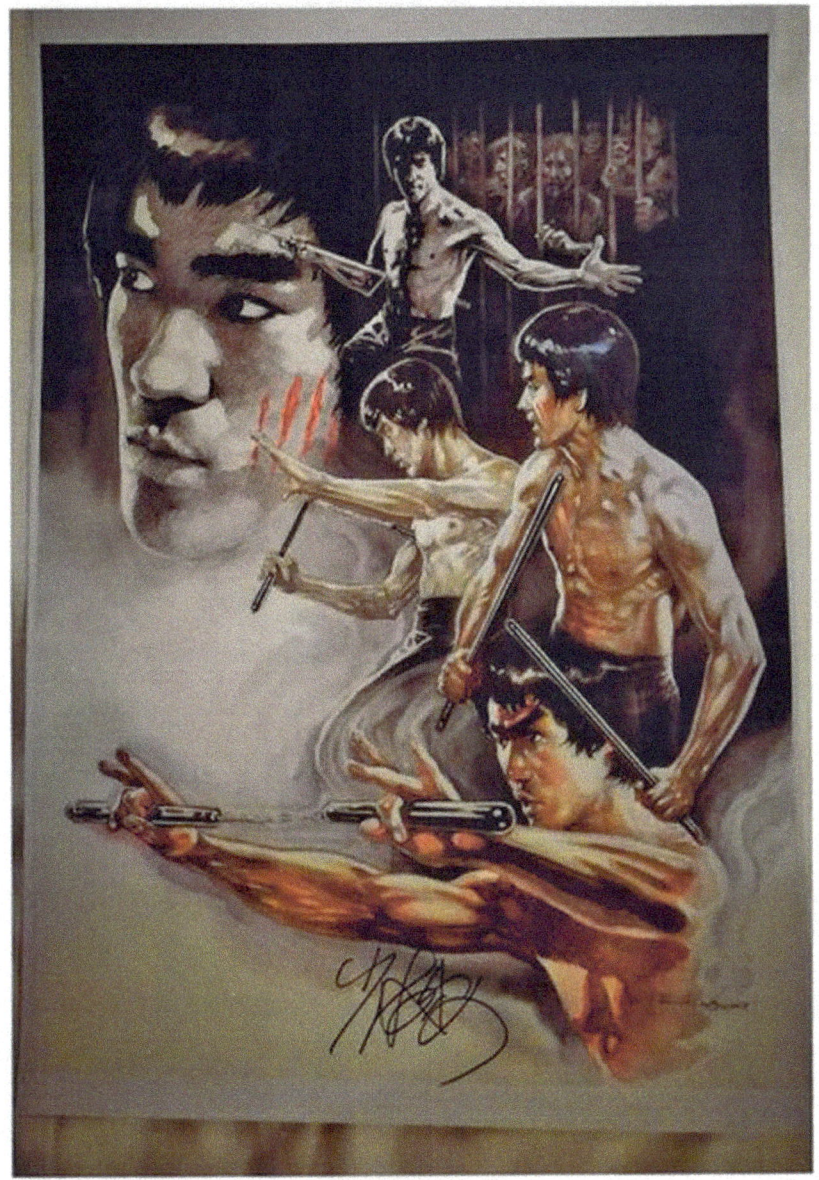

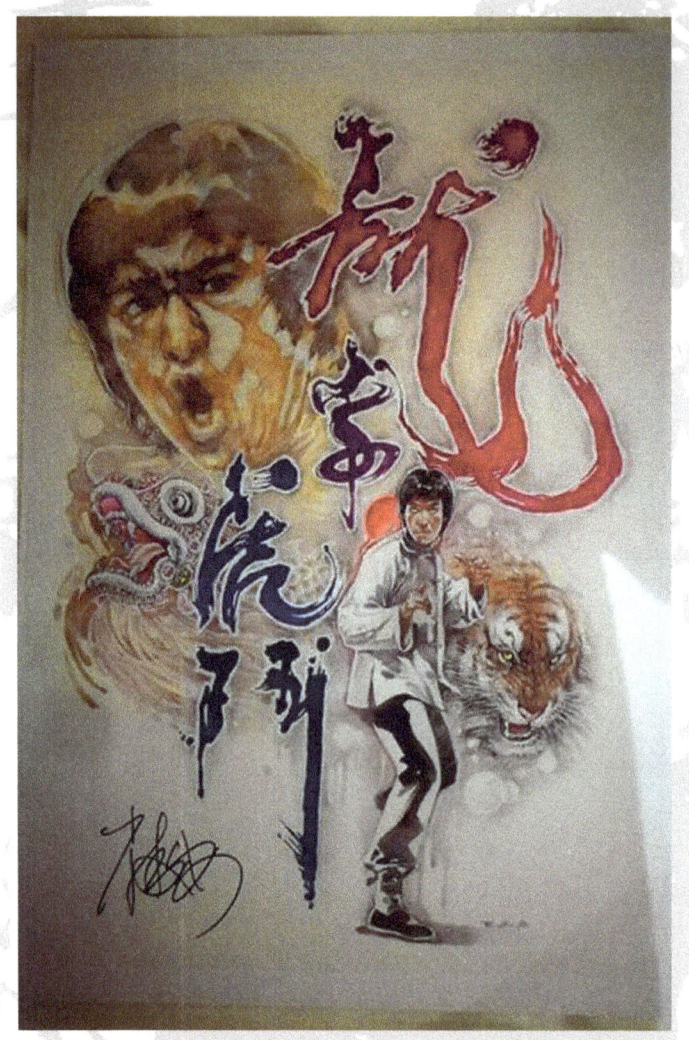

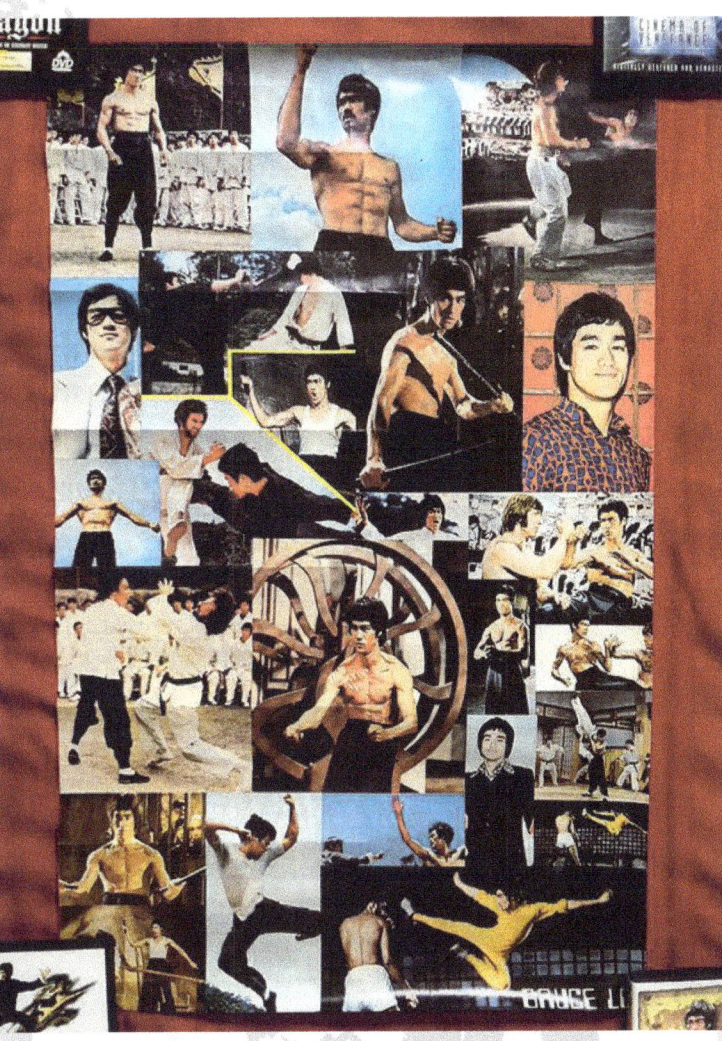

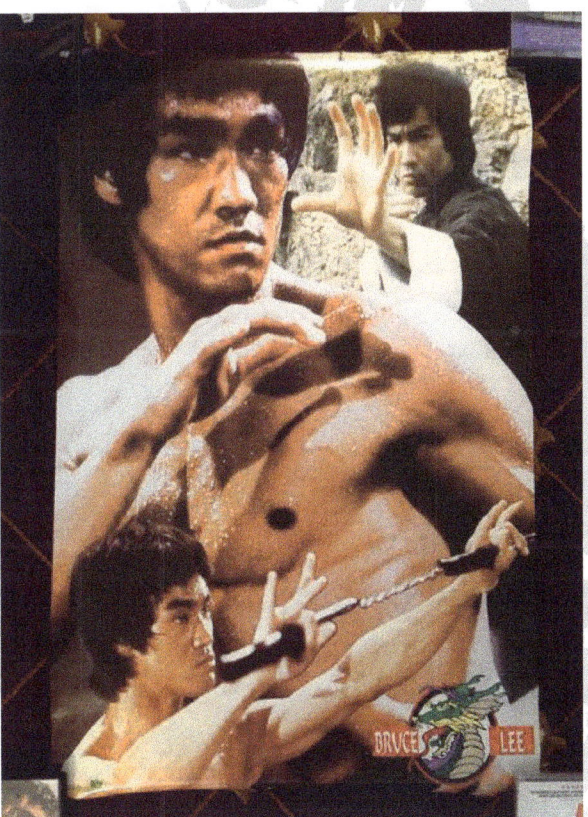

KUNG-FU ACTION—DEATHLY DRIVING SKILLS IN THE TOUGHEST DOUBLE BILL AROUND!
THE LEGENDARY
BRUCE LEE
Enter The Dragon
X
AND
DAVID CARRADINE
DEATH RACE 2000
X
BRUCE LEE · JOHN SAXON · AHNA CAPRI
in "ENTER THE DRAGON"
Co-Starring BOB WALL · SHIN KIEN
and Introducing JIM KELLY
Music: Lalo Schifrin · Written by Michael Allin
Produced by Fred Weintraub and Paul Heller
in association with Raymond Chow · Directed by Robert Clouse
PANAVISION · TECHNICOLOR
DAVID CARRADINE SYLVESTER "ROCKY" STALLONE
"DEATH RACE 2000" SIMONE GRIFFETH
ROBERT THOM CHARLES B. GRIFFITH · IB MELCHIOR · ROGER CORMAN · PAUL BARTEL
Brent Walker

EL CARTEL DE
KUNG FU
En Mágico Color un Explosivo y Violento Poster de...
BRUCE LEE
(El Rey del Kung Fu)

李小龍

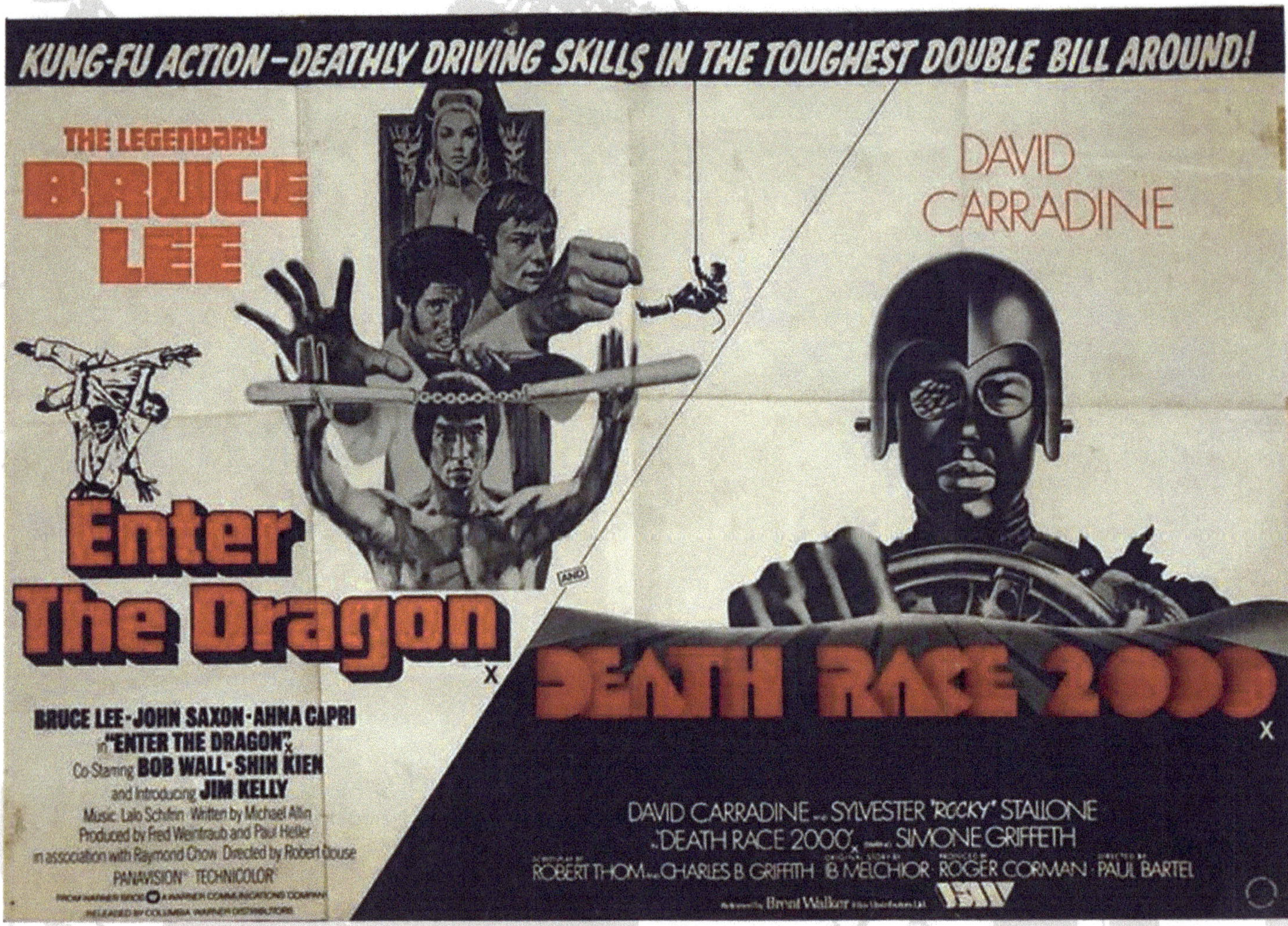

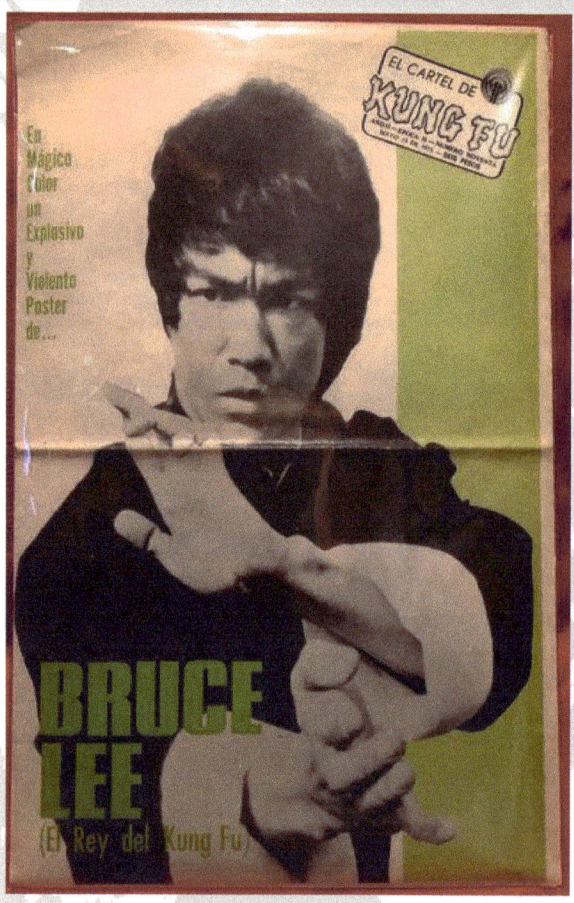

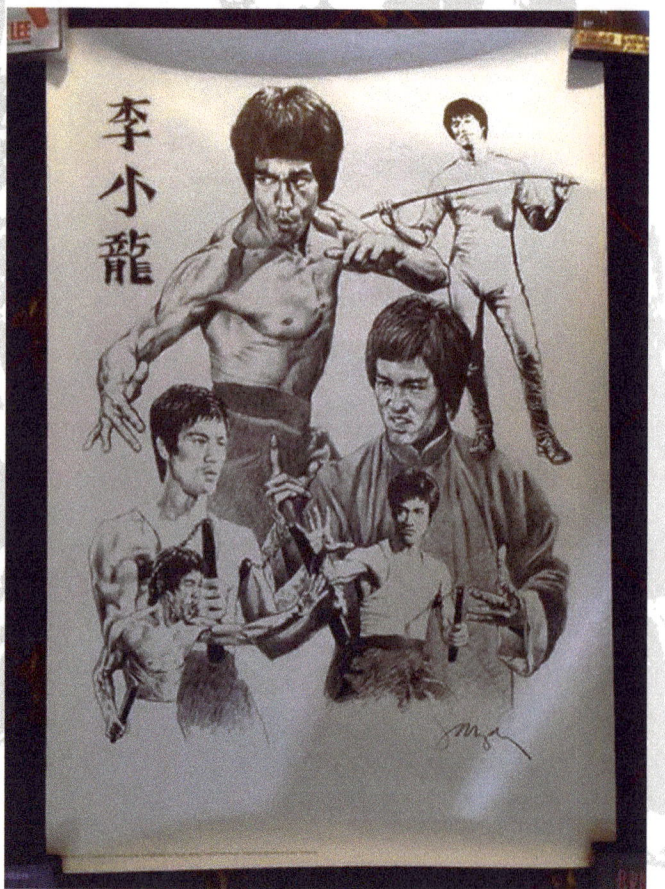

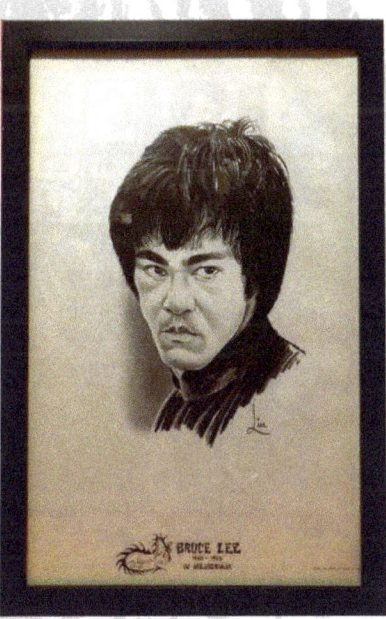

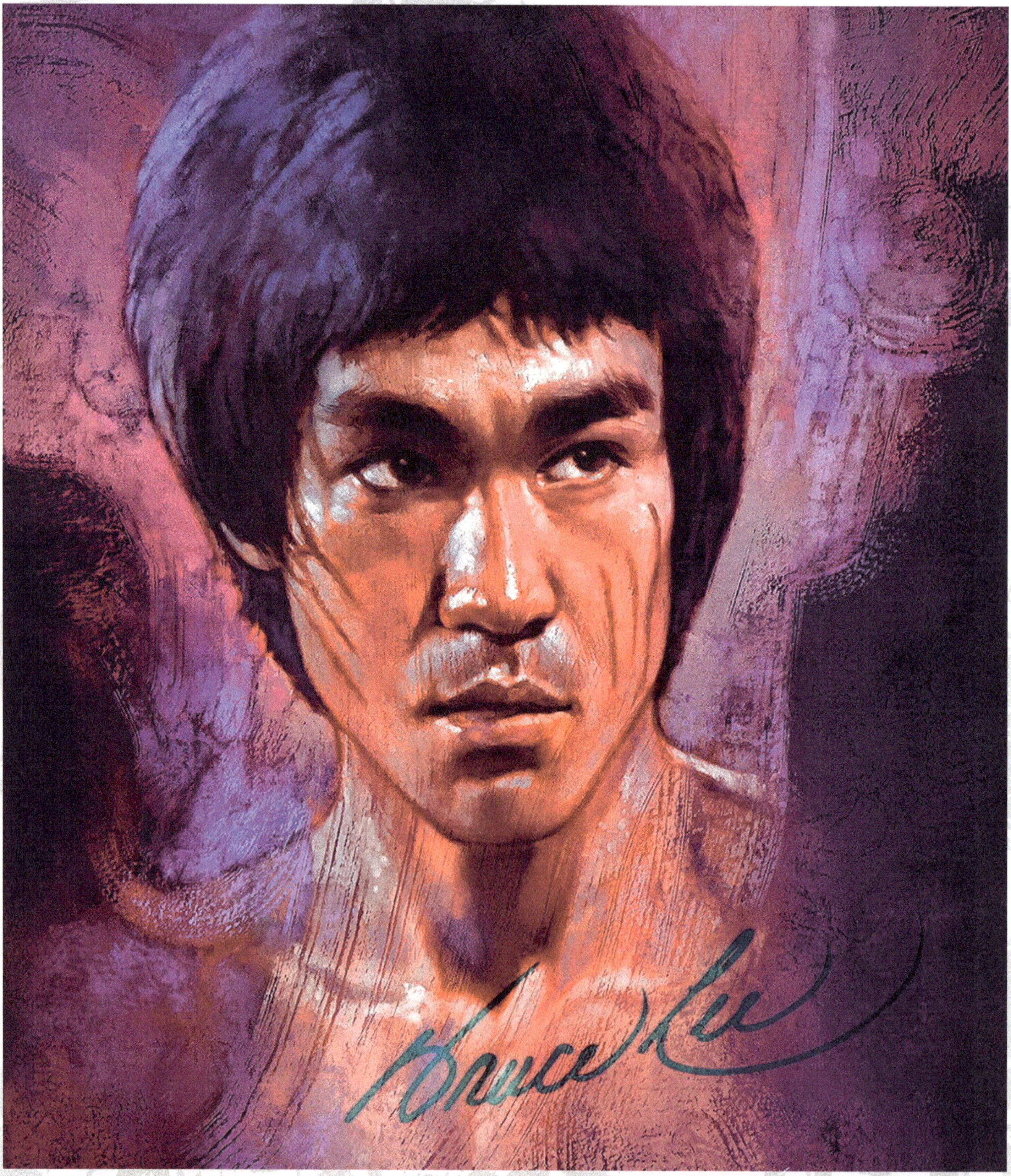

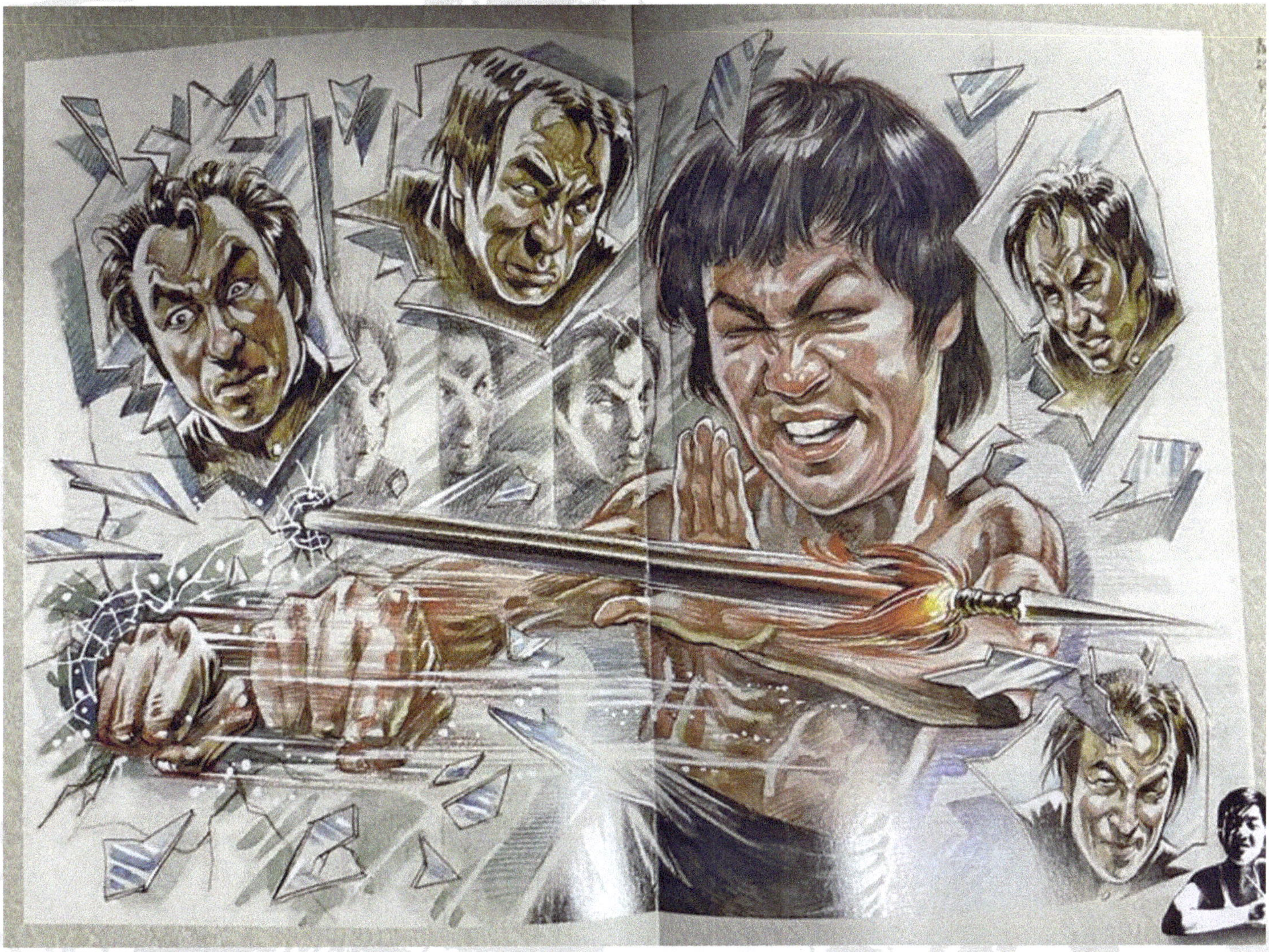

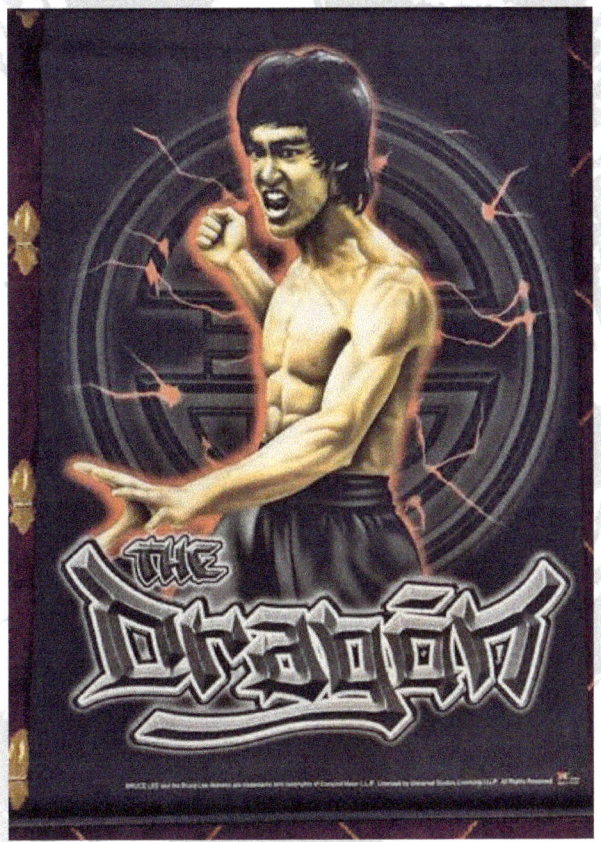

BRUCE LEE
1940-1973

BRUCE LEE

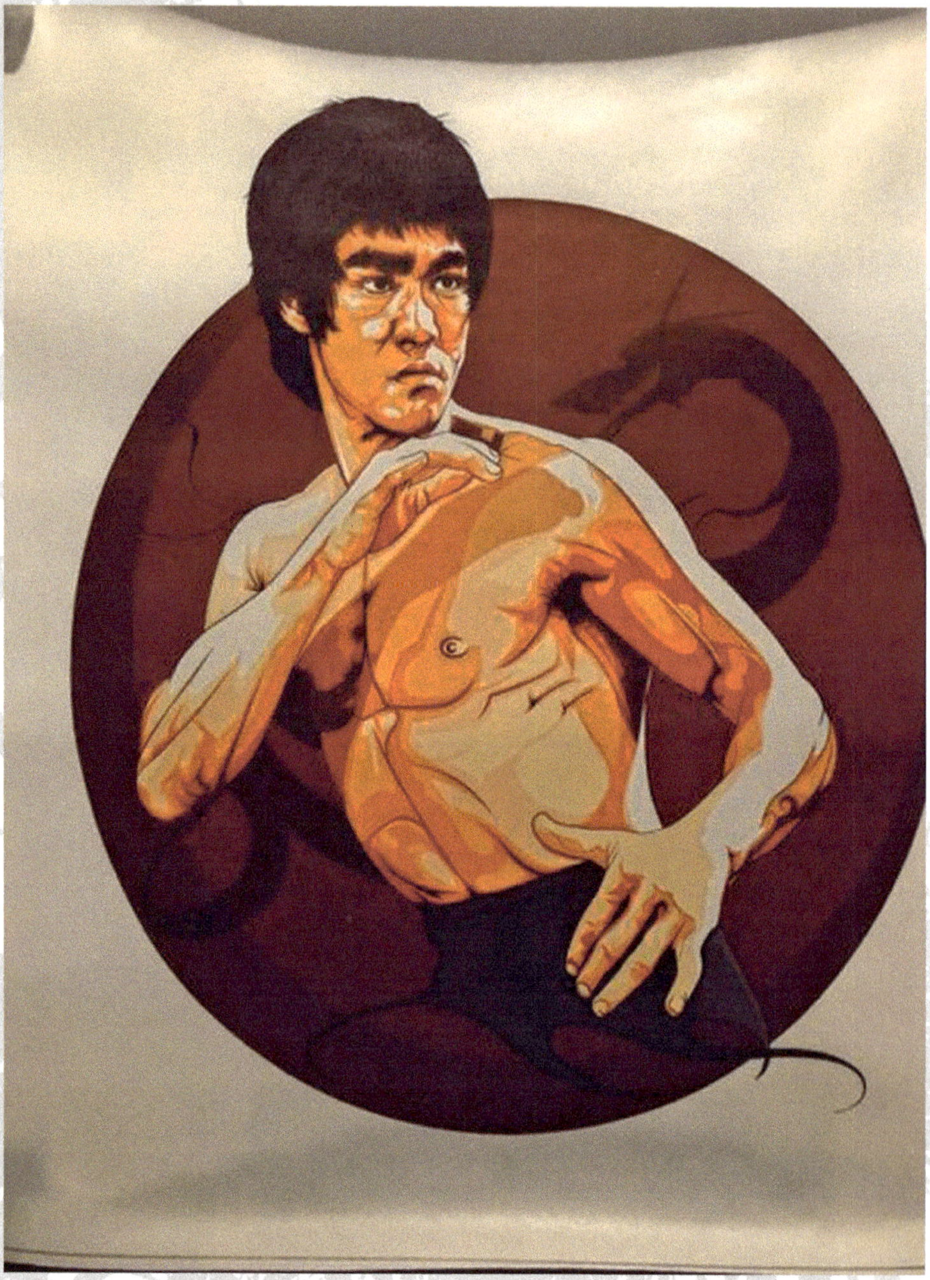

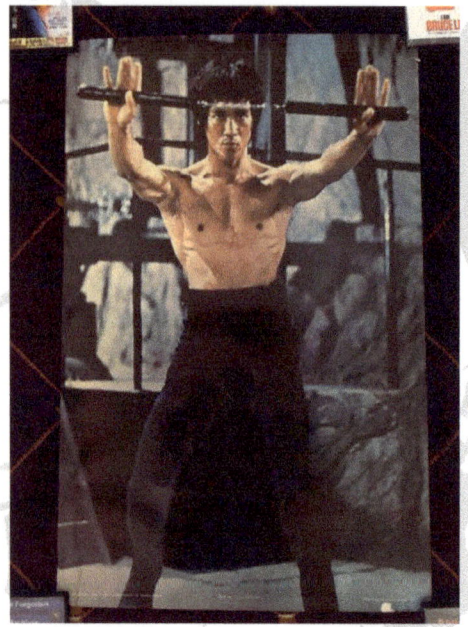

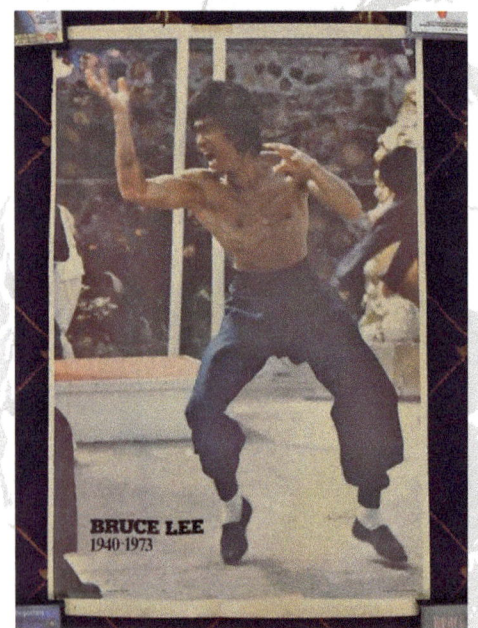

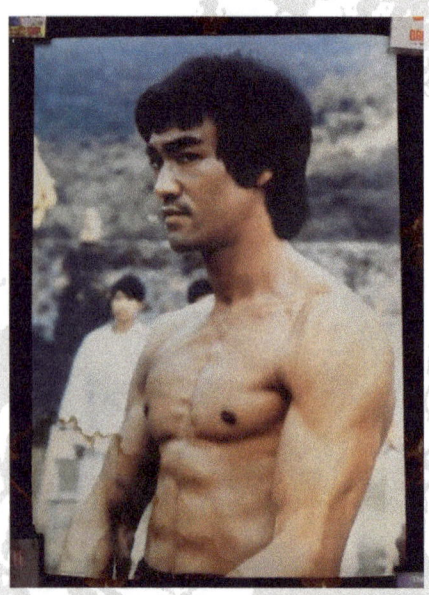

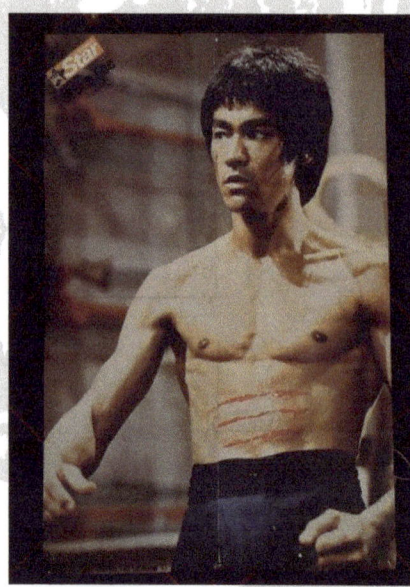

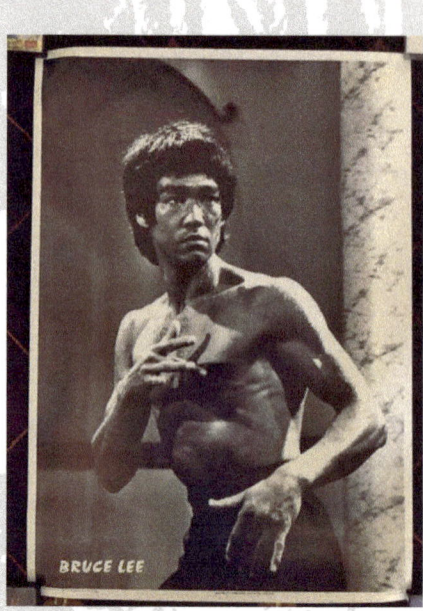

Samurai

JUDO - KARATE - KUNG-FU

periodico mensile
anno I - n. 6 - lire 500
agosto 1976

Spedizione in abbonamento postale Gruppo III

arti marziali e cultura orientale

LA BOXE TAILANDESE

il personaggio
CARLO FUGAZZA

la leggenda di
BRUCE LEE

10 domande
alle ragazze del judo

INSERTO SPECIALE: KUNG-FU

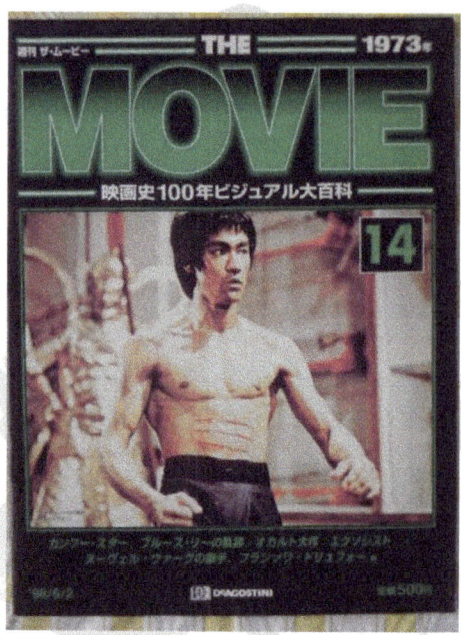

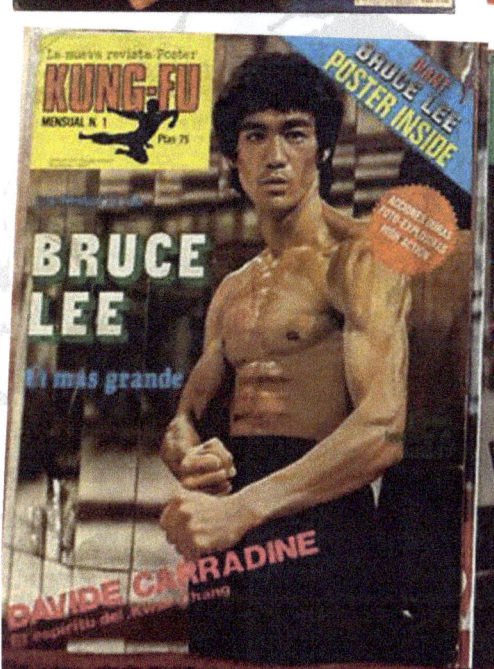

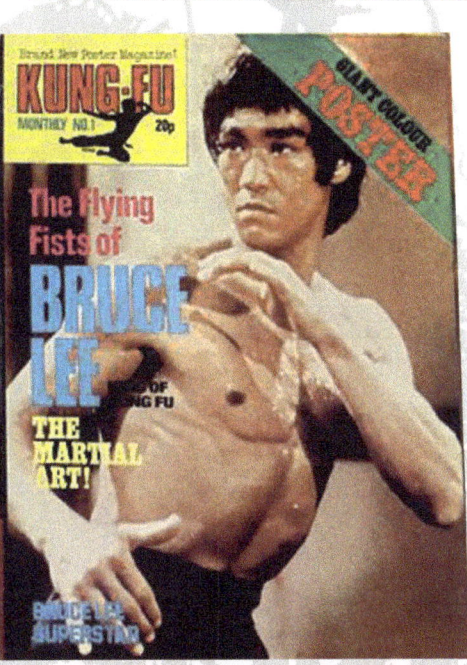
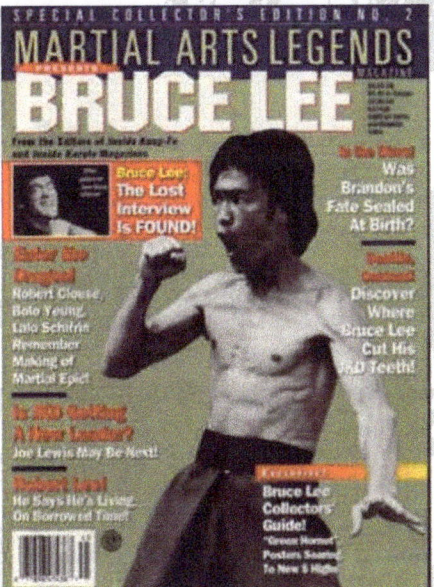

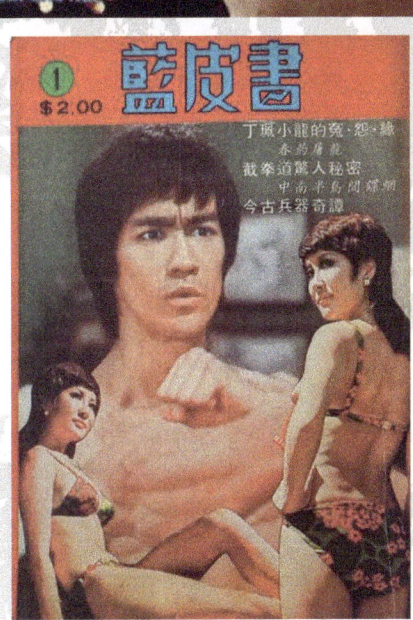

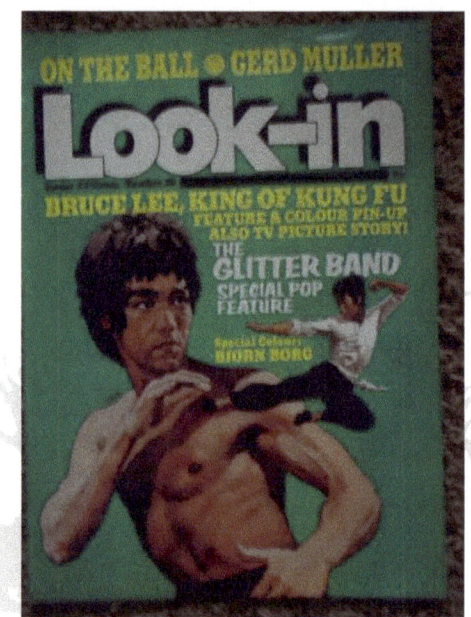

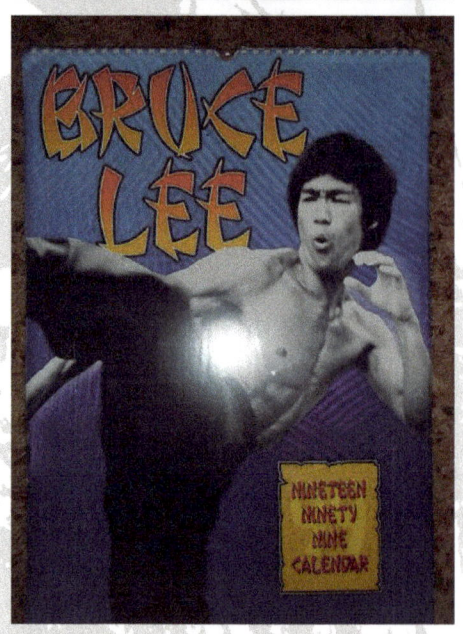
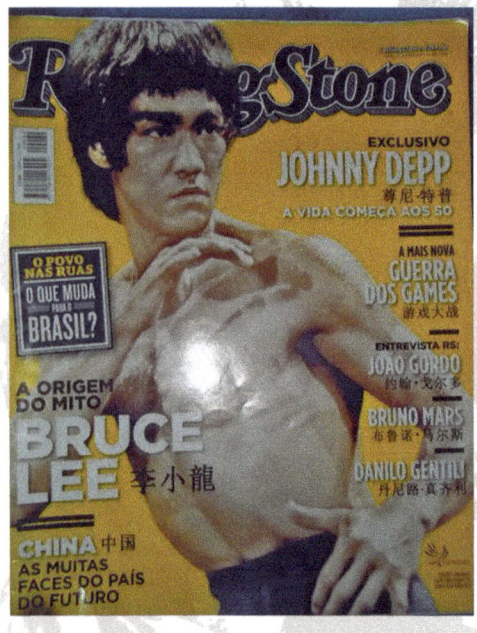

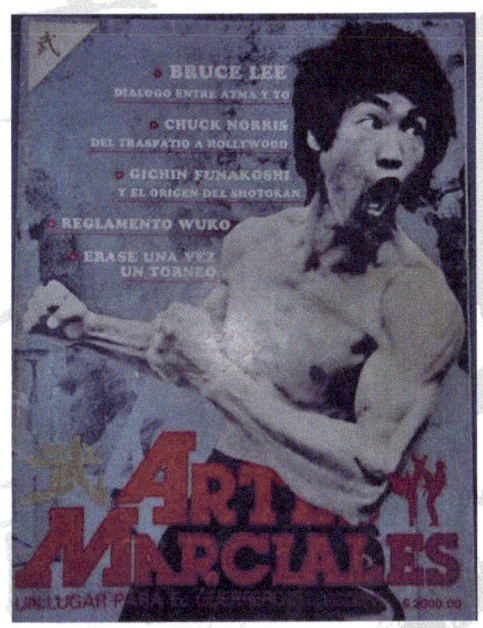

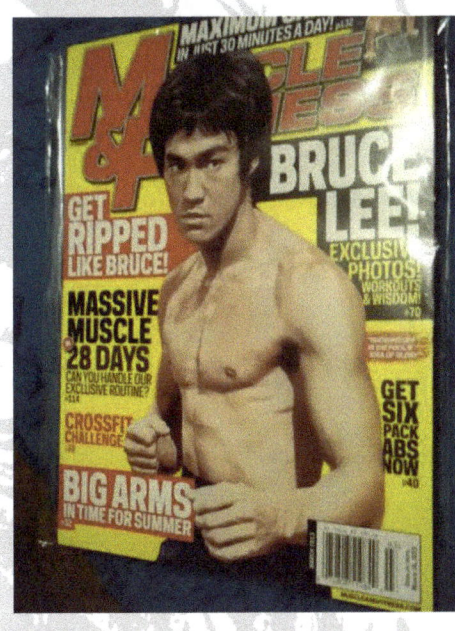
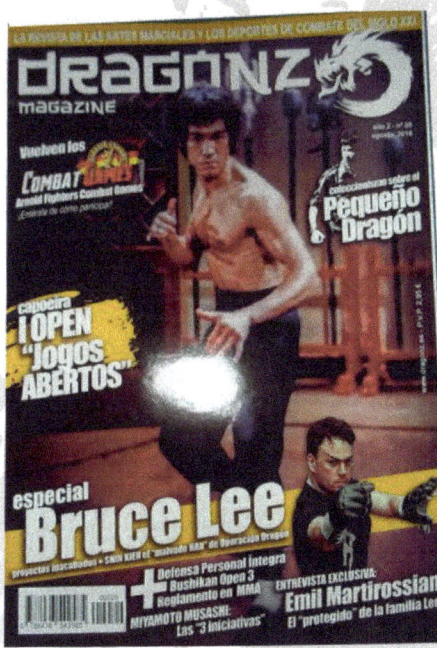

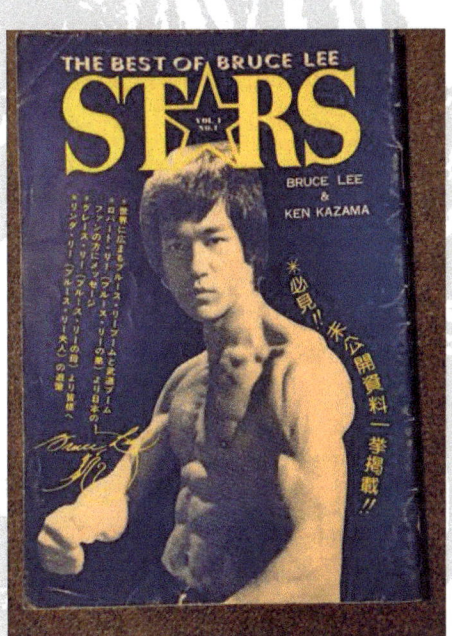

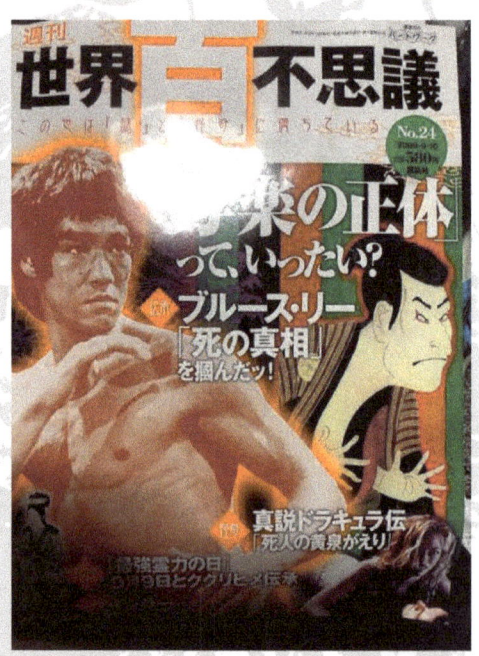
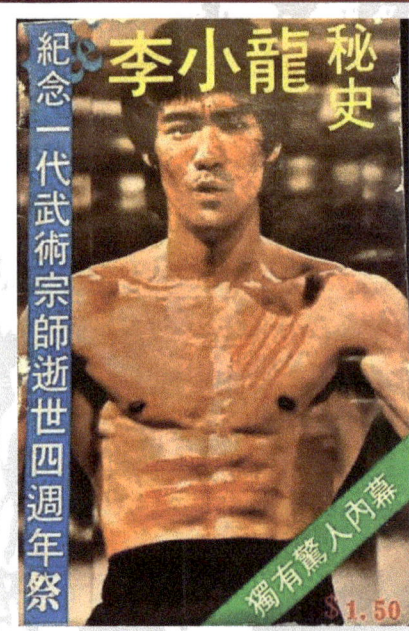

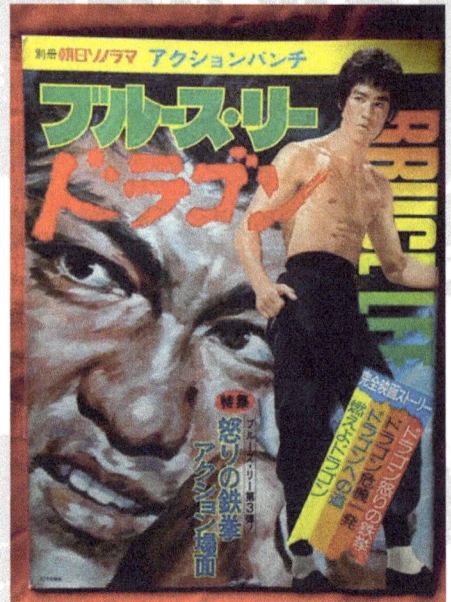

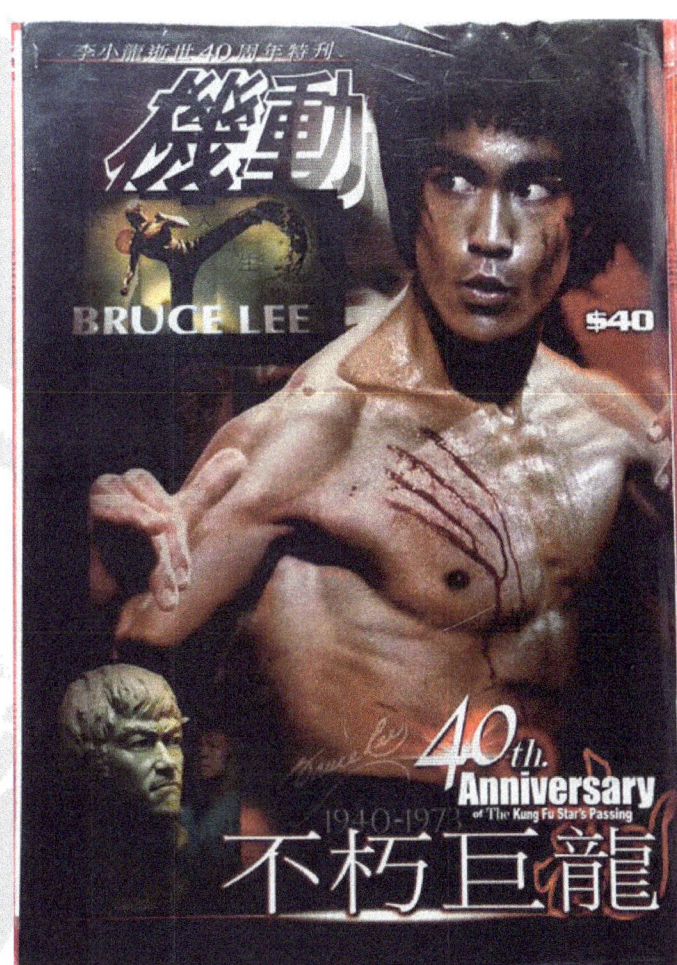
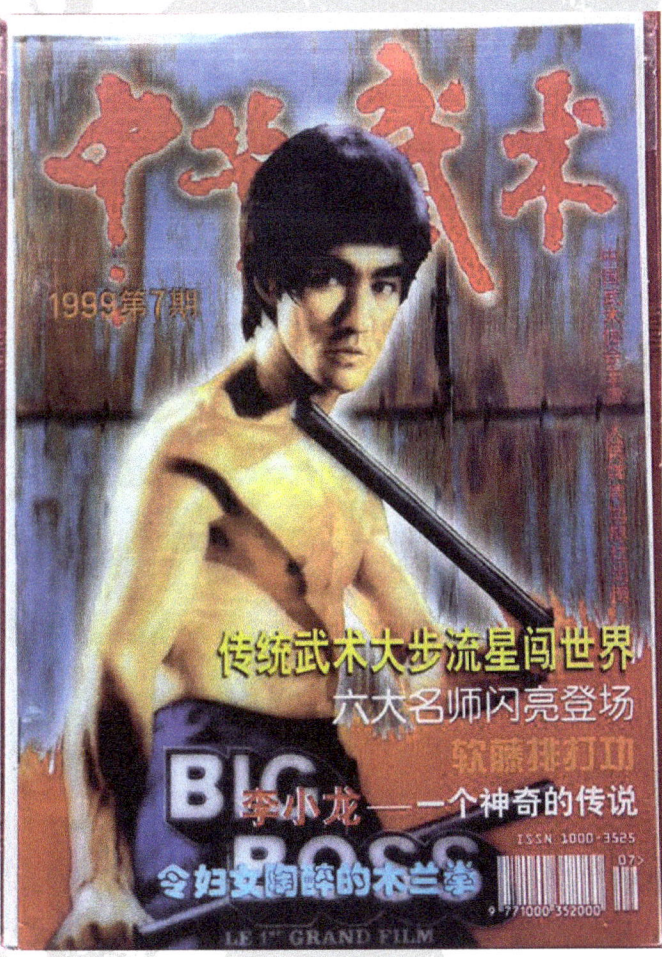

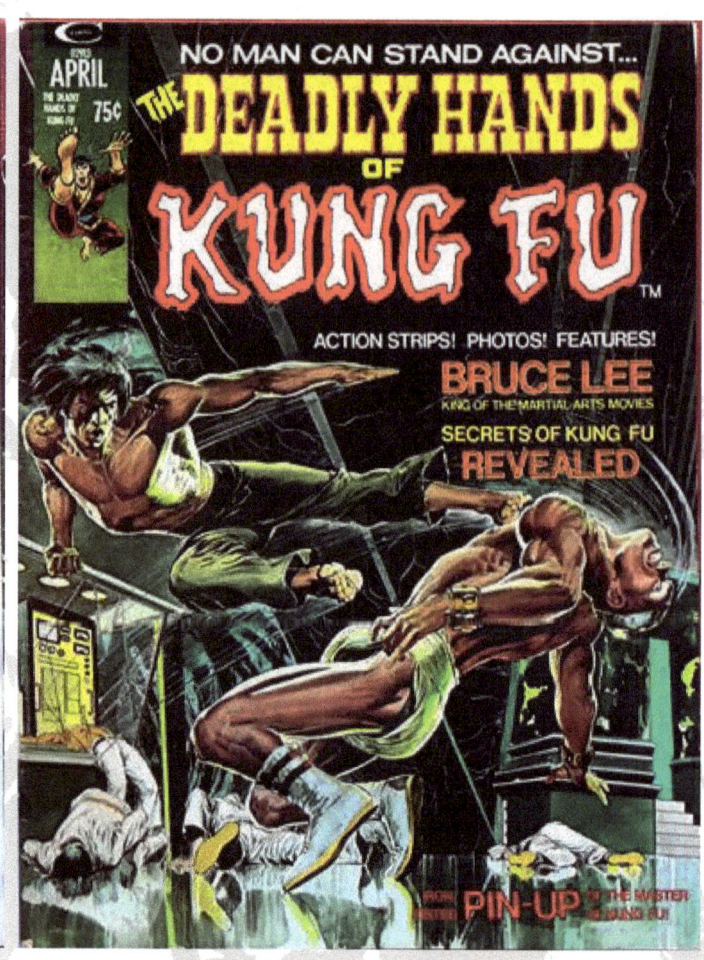
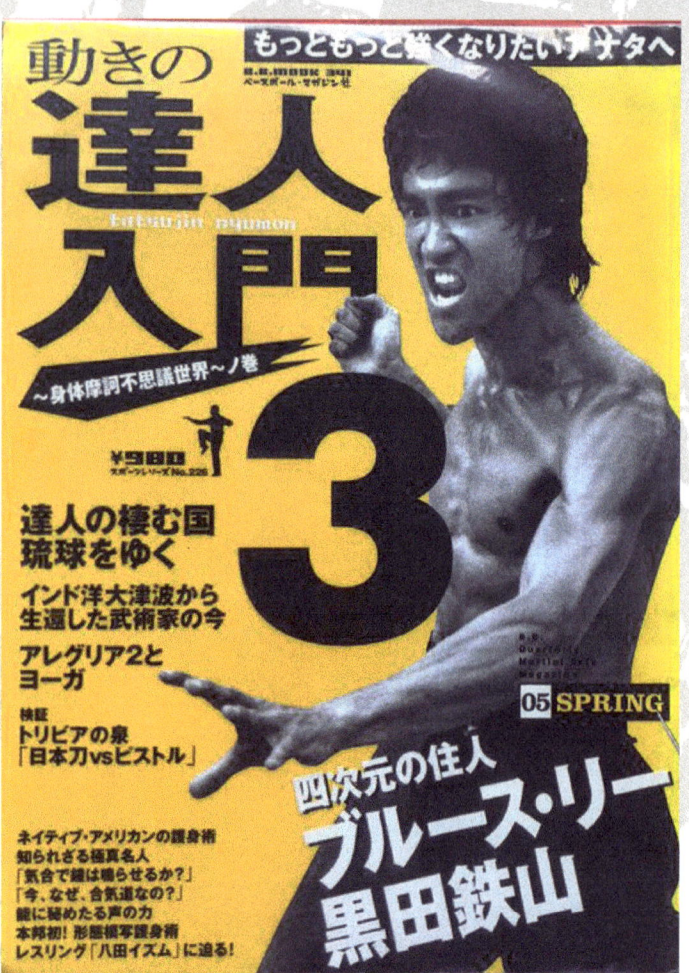

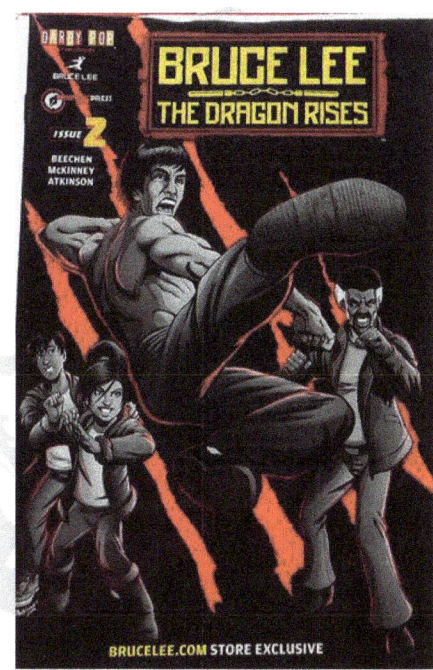

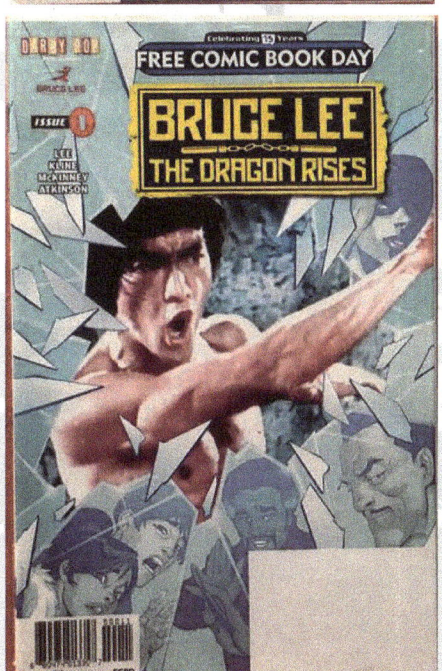

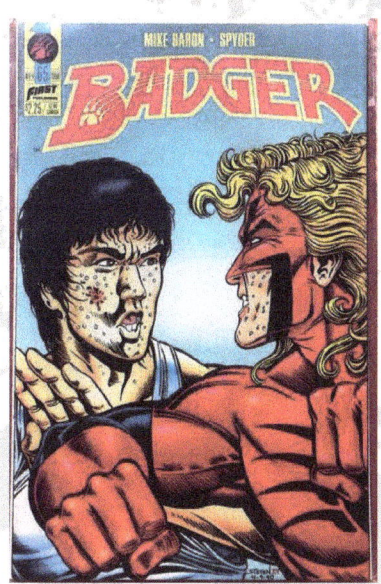

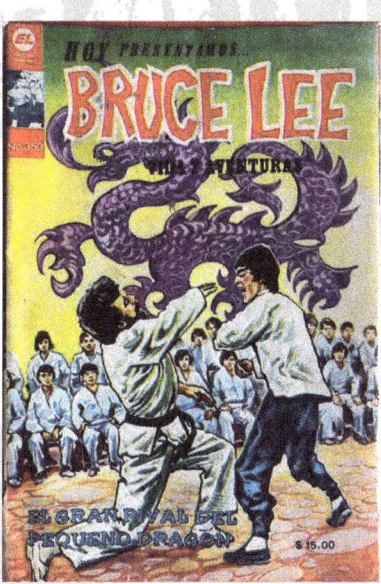

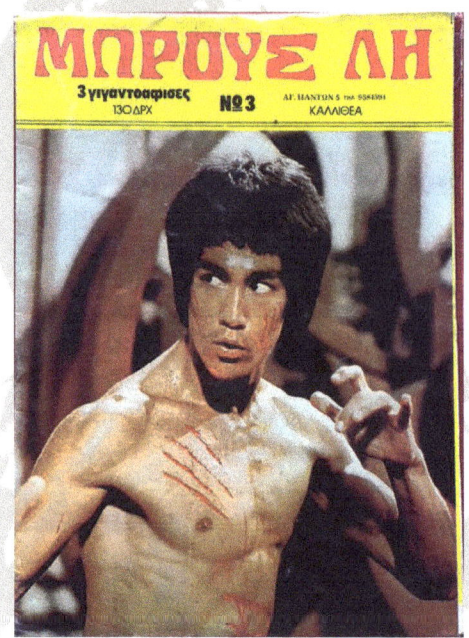

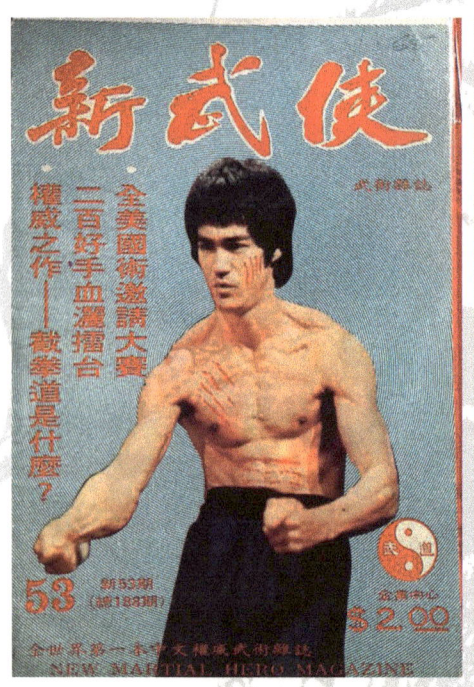

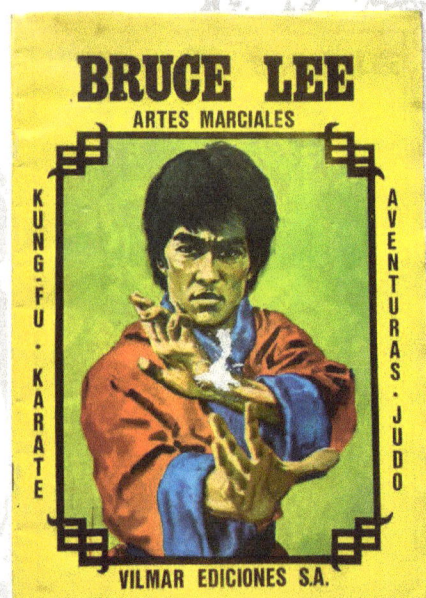

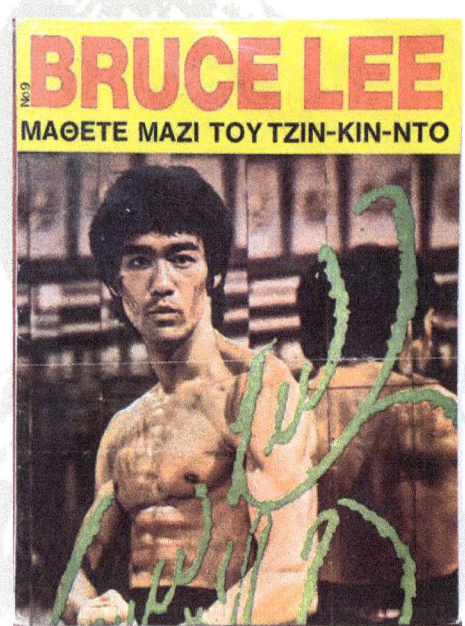
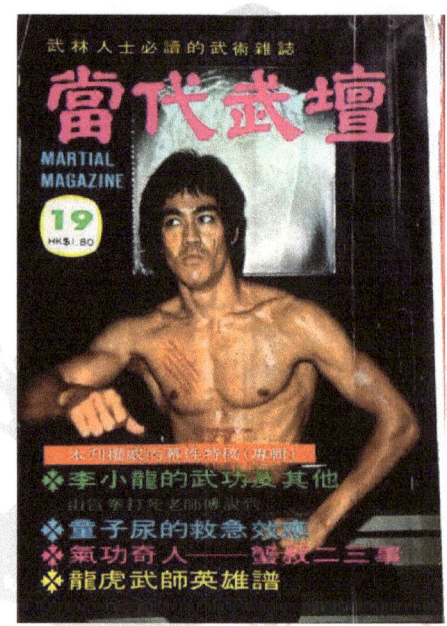
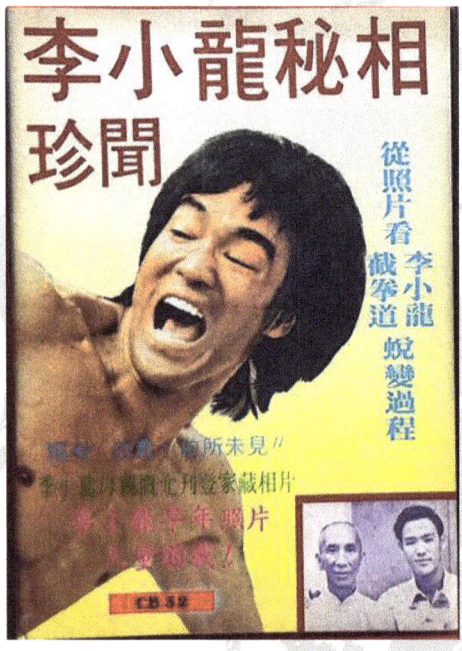
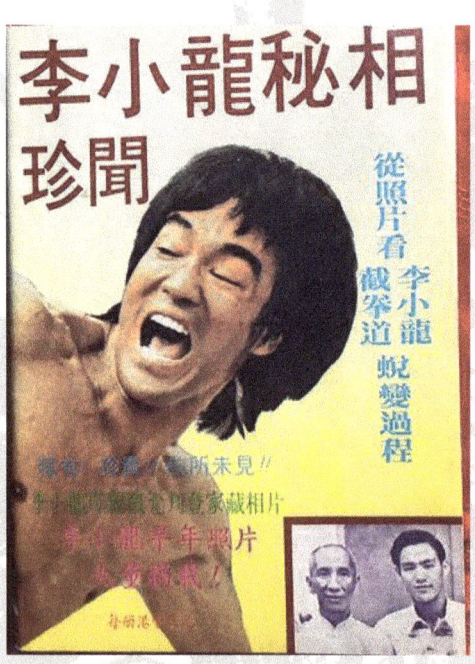
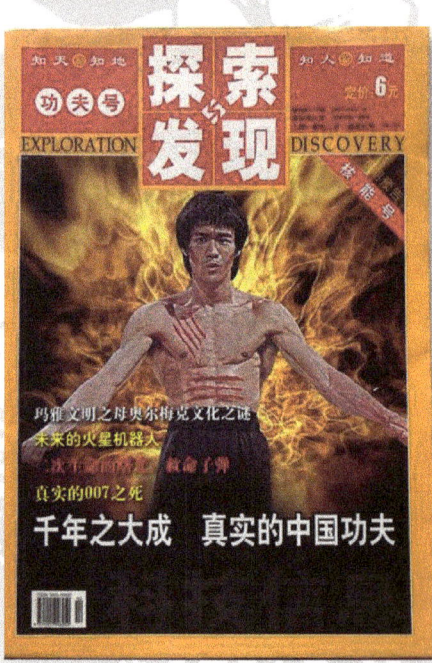
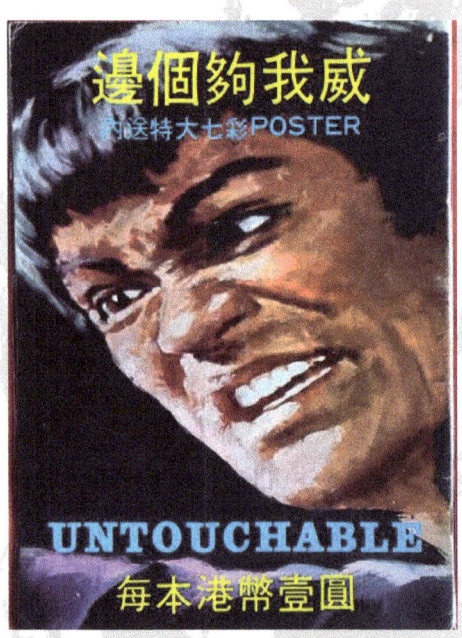

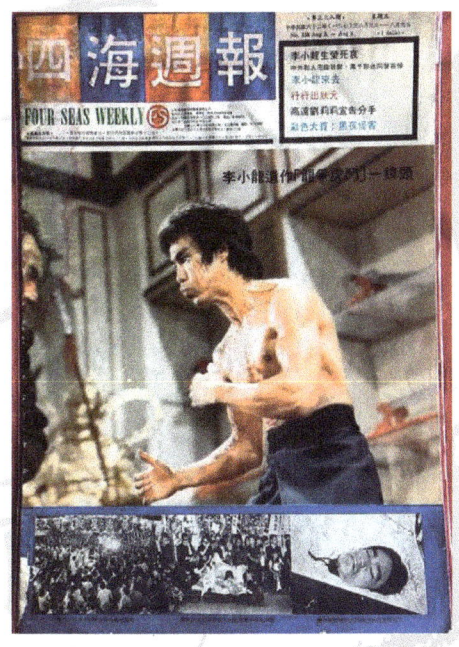
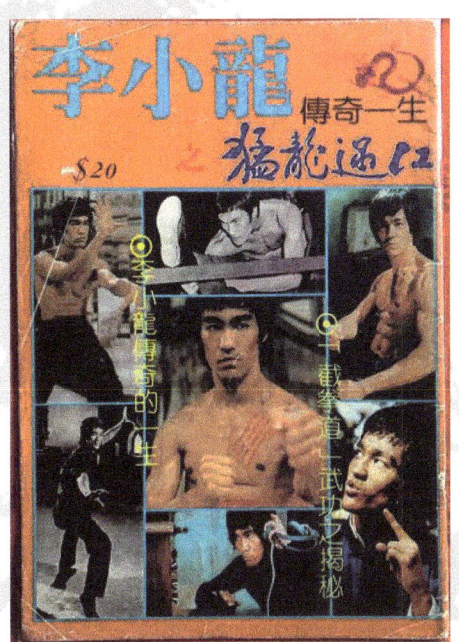
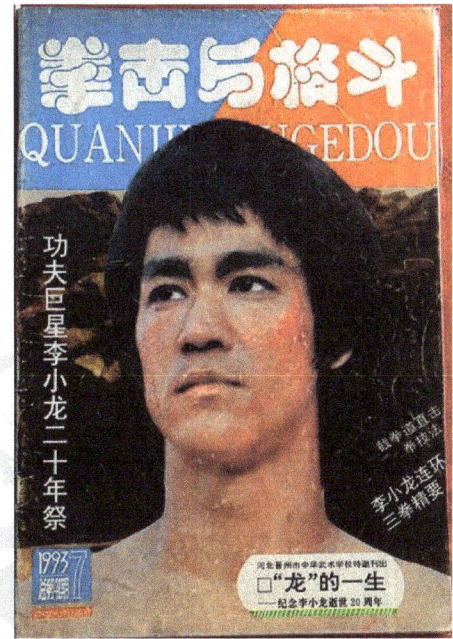

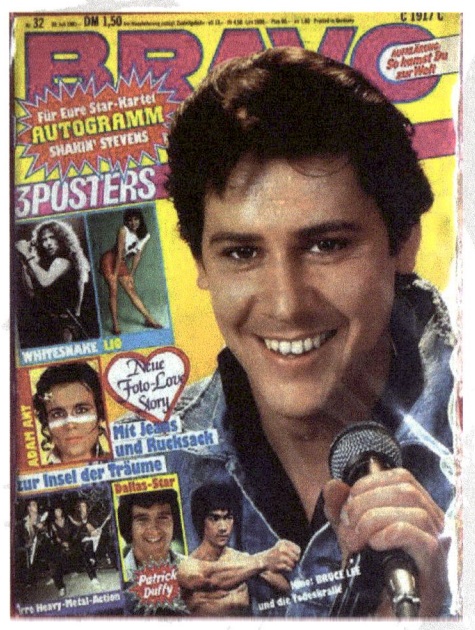

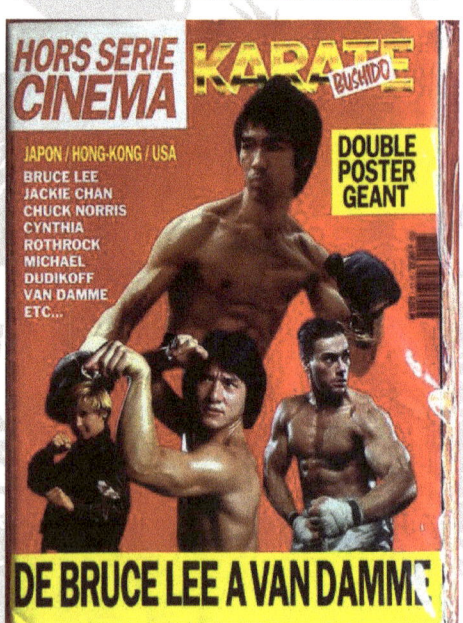

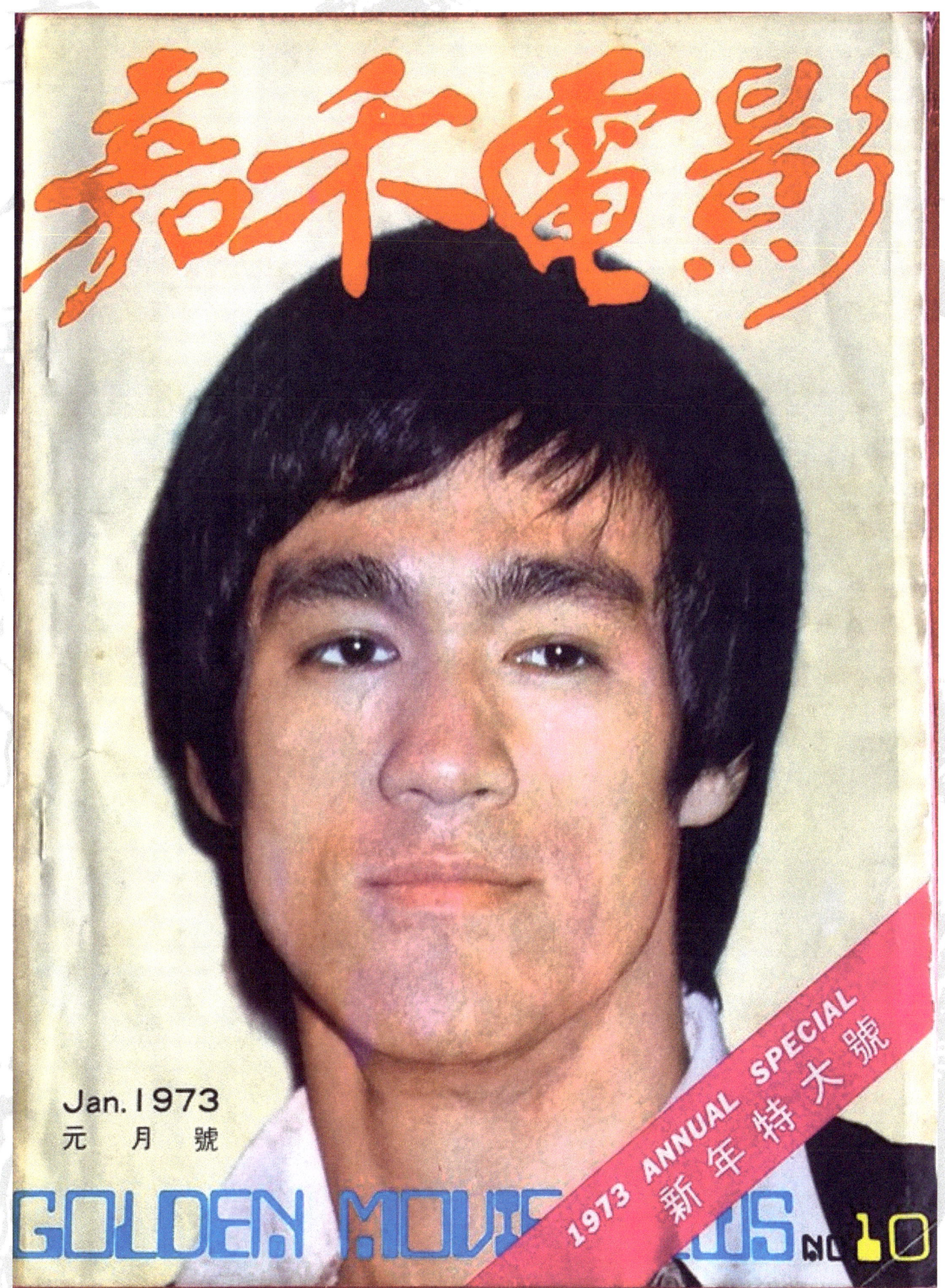

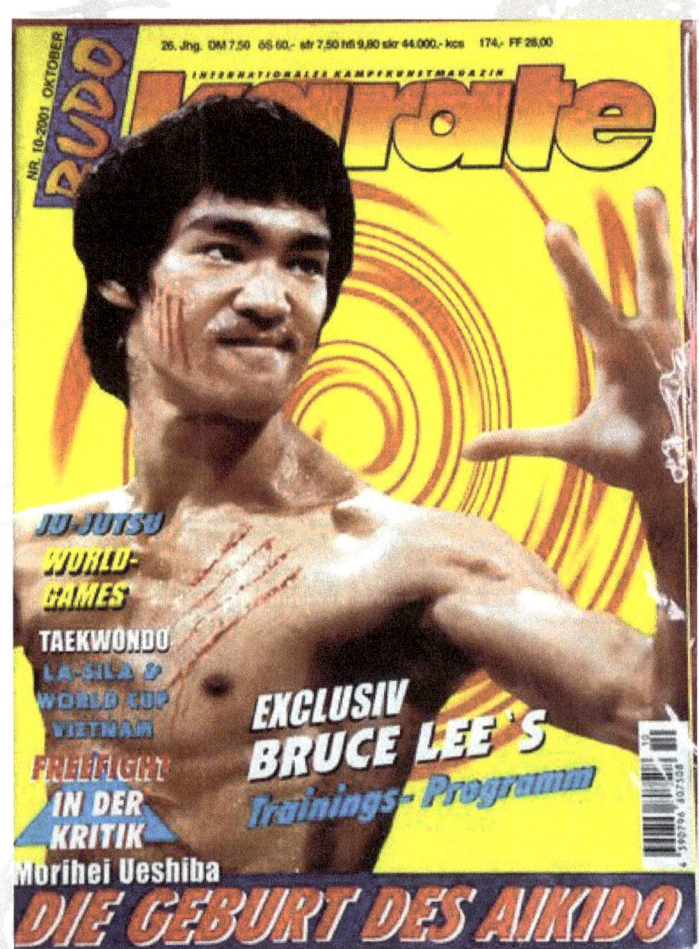

BRUCE LEE'S NUNCHAKU
IN ACTION
COMPLETE NUNCHAKU KNOW-HOWS PRESENTED BY BRUCE LEE
17 DIFFERENT TECHNIQUES FOR YOU STUDY AT HOME
INSTANT SUCCESS GUARANTEE

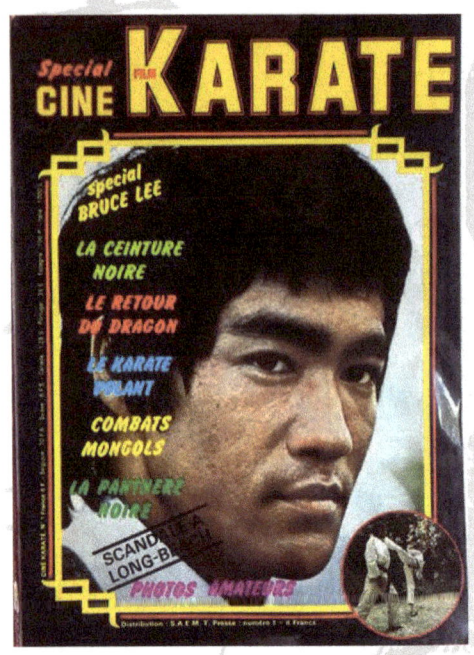

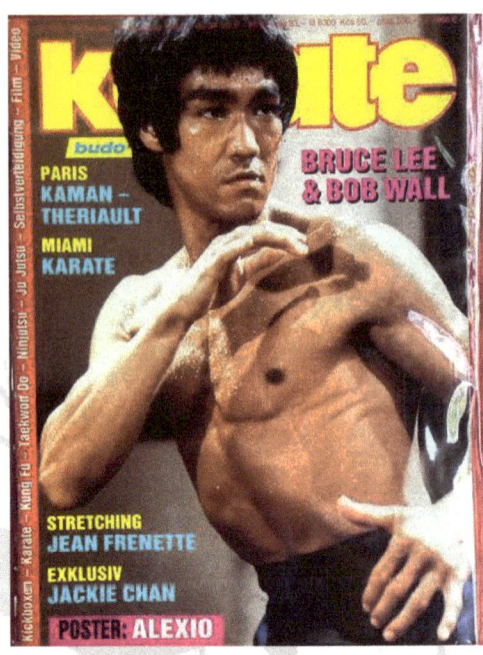

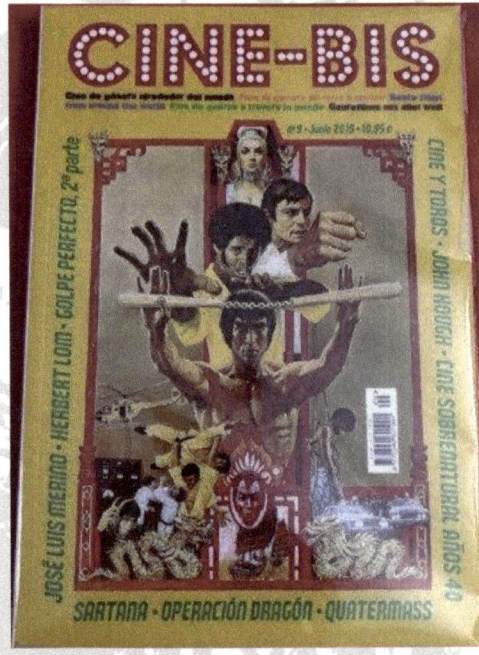

FIGHTING ST★RS

CELEBRITIES IN THE ART OF SELF-DEFENSE

AUG. '75   75 CENTS   47479

BRUCE LEE ROLE UP FOR GRABS
Hollywood search for look-alike

JAPAN'S NUMBER ONE — TAKAKURA KEN
YAKUZA'S star ready for more U.S. film

ROMAN GABRIEL AND THE EAGLES IMPROVE WITH KUNG-FU

ODD JOB — BOND'S EXECUTIONER

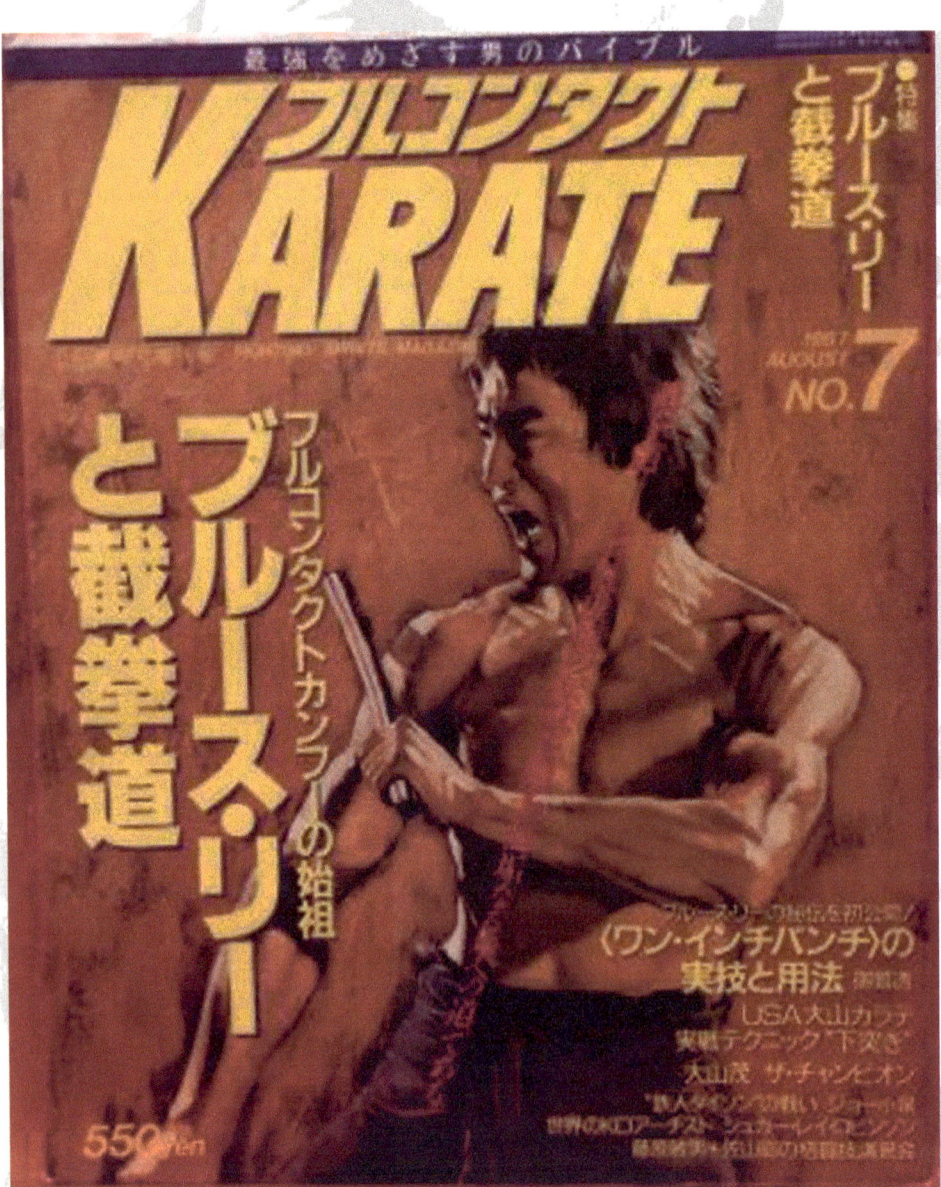

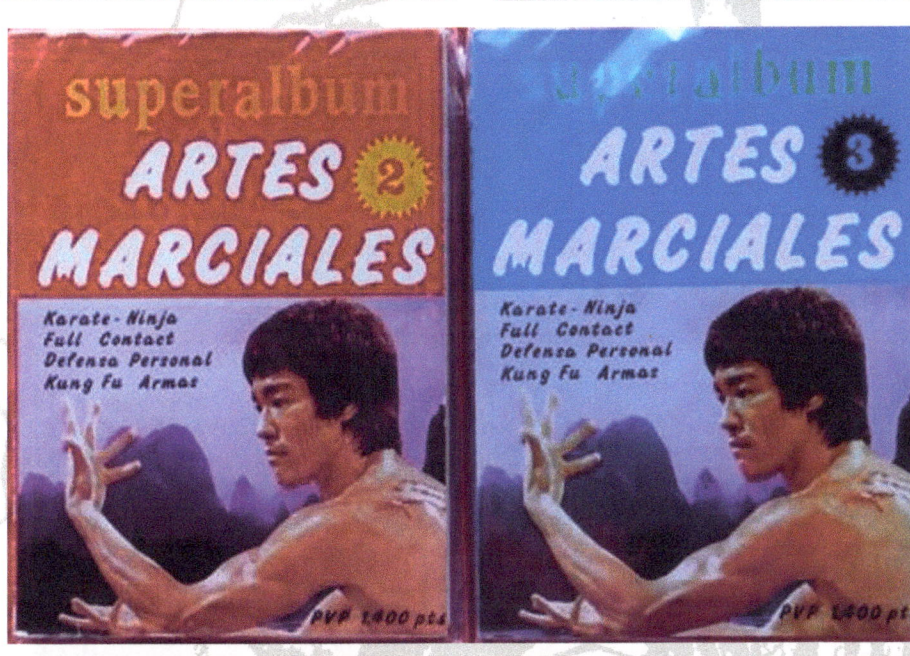
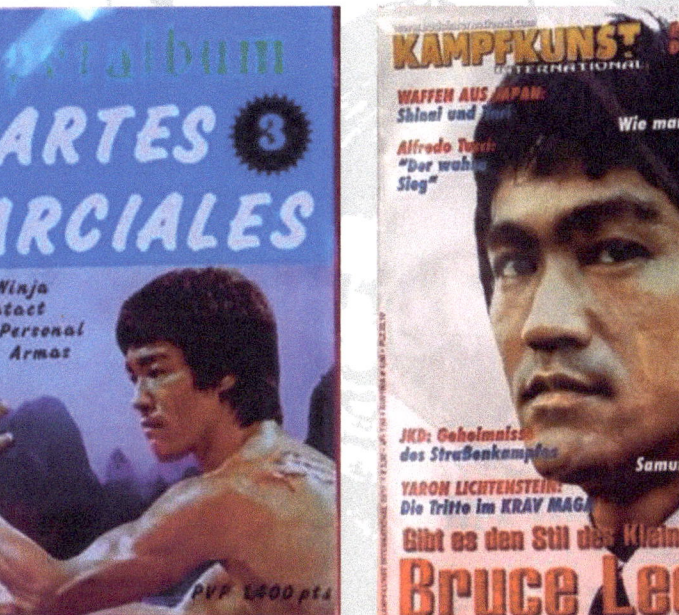
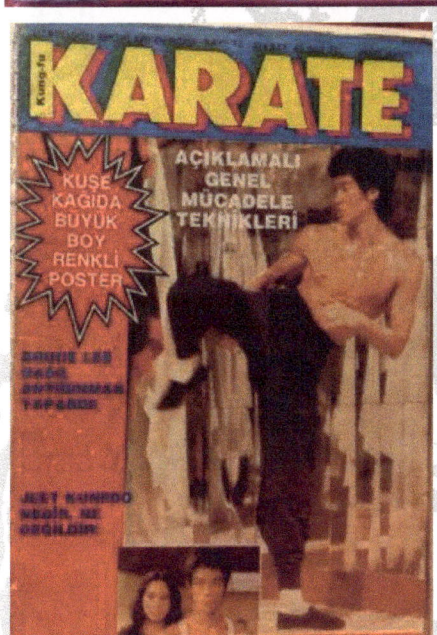

フルコンタクトKARATE
5月号別冊

それゆけ！フルコン探偵団

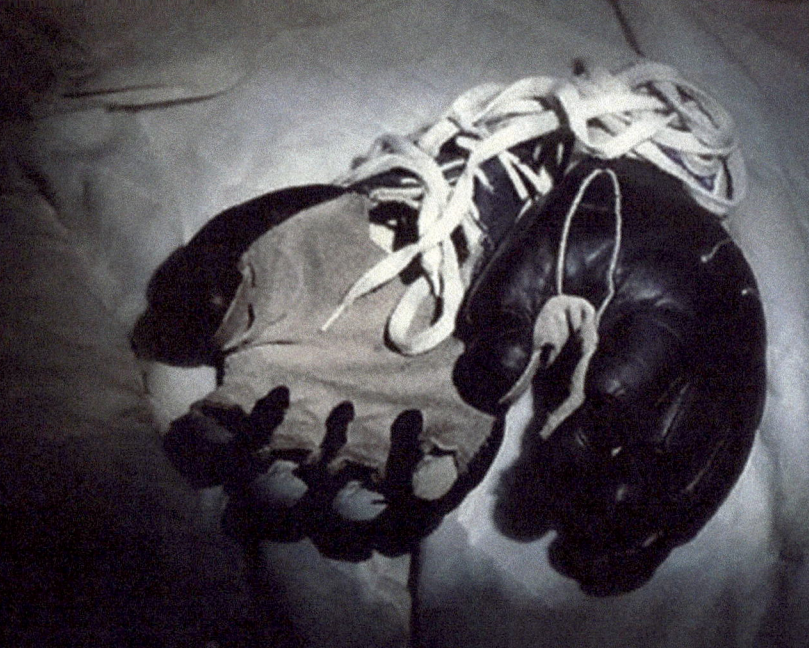

格闘技探偵の事件簿
探偵★岡本典久／下村敦夫

格闘技をこよなく愛し、不正を憎み、人智では解明できぬミステリーに、
勇気と情熱をもって挑み続ける不屈の探偵たち。
人は彼らを、フルコン探偵団と呼ぶ。

福昌堂　　　　　　　　　　　定価1200円（本体1165円）

FIGURES

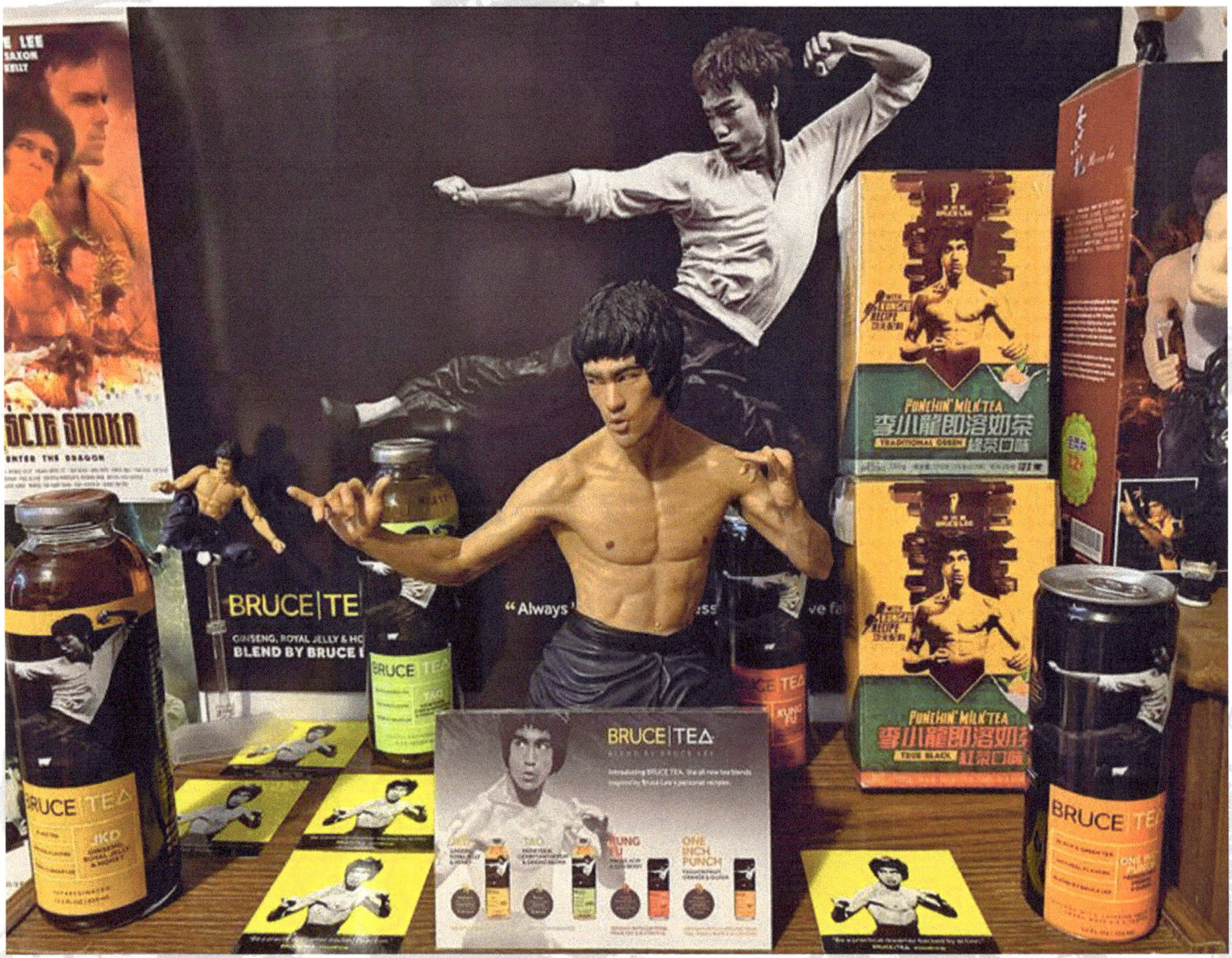
ENTER THE DRAGON
BRUCE|TEA
BRUCE|TEA
JKD
TAO
KUNG FU
ONE INCH PUNCH
PUNCHIN' MILK TEA
李小龍即溶奶茶
TRADITIONAL GREEN
PUNCHIN' MILK TEA
TRUE BLACK
BRUCE|TEA

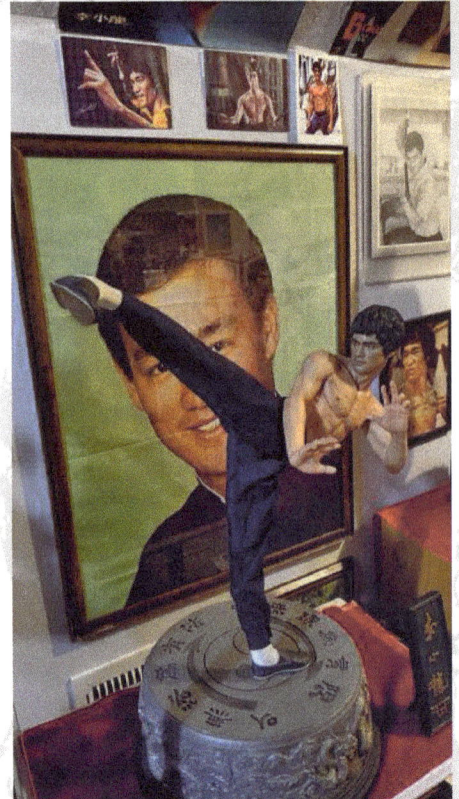

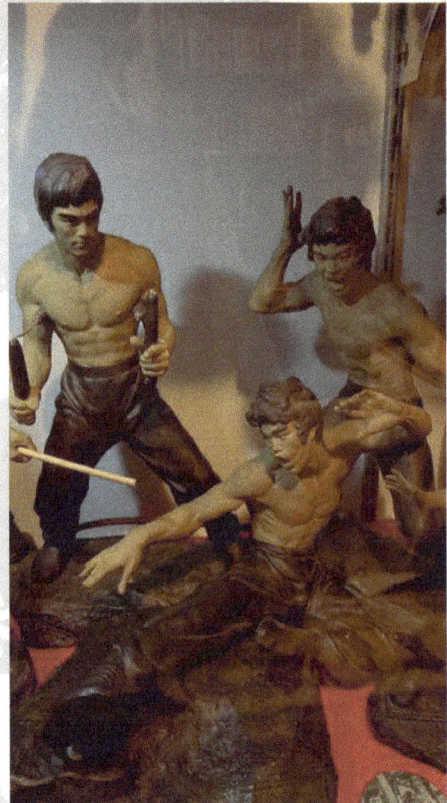

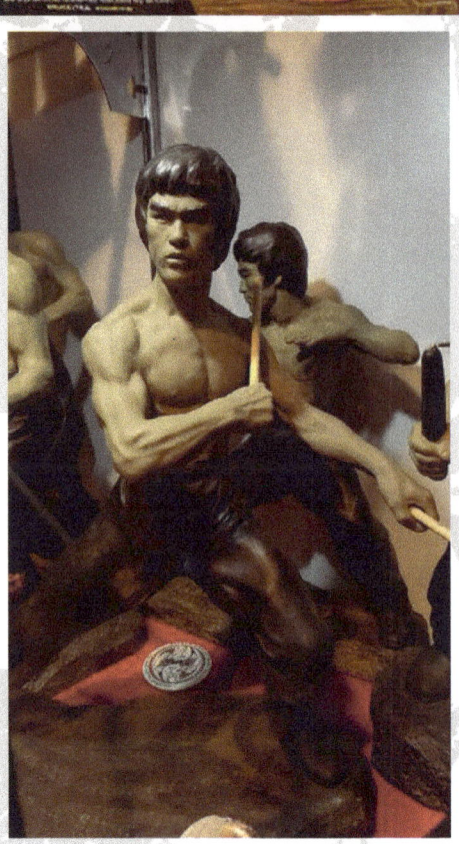

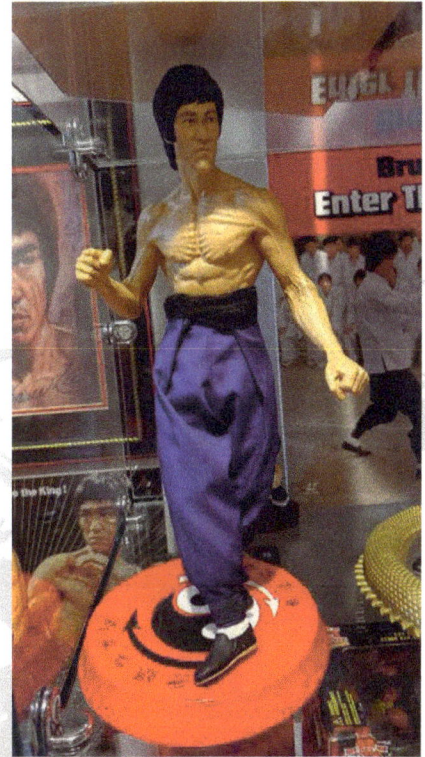
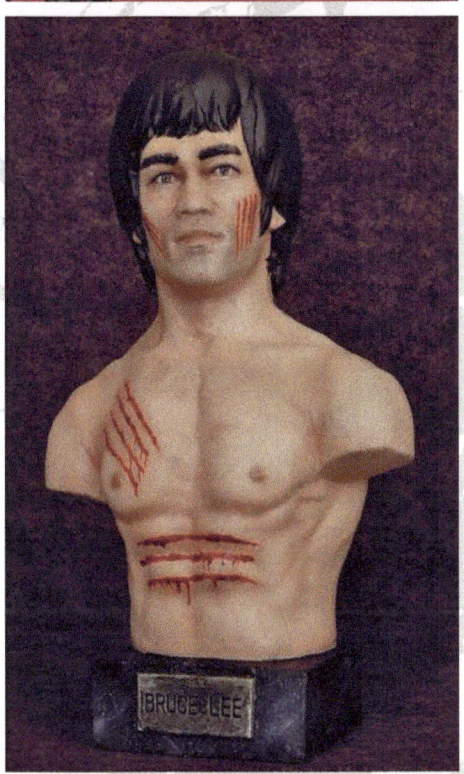

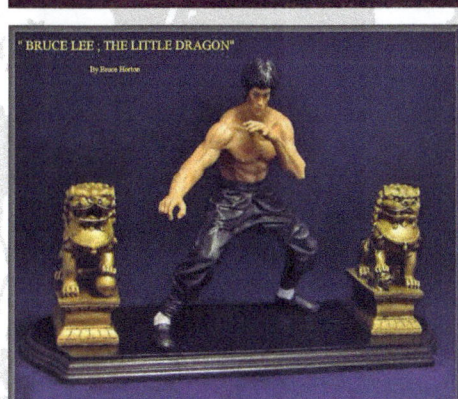

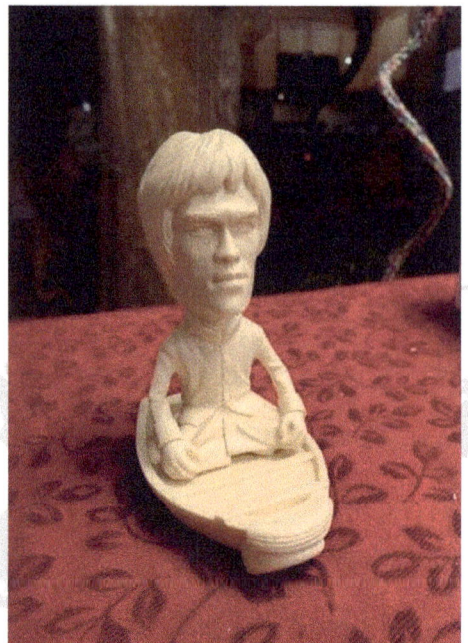

MISCELLANEOUS

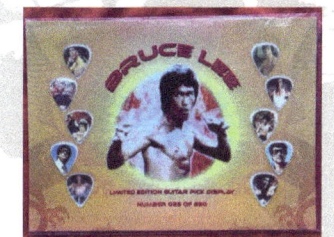
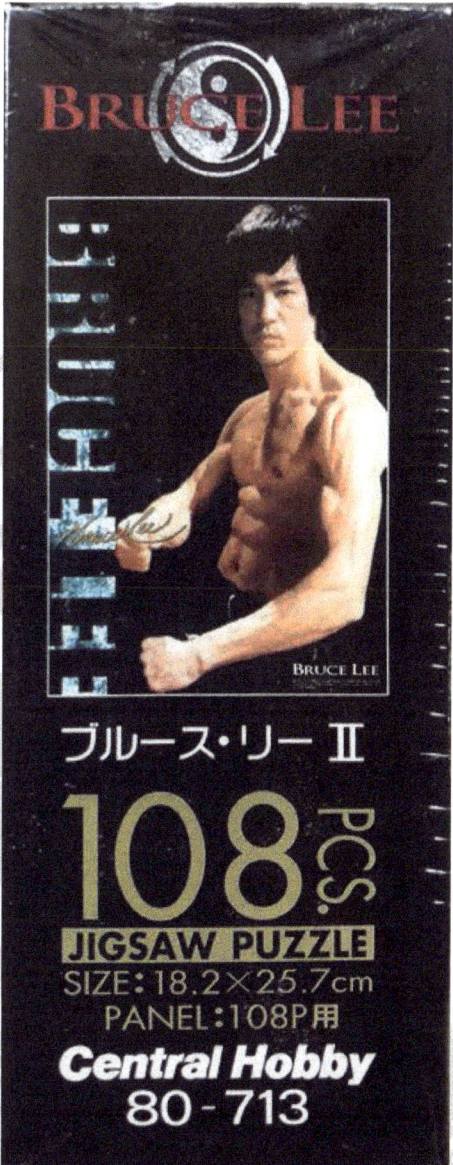

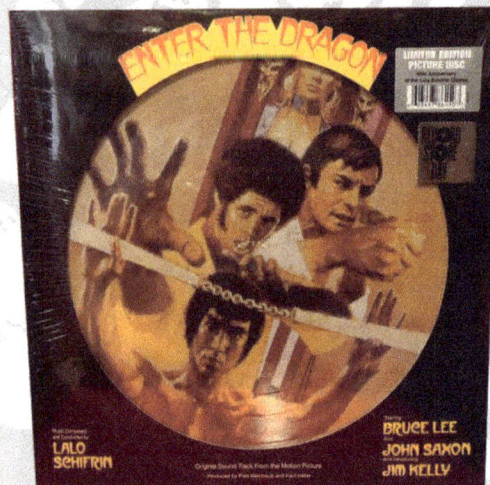
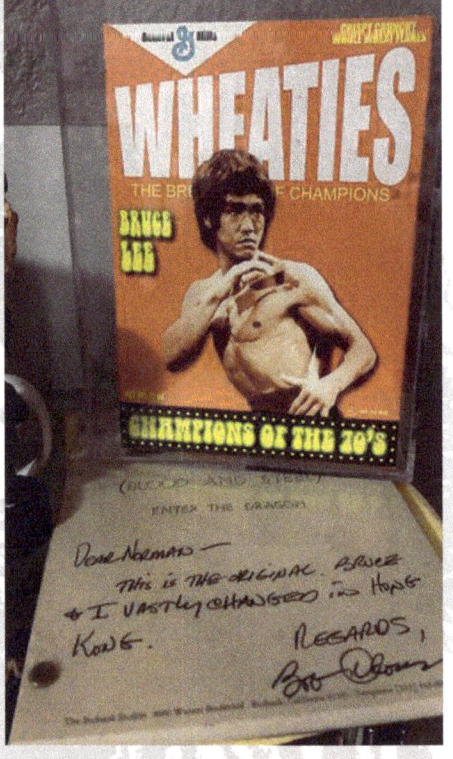

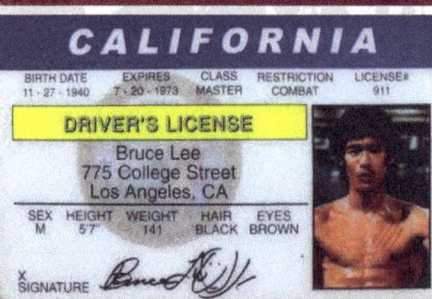
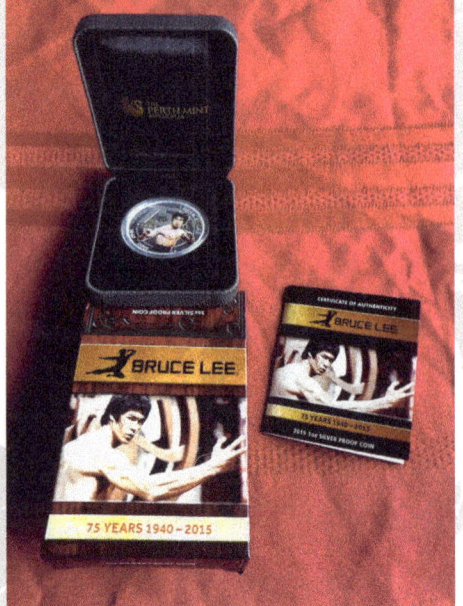

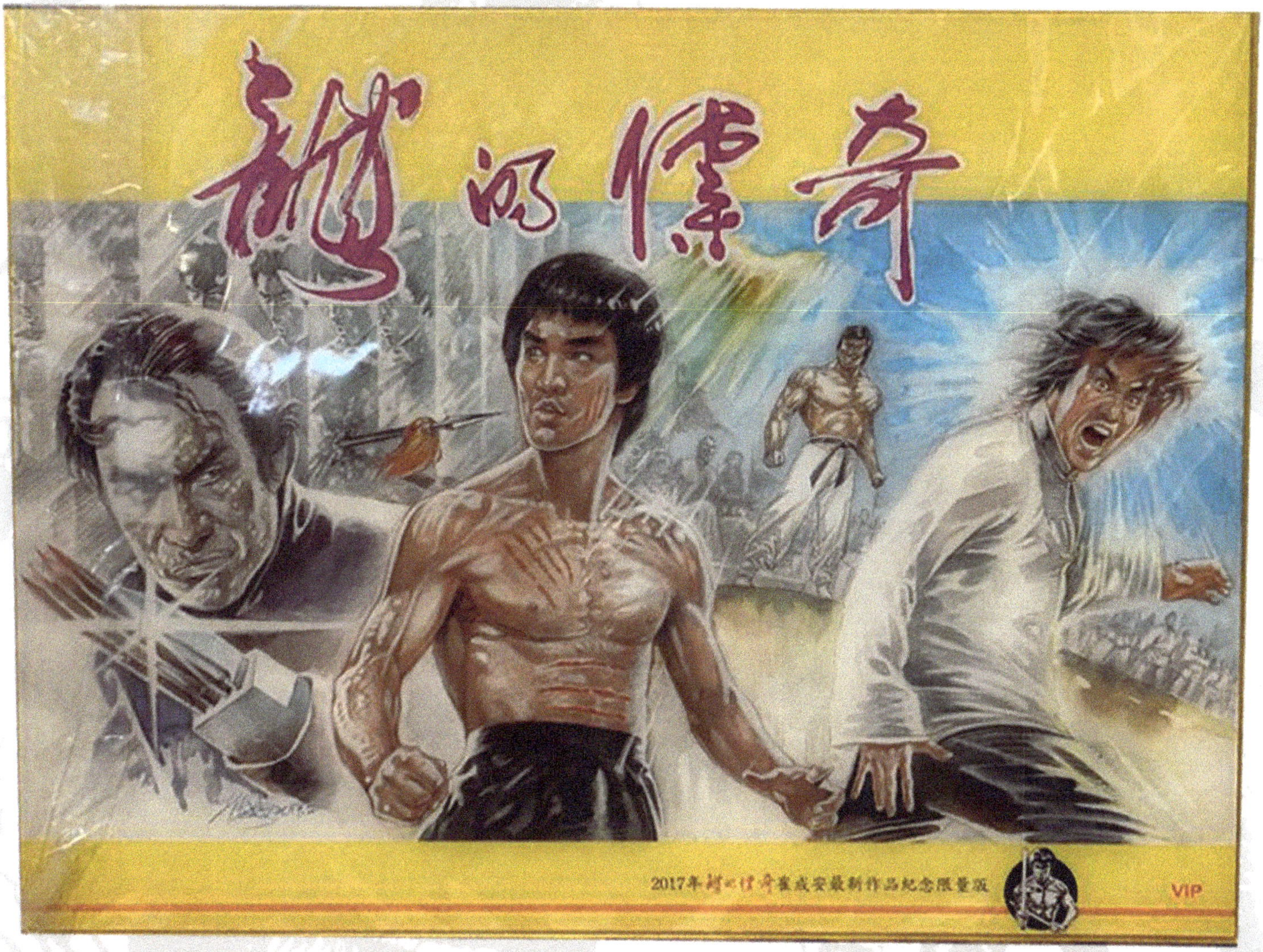
VIP

Bruce Lee
BRUCE LEE
SEE YOU AT
BRUCE LEE
CONVENTION
BRUCE LEE SOCIETY
BRUCE LEE SOCIETY
The Dragon

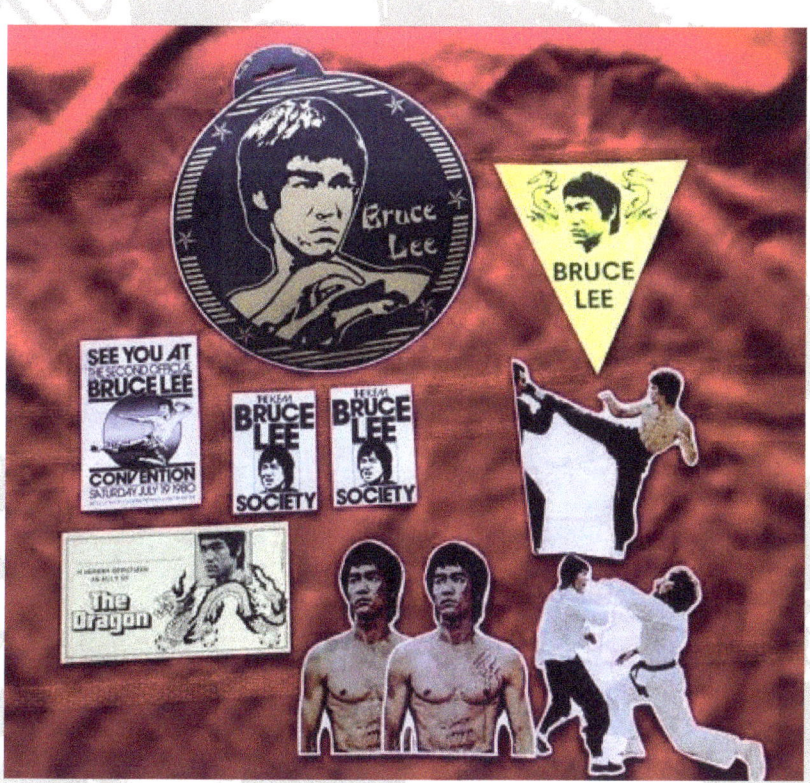

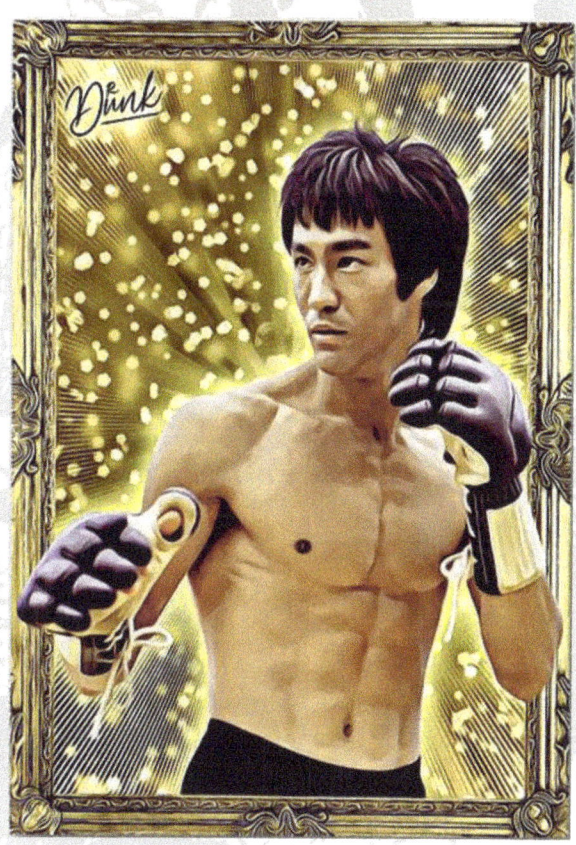

THE MARTIAL ARTS
THIS WEEK IN THE
Sunday Sun

BRUCE LEE

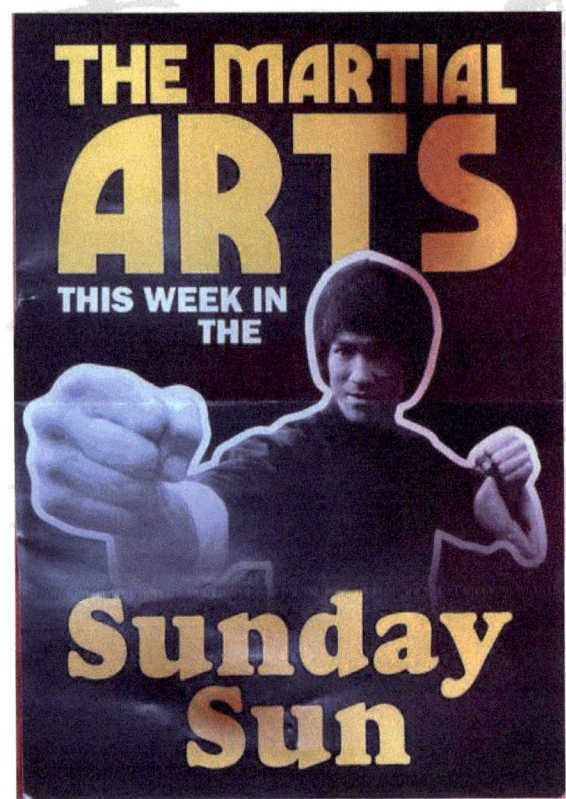

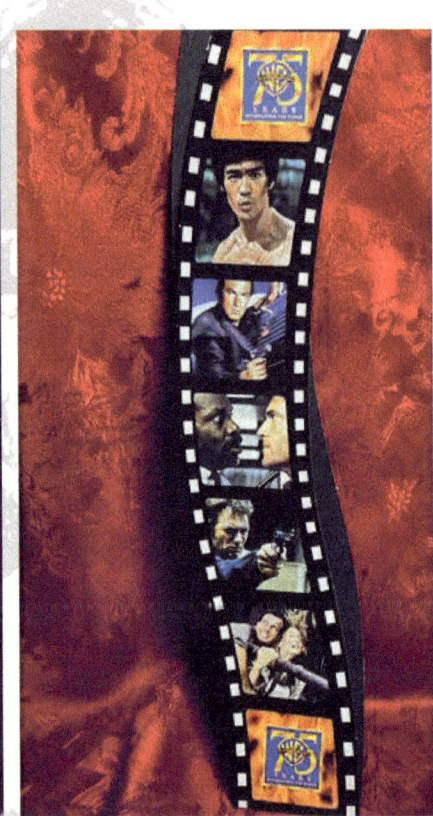

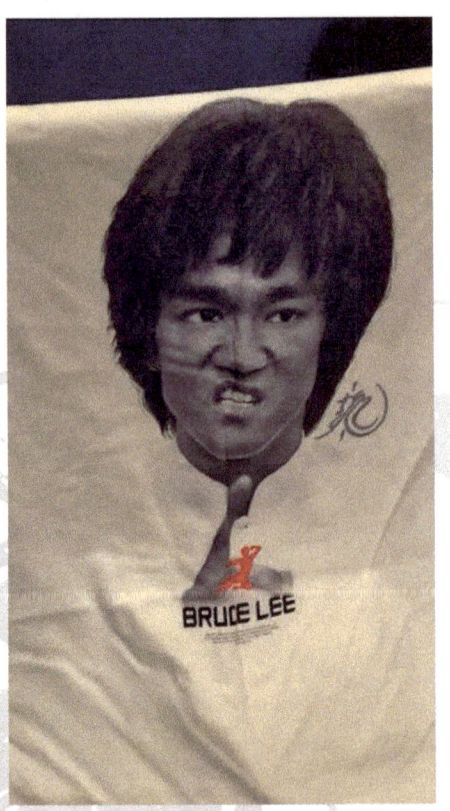

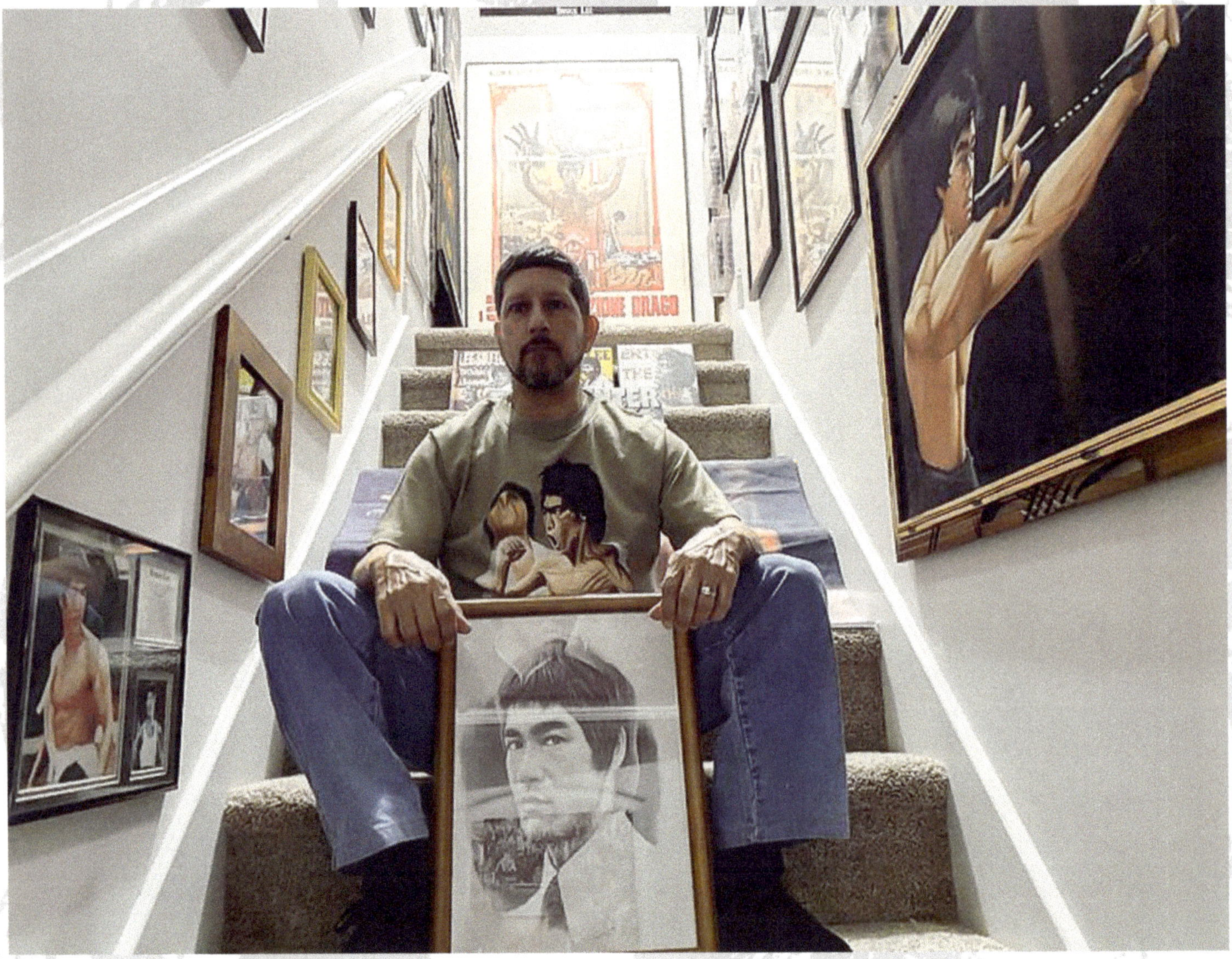

THANK YOU'S

Publisher: Rick Baker
Editor in Chief: Rick Baker
Designer: Tim Hollingsworth

Special Thank you
Johnny Burnett
youtube.com/@thefanaticaldragon

Mike Nesbitt (UK)
Dalton Regit (Canada)
Simon Pritchard (UK)
Thomas Gross (Germany)
John Negron (USA)

www.ingramcontent.com/pod-product-compliance
Lightning Source LLC
Chambersburg PA
CBHW061125170426
43209CB00013B/1674